422135

D0303594

The Contradiction Between Form and Function in Architecture

Continuing the themes that have been addressed in *The Humanities in Architectural Design* and *The Cultural Role of Architecture*, this book illustrates the important role that a contradiction between form and function plays in compositional strategies in architecture. The contradiction between form and function is seen as a device for poetic expression, for the expression of ideas, in architecture.

Here the role of the terms "form" and "function" are analyzed throughout the history of architecture and architectural theory, from Vitruvius to the present, with particular emphasis on twentieth-century functionalism. Historical examples are given from Ancient, Classical, Islamic, Christian, Byzantine, Gothic, Renaissance, Mannerist, and Neoclassical architecture, and from movements in the twentieth century to the present.

In addition philosophical issues such as lineamenti, Vorstellung, diffé- rance, dream construction, deep structure and surface structure, topology theory, self-generation, and immanence are explored in relation to the compositions and writings of architects throughout history.

This book contributes to the project of re-establishing architecture as a humanistic discipline, to re-establish an emphasis on the expression of ideas, and on the ethical role of architecture to engage the intellect of the observer and to represent human identity.

John Shannon Hendrix is Professor of Architectural History at the University of Lincoln, UK, and Adjunct Professor at Roger Williams University and at Rhode Island School of Design, USA.

The Contradiction Between Form and Function in Architecture

John Shannon Hendrix

 Routledge
Taylor & Francis Group

LONDON AND NEW YORK

First published 2013
by Routledge
2 Park Square, Milton Park, Abingdon, Oxon OX14 4RN

Simultaneously published in the USA and Canada
by Routledge
711 Third Avenue, New York, NY 10017

Routledge is an imprint of the Taylor & Francis Group, an informa business

© 2013 John Shannon Hendrix

The right of John Shannon Hendrix to be identified as author of this work
has been asserted by him in accordance with sections 77 and 78 of the
Copyright, Designs and Patents Act 1988.

All rights reserved. No part of this book may be reprinted or reproduced or
utilised in any form or by any electronic, mechanical, or other means, now
known or hereafter invented, including photocopying and recording, or in
any information storage or retrieval system, without permission in writing
from the publishers.

Trademark notice: Product or corporate names may be trademarks or
registered trademarks, and are used only for identification and explanation
without intent to infringe.

British Library Cataloguing in Publication Data
A catalogue record for this book is available from the British Library

Library of Congress Cataloging in Publication Data
Hendrix, John.
The contradiction between form and function in architecture / John
Shannon Hendrix.
pages cm
Includes bibliographical references and index.
1. Architecture—Philosophy. I. Title.
NA2500.H386 2013
720.1—dc23
2012029137

ISBN: 978-0-415-63913-2 (hbk)
ISBN: 978-0-415-63914-9 (pbk)
ISBN: 978-0-203-07093-6 (ebk)

Typeset in Univers LT Std 8.5/12.5pt
by Fakenham Prepress Solutions, Fakenham, Norfolk NR21 8NN

WITHDRAWN FROM STOCK

MIX
Paper from
responsible sources
FSC
www.fsc.org   FSC® C004839

Printed and bound in Great Britain by
TJ International Ltd, Padstow, Cornwall

720.
1
HEN

422135

Contents

Acknowledgments

The project benefited from the support of Dean Stephen White at Roger Williams University and extended discussions with colleagues, including Andrew Thurlow and Arman Bahram, and students, including Amy Lewis. Amy Lewis contributed images, along with Tom Sherman, Walker Shanklin, and Rebecca Sargent. Thanks also to Artists Rights Society and Bastin & Evrard for permissions. In the past few years I have taught several classes in Early Modern Architecture, Modern Architecture, and Theory of Architecture, along with Classical Art and Architecture, Medieval Art and Architecture, and Renaissance Art and Architecture. The lectures and discussions in the classes were instrumental in developing the ideas presented. Discussions with colleagues at the University of Lincoln have also benefited greatly, especially with Nicholas Temple, Jane Lomholt, and Nader El-Bizri. Many of the ideas were developed for conference papers presented at the University of Lincoln over the past five years, conferences on "The Role of the Humanities in Design Creativity," "Architecture and Justice," "The Cultural Role of Architecture," "Redefining the Sketchbook," "Architecture as Cosmology," and "Architecture and Its Geographical Horizons." The present volume was largely influenced by two publications from those conferences: *The Humanities in Architectural Design*, and *The Cultural Role of Architecture*. The ideas in this volume have been developed through twenty years of research, and the groundwork for the ideas can be found in previous publications: *The Relation Between Architectural Forms and Philosophical Structures in the Work of Francesco Borromini in Seventeenth-Century Rome*, *Architectural Forms and Philosophical Structures*, *Platonic Architectonics*, *Aesthetics and the Philosophy of Spirit*, *Architecture and Psychoanalysis*, and most recently at Lincoln, *Architecture as Cosmology*. I would especially like to thank Raymond Quek and Nikolaos-Ion Terzoglou for their feedback, along with the anonymous readers for Routledge. I would like to thank Francesca Ford at Routledge for her support of the project, and Laura Williamson for her help.

Introduction

Exposition of the thesis

The thesis is that the contradiction between form and function should be seen as an important element in architecture. The contradiction between form and function in architecture is proposed as a historical architectural construction that has not been theorized, a historical philosophy underlying theories of architectural practice that has not been articulated. By "form" is meant the visual appearance of a building (line, outline, shape, composition); by "function" the structural and functional requirements of a building (construction, shelter, program, organization, use, occupancy, materials, social purpose). Form of course can be said to have a metaphysical "function" to represent or express an idea, but that sense of the word is not used here. Both terms have modern connotations, related to the dictum "form follows function," but both have also played a role in architecture throughout history. In the twentieth century, form is the visual shape or appearance of a building. This is made clear in books ranging from Paul Frankl's *Principles of Architectural History*, to Rudolf Arnheim's *The Dynamics of Architectural Form*, to Peter Eisenman's *The Formal Basis of Modern Architecture*.

Form as appearance goes back to the Classical distinction between *eidos* and *hyle*, form and matter. Plato defined *eidos* or *idea* as an archetype, separate from matter. Aristotle maintained the distinction, but said that *eidos* participates in *hyle*, and is in fact the *ousia* or being of the natural world. The Latin *forma* was used by the Romans as a synonym for both *eidos* (conceptual form) and *morphe* (sensual or sensible form). Vitruvius, in *De architectura* in the first century BC, used the words *imago*, *idea*, *species*, and *eurhythmia*, all referring to form or visual appearance (either conceptual or sensible). He distinguished between *ratiocinatio*, the intellectual apprehension of architecture, and *fabrica*, the craft of architecture. In *dispositio* (arrangement), *orthographia* is the image (*imago*) of a building, and the result of *cogitatio* is the visual effect. The elements of *dispositio*—*ichnographia* (plan), *orthographia* (elevation), and *scenographia* (perspective)—are described as *ideae* (*eidos* or *forma*). *Eurhythmia* is *venusta species* (beautiful form); *eurhythmia* is derived from *rhythmos*, or form.

The Aristotelian commentators and scholastics distinguished between sensible form (*morphe*, *species sensibilis*) and intelligible form (*eidos*, *species apprehensibilis*), form as property of the object and form as a product of the mind, as an incorporeal likeness of matter. Kant defined form as an a priori intuition, a transcendental idea, of phenomena. The distinction between sensible and intelligible is related to the distinction between signifier and signified in language or rhetoric, which also has a modern connotation, in twentieth-century structural linguistics, but has played a role in visual theory since Vitruvius. According to Vitruvius, architecture consists of "that which signifies and that which is signified" (*quod significatur et quod significat*, in *De architectura* I.I.3) (Vitruvius 1931 [27 BC]). That which signifies is the *verba* or words in rhetoric (the material vocabulary of architecture), and that which is signified is the *res* (proposed thing, relation). As Leandro Madrazo Agudin says in *The Concept of Type in Architecture: An Inquiry into the Nature of Architectural Form*, "the concept of Form in architecture will reveal itself as permanent and ubiquitous" (Agudin 1995: 51), and the three kinds of form defined by Vitruvius—structural, sculptural, and geometric—"exist in architectural works of all times" (p. 81).

The modern connotation of the function of a building is related to its use or utility (as defined, for example, by Hitchcock and Johnson in *The International Style*, 1932). This concept also goes back to Vitruvius, in that a building must have *utilitas* (usefulness), *firmitas* (firmness), and *venustas* (beauty), and these have also played a role throughout the history of architecture, with different cultural and historical nuances. According to Edward Robert de Zurko in *Origins of Functionalist Theory*, "Functionalism is generally associated with … the practical, material needs of the occupants of the building and the expression of structure" (Zurko 1957: 7). As Peter Eisenman wrote, in "Notes on Conceptual Architecture," "there is no conceptual aspect in architecture which can be thought of without the concept of pragmatic and functional objects" (Eisenman 2004c: 16). But as Le Corbusier wrote in the early twentieth century, "Architecture has a different meaning and different tasks from showing constructions and fulfilling purposes. Purpose is here understood as a matter of pure utility, of comfort, and of practical elegance" (Behne 1996 [1926]: 134). While the emphasis in the functionalism of the twentieth century has been on utility and program, structure plays a role as well, and each has been present throughout the history of architecture in various ways. In the nineteenth and twentieth centuries, geometrical form replaced sculptural form, and "functional goals merely replaced the orders of classical composition as the starting point for architectural design," as Eisenman wrote in "The End of the Classical" (Eisenman 2004b: 154).

There are many examples in the history of architecture which display the contradiction between form and both structure and program. The goal of this thesis is not to challenge or criticize the legitimacy of functionalism in architecture. The synthesis of form and function plays a dominant and valuable role in architectural design. The present thesis is only intended to add another dimension to architectural composition and expression, without diminishing the importance of functionalism. In fact, successful contradiction between form and function can only be achieved after the functional requirements are fully understood. If the definitions of the terms throughout the history of architecture are examined, it can be seen that a contradiction between form and function is often present in architecture.

The distinction between form and function is related to what are seen as the "communicative" roles of architecture, in expression or representation, and the "instrumental" roles of architecture, in utility and technology; this distinction can in turn be related to the distinction between "culture" and "civilization," described by various authors, including C.P. Snow in *The Two Cultures*, and Nikolaos-Ion Terzoglou in "Architectural Creation between 'Culture' and 'Civilization'" in *The Cultural Role of Architecture*. According to Christian Herrmann, the duality of form and utility plays a role in every aspect of human life, including the life of the soul. Architecture has a role, as a work of art, to express a metaphysical or transcendental idea which is not connected to its material presence. This is the definition of art. The transcendental can be the formal, conceptual, expressionistic, intellectual, numinous, spiritual, or aesthetic aspect of architecture.

According to Friedrich Schelling, in *The Philosophy of Art* (1859), because architecture is always necessarily tied to the material, to its physical and structural requirements, in order for architecture to be art, to communicate an idea not connected to its material requirements, architecture must be the "imitation of itself as the art of need" (Schelling 1989 [1859]: §111), that is, its visual appearance must contradict its physical requirements, its form must contradict its function. As Karl Friedrich Schinkel said, "Two elements must be distinguished precisely" in architecture: "the one intended to work for practical necessity and the one that is meant only to express directly the pure idea" (Behne 1996 [1926]: 88).

As twentieth-century architectural discourse was dominated by the idea that there should be a causal relation between form and function in architecture, that "form follows function," the purpose of this thesis is to suggest that the contradiction between form and function also plays a role in architecture. As Madrazo Agudin points out, "in spite of their adherence to functionalism, the architects of the Modern Movement did not leave out the aesthetic significance of form. As a matter of fact, functionalism alone cannot explain the forms of modern buildings" (Agudin 1995: 380). As Rudolf Arnheim asserted in *The Dynamics of Architectural Form*, "Physical function does not sufficiently determine form and no such determination explains why a visible kinship should result between function and expression" (Arnheim 1977: 256). With expression based in form, "expression is not identical with a building's physical properties: a building may be soundly built yet look flimsy and precarious. Nor is expression identical with what the viewer, rightly or wrongly, believes the physical structure of a building to be" (p. 254).

According to Adolf Behne in *The Modern Functional Building*, while function is the consequence of individual need, form is "the consequence of establishing a relationship between human beings" (Behne 1996 [1926]: 137). Architecture in its form is an expression of human identity and the human condition, a poetic expression of the human spirit. The juxtaposition of function and form stages a dichotomy between the material and transcendent, the real and the ideal, matter and mind, the instrumental and the communicative, which results in artistic expression and communication.

Geoffrey Scott, in *The Architecture of Humanism*, defined the humanism of architecture as the "tendency to project the image of our functions into concrete forms" (Scott 1980 [1914]: 213). In *The Architecture of Humanism*, there are examples given throughout history in which the appearance of structure in a building contradicts the fact of structure, the form of a building is unrelated to its social purpose, aesthetics are unrelated to construction, forms are produced irrespective of mechanical means or materials, forms are designed in excess of structural requirements, and the art of architecture is detached from mechanical science, all of which results in a humanistic architecture. An architecture that displays the contradiction between form and function is a humanistic architecture— an architecture that reveals the relationship between the human mind and the material world. Form is a product of the mind, while function is a product of matter.

Summary of chapters

The first chapter in the historical survey of the contradiction between form and function in architecture, "Ancient and Classical: Egypt, Greece, and Rome," examines the symbolism of the pyramids in the Funerary Texts and the Book of the Dead, and discusses Egyptian theology in relation to Plato, Plotinus (*Enneads*), and Christianity. The symbolism of the pyramids (Giza, 2589–2504 BC, Figure 1.1) can be seen in contradiction to their structure and accommodation of funerary programs. The chapter also discusses the symbolism of the pyramids in relation to Renaissance theories of vision (Marsilio Ficino, *Theologia Platonica*; Leon Battista Alberti, *De pictura*; Piero della Francesca, *De prospectiva pingendi*; Nicolas Cusanus, *De coniecturis*; Athanasius Kircher, *Prodromus Coptus Sive Aegyptiacus*, *Oedipus Aegyptiacus*; Robert Fludd, *Microcosmi Historia*), and theories of vision in the *De anima* of Aristotle and the *De intellectu* of Abu Nasr Alfarabi.

The non-structural role of peripteral colonnades on Classical Greek temples (Parthenon, 438 BC, Figure 1.2), and optical adjustments to the temples, such as entasis, can be seen in relation to the deceptive nature of the objects of sense perception in the Allegory of the Cave in the *Republic* of Plato, and the conceptions of optics and perspective found in the *De architectura* of Vitruvius, and the *Enneads* of Plotinus. Optical refinements to the Greek temple, discovered in around 1837 by John Pennethorne and Joseph Hoffer, include horizontal curvatures of the stylobate, entablature, and gable; the leaning of columns, walls, antae, architrave, and frieze; and unequal sizing and spacing of columns and capitals. As Geoffrey Scott wrote in *The Architecture of Humanism*, "The Parthenon deceives us in a hundred ways, with its curved pediment and stylobate, its inclined and thickened columns" (Scott 1980 [1914]: 157). The Doric column itself, he pointed out, "provides a support immeasurably in excess of what is required" (p. 102).

Theories of *natura naturans* (imitation of the forming principles of nature) versus *natura naturata* (mimesis of natural forms) in Classical architecture, involving the distinction between *eidos* and *morphe*, intelligible form and sensible form, are developed in the writings of Johann Joachim Winckelmann (*History of the Art of Antiquity*), Francesco Algarotti (*Saggio sopra l'architettura*), Antoine Chrysostome Quatremère de Quincy (*Encyclopédie méthodique*, *De l'architecture égyptienne*), and Marc Antoine Laugier (*Essai sur l'architecture*). According to Johann Joachim

Winckelmann in *History of the Art of Antiquity* (2006 [1764]), architecture is more "ideal" than the other arts because it does not imitate objects in nature; its forms are rather derived from the rules and laws of proportion, which are abstract concepts. Francesco Algarotti, in *Saggio sopra l'architettura* (1784), explained that architecture "must raise itself up with intellect and must derive a system of imitation from ideas about things that are the most universal and farthest from what can be seen," that is, perceived by the senses, and thus "architecture is to the arts what metaphysics is to the sciences" (Lavin 1992: 107). Architecture is necessarily metaphysical, because its design is derived from systems which are not directly connected to sensible perception.

According to Quatremère de Quincy, in the *Encyclopédie méthodique* (1788), Classical Greek architecture was based on an underlying conceptual organization of abstracted forms and principles from nature, but it required in addition a dressing or costume that was completely disconnected from the forms of nature, and was purely ideal. The result is that the "imitative system disguises the object imitated under a veil of invention and masks the truth with the appearance of fiction" (1:467) (Lavin 1992: 111). The imitation of imitation was necessary because of the transposition of the forms of the primitive hut from wood to stone. According to Quatremère, architecture has a moral responsibility to present the relation between human reason and nature as false, in the deliberate artificiality of its imitation. The contradiction between form and function in architecture can be found in the Tabularium Motif in Roman architecture (Colosseum, 80, Figure 1.3), and the construction of the Pantheon (128, Figure 1.4).

In Chapter 2, "Medieval: Byzantine, Islamic, Gothic," the contradiction between physical and spiritual worlds is examined in the symbolism of Christian and Byzantine architecture, the iconostasis, and Byzantine mosaics (Hagia Sophia, 537, Figure 2.1). The compositions of the mosaics are discussed in relation to the *Enneads* of Plotinus. The squinch dome operates both structurally and symbolically, in the mediation between the physical and spiritual worlds (Katholikon, Hosios Loukas, 1012, Figure 2.2). The geometries of Islamic architecture communicate in contradistinction to the structure of the building (muqarnas dome, Alhambra, 1391, Figure 2.3). The geometrical symbolism in Islamic architecture is discussed in relation to the writings of Alfarabi (*al-Madina al-Fadila*) and Avicenna (*Liber Naturalis, Shifā: De anima*).

The contradiction between form and structure can be seen in English Gothic architecture in the development of the rib vault beginning at Durham Cathedral (1104, Figure 2.4). According to Paul Frankl in *Gothic Architecture*, the Gothic style began when diagonal ribs were added to the Romanesque groin vault, the rib being defined as an arch added to the surface of the vault. The Gothic is thus defined as involving the articulation of structure, beyond structure itself. The rib can be seen as a signifier for structure, a linguistic element in architecture, which removes the reading of the form of the architecture from the immediate presence of the architecture, in its structure or function, in the same way that language functions as a system of signifiers which is removed from that which it purports to signify.

The undermining of the French Gothic system began at Canterbury Cathedral, in the work of William of Sens and William the Englishman, which resulted in contradictions between form and structure; for example, the non-structural springer shafts, hidden buttresses, or the excessive mass of the triforium (Canterbury choir, 1179, Figure 2.5). The contradiction in the architecture is related to the contradiction between reason and faith in the dialectical process of the scholasticism of Anselm of Canterbury (*Monologion*, *Oratio ad sanctum Nicolaum*), the "Father of Scholasticism." In the architecture, the sensible form, the design of the elevation, contradicts the intelligible form, the structural logic of the building. In the dialectic, the intelligible can be represented in terms of vision, "by the progress of sight from shadows" (Plato 1955: 532), from the dark beyond human understanding, as described by Anselm in his *Oratio ad sanctum Nicolaum*. The exercise of the dialectic is ultimately carried out by reason in the realm of faith without the aid of the senses, and culminates in pure thought, *noesis*, the "summit of the intellectual realm."

The contradiction between form and structure in the asymmetrical vaulting of St. Hugh's Choir at Lincoln Cathedral (1200–39, Figure 2.6), possibly designed by Geoffrey de Noyers, can be seen in relation to precedents at Canterbury and possible symbolic purposes relating to the mathematical and geometrical organization of the architecture. The vault is composed of non-structural ribs: the ridge pole and tiercerons, forming triradial ribs. Nikolaus Pevsner, in *An Outline of European Architecture*, called the vault "the first rib-vault with purely decorative intentions" (Pevsner 1943: 207), as it is composed of non-structural geometries posing as structural elements.

The mathematical and geometrical symbolism can be understood in relation to the writings of Robert Grosseteste, Bishop of Lincoln 1235–53. The geometries used in the architecture at Lincoln Cathedral—bent and curved lines of varying lengths, conic sections, convex and concave surfaces—correspond to the geometries described by Grosseteste in his treatises on light and optics, *De Luce* and *De Lineis, Angulis et Figuris*. The geometries are described by Grosseteste for the purpose of explaining the functioning of natural phenomena, in particular the diffusion and rarefaction of light. Grosseteste's description of the functioning of natural phenomena in geometrical terms is an architectonic catechism which corresponds to the architecture of the cathedral, the form of which represents the scholastic understanding of the structure and function of the natural world, as a cosmology, in contradiction to the actual structure of the building.

Contradictions in English Gothic architecture are related to the contradiction between the organic and the inorganic in architecture as discussed by Georg Wilhelm Friedrich Hegel (*Introductory Lectures on Aesthetics*) and Friedrich Wilhelm Joseph von Schelling (*The Philosophy of Art*) at the beginning of the nineteenth century. A call for the necessity of the contradiction between form and function in architecture is found in the writings of Hegel and Schelling, in order for architecture to be art. According to Hegel, the art form "refers us away from itself to something spiritual which it is meant to bring before the mind's eye" (Hegel 1993

[1886]: XV), and the forms of architecture are "merely set in order in conformity with relations of the abstract understanding" (CIX), in mathematics and geometry, rather than material function. The beauty of art is beauty that is born "of the mind" (I, II), and not of the material. According to Schelling, "Architecture can appear as free and beautiful art only insofar as it becomes the expression of *ideas*, an image of the universe and of the absolute" (Schelling 1989 [1859]: §107), as architecture must be the "imitation of itself as the art of need" (§111). Architecture cannot be organic form, so it must represent organic form in the idea, as in the vaulting of English Gothic architecture, to which Nikolaus Pevsner refers as "palm-fronds" (Lincoln Cathedral nave, 1245, Figure 2.7). The symbolic contradicts the organic as the human mind contradicts nature. The symbolic is the self-realization of the artificial construction of meaning. Philosophy is "symbolic science," as described by Schelling, as seen in scholasticism.

How architecture is perceived (in the apperception of intelligible form as opposed to perception of sensible form) and the contradiction between sensible forms and intelligible forms in perception and intellection can be found in the writings of Aristotle, Plotinus, Grosseteste, Leon Battista Alberti, Gottfried Wilhelm Leibniz, Immanuel Kant, Rudolf Arnheim, and Peter Eisenman, to name a few. As Rudolf Arnheim asserted, a view of a building is synthesized from a multiplicity of views, and a work of architecture is "a mental image synthesized with greater or lesser success from partial views" (Arnheim 1977: 111), leading Arnheim to conclude that "expression is not identical with a building's physical properties," nor its physical structure, as is the case in English Gothic architecture.

In Chapter 3, "Renaissance and Baroque: architectural theory and form," the contradictions between the façades and the structures and symbolic programs of the buildings in the architecture of Leon Battista Alberti (Palazzo Rucellai, 1455; Santa Maria Novella, 1470; Sant'Andrea in Mantua, 1476), and Alberti's designs based in syncretic combinations and underlying proportioning systems, can be understood in relation to the writings of Alberti (*De re aedificatoria*) and Marsilio Ficino (*De amore*), for example, derived from Classical sources (Plato, *Timaeus*, *Phaedrus*; Aristotle, *De anima*; Vitruvius, *De architectura*; Plotinus, *Enneads*; Proclus, *Elements of Theology*). The writings include Alberti's distinction between lineament (the line in the mind of the architect) and matter, and his theory of *concinnitas* or visual harmony. Lineaments are the outline of a building, consisting of lines and angles, as conceived in the mind (as *eidos* or *species apprehensibilis* in intellect and imagination), separate from matter, as in the *ratiocinatio* of Vitruvius. In the *De re aedificatoria*, "It is quite possible to project whole forms in the mind without any recourse to the material" (Alberti 1988 [1452]: I.1). *Concinnitas* is defined as the "form and figure" of a building, that which is "pleasing to the eyes," and is "the main object of the art of building" (IX.5). Alberti followed Vitruvius in his definition of *concinnitas* or beauty in *De re aedificatoria*: "It is the task and aim of *concinnitas* to compose parts that are quite separate from each other by their nature, according to some precise rule, so that they correspond to one another in appearance" (VII.4). *Concinnitas*, like apperception, transforms disparate and unrelated sensible perceptions into a coherent whole, in a disjunction between perception and what is perceived, a contradiction between visual form and material function.

On the façade of the Palazzo Rucellai (1455, Figure 3.1), the forms of structural Classical columns perform no structural function, and the bays of the façade do not correspond to the structure of the building. On the façade of Sant'Andrea in Mantua (1476, Figure 3.2), the forms of a Greek temple front and Roman triumphal arch are combined for a Catholic church, a contradiction in representation and purpose. The trabeated elevations on the interior of the basilica conceal Gothic-style buttressing in the bays, as at St. Peter's in Rome. The contradiction between the lineament (as *archê* or archetypal principle) and matter is expressed in Renaissance painting as well, and is found in the theories of vision of Ficino (*De amore*, *Theologia Platonica*) and Alberti (*De pictura*). As Alberti explained in the *De re aedificatoria*, a building consists of "lineaments and matter, the one the product of thought, the other of Nature; the one requiring the mind and the power of reason, the other dependent on preparation and selection" (Alberti 1988 [1452]: Prologue), in the realms of form and function.

According to Geoffrey Scott in *The Architecture of Humanism*, the humanistic architecture of the Renaissance, and the visual expression of humanistic ideals, entailed a contradiction between form and function. The form of the building was often "disproportionate, and even unrelated, to the social purpose it ostensibly fulfils" (Scott 1980 [1914]: 26). The decorative use of the Orders did not express structure and was contrary to construction. Forms in architecture were not used in relation to "the mechanical means by which they were produced," the "materials out of which they were constructed," or "the actual purposes they were to serve" (p. 32). Arches and pilasters on Renaissance buildings were employed in ways that contradicted the structural purpose for which they were designed, a phenomenon that can be found throughout Renaissance, Baroque, and Neoclassical architecture.

Alberti's theory of vision was applied to his prescriptions for composition in painting and architecture. The contradiction between form and function can be seen in Donato Bramante's trompe l'oeil compositions in Milan, where trompe l'oeil space contradicts real space, as in the trompe l'oeil perspective devices in the paintings of Andrea Mantegna and Leonardo da Vinci. The contradiction between form and structure is seen in the mannerist devices of Michelangelo (Laurentian Library, 1525; Porta Pia, 1562, Figure 3.3) and Giulio Romano (Palazzo del Tè, 1527, Figure 3.4). The contradiction between form and structure in the mannerist devices of Giuilo Romano is related to the architectural use of tropes or figures of speech and to the inherent contradictions in rhetorical language. Tropes in poetic language, such as metaphor, metonymy, or synecdoche, contradict the ability of the language to convey literal meaning, but result in poetic expression. In language or architecture, poetic expression requires the contradiction between form and function. Mannerist compositions culminate in the architecture of Federico Zuccari in Rome (Palazzo Zuccari, 1592, Figure 3.5), which is related to the theoretical discussions of the Accademia di San Luca (Federico Zuccari, *L'Idea de' pittori, scultori ed architetti*; Romano Alberti, *Origine et Progresso dell'Academia del Disegno*; Pietro da Cortona,

Trattato della Pittura e Scultura), and in particular the distinction between *disegno interno* (the design in the mind of the artist, *eidos*) and *disegno esterno* (the physical design, *morphe*).

The contradiction between form and structure abounds in the architecture of Francesco Borromini (San Carlo alle Quattro Fontane, 1638, Figure 3.6), influenced by Classical philosophy, Renaissance humanism, the Accademia di San Luca, and the mysticism of the Counter Reformation. At San Carlo, the trabeated elevations again conceal structural buttressing; an exhaustive structural system is presented which serves no structural purpose, as if it were shadows on the wall of the cave in the *Republic* of Plato. Balusters are turned upside down, volutes are inverted, and straight and concave entablature sections alternate, without apparent rational purpose. But the seemingly bizarre formal juxtapositions have underlying rational explanations. Borromini's architectural forms can be related to the contradiction between dream thoughts and dream images in Sigmund Freud's *The Interpretation of Dreams* (1900), and the *coincidentia oppositorum*, or coincidence of opposites, which is found in philosophy, language, and psychoanalysis. According to Freud, while "little attention is paid to the logical relations between the thoughts, those relations are ultimately given a disguised representation in certain formal characteristics of dreams" (Freud 1965 [1900]: 544–5), as rational structures are disguised by Borromini's forms. As Freud describes, "Dreams feel themselves at liberty ... to represent any element by its wishful contrary" (p. 353), as in the forms of Borromini, which contradict their functions.

Chapter 4, "Enlightenment and idealism," discusses elements of the architecture of Karl Friedrich Schinkel (Schauspielhaus, Berlin, 1821, Figure 4.1) in relation to the writings of Friedrich Wilhelm Joseph von Schelling and Georg Wilhelm Friedrich Hegel. The ideas of Immanuel Kant (*Critique of Pure Reason*), Johann Gottlieb Fichte, Schelling (*The Philosophy of Art*), and Hegel (*Introductory Lectures on Aesthetics*) were understood by Schinkel through his friends Karl Wilhelm Ferdinand Solger and Wilhelm von Humboldt. Schinkel saw architecture as a theatrical stage set, and as a representation of the true underlying structure of reality, in contradiction to perceived reality. As Schinkel said, "Two elements must be distinguished precisely: the one intended to work for practical necessity and the one that is meant only to express directly the pure idea" (Behne 1996 [1926]: 88). The trabeated façade of the Schauspielhaus in Berlin contradicts the structure and program of the building; according to Schelling, architecture must contradict itself in its form in order to express an idea and in order to be art. The transcendental idealism of Schinkel's architecture would influence the architecture of Ludwig Mies van der Rohe in the twentieth century, in the contradiction between mind and perception, form and function.

In the *Critique of Pure Reason* (1781) of Kant, space and time, and geometry and mathematics in architecture, are transcendental a priori categories of mind which do not exist in the world of matter as given by perception, but are applied by experience, as influenced by the thought of George Berkeley. The form of architecture is an a priori representation in relation to its structure and program. As

Kant wrote, when "I make the empirical intuition of a house by apprehension of the manifold contained therein into a perception, the *necessary unity* of space and of my external sensuous intuition lies at the foundation of this act" (Kant 1990 [1781]: 92). Without the a priori intuition, apperception, cognition, and discursive reason would not be possible. The form of the house is drawn according to the synthetic unity of the manifold in space, which does not exist in material phenomena, but rather only in the mind.

As geometry and mathematics, as a language or a form of representation, architectural form mediates between thought and the sensible world given by perception. Objects of perception are given by signs or representations in the thought of Berkeley (*An Essay Toward a New Theory of Vision*; *Alciphron*; *The Theory of Vision or Visual Language Vindicated and Explained*), and words in language as signs do not correspond to the objects they signify according to René Descartes (*The World, or a Treatise on Light and the Other Principal Objects of the Senses*). The relation between the signifier and the signified in language is arbitrary, corresponding to a contradiction between form and function in the language of architecture, and anticipating the theories of structural linguistics and deconstruction in the twentieth century.

Chapter 5, "Modernism: structural rationalism to structural linguistics," begins with a discussion of the concept of style as a conception of the mind, rather than a physical quality of a building, in the structural rationalism of Eugène-Emmanuel Viollet-le-Duc (*Dictionnaire raisonné de l'architecture*, 1854–68). Style in art is "the manifestation of an ideal based on a principle" (Viollet-le-Duc 1990: 232), a manifestation of *eidos* rather than *morphe*, of form rather than function. The terra cotta ornament designed by Louis Henry Sullivan (Wainwright Building, 1890, Figure 5.1), contradicts the dictum for which Sullivan is known, that "form ever follows function," in "The Tall Office Building Artistically Considered" (Sullivan 1947: 208). Sullivan said that form should follow function in the creative process of the architect, and that "the essence of things is taking shape in the matter of things" in nature, but he did not say that the form of the building should follow the function of the building, its functional or structural requirements. As Robert Woods Kennedy wrote in the *Journal of the American Institute of Architects* in 1950, the dictum "was not interpreted by him as it was by the functionalists. He considers the business of properly relating them a matter of *professional technique*, not an end in itself" (Kennedy 1950: 199), in the design of the building. As Marcel Breuer said, "Sullivan did not eat his functionalism quite as hot as he cooked it" (Blake 1974: 16). Sullivan's causal relation is an example of organic functionalism, but as Richard Neutra suggested in *Survival Through Design*, operation also can follow appearance in nature, so function can follow form as well.

The relation between form and function in architecture for Sullivan is a dialectical relation, between the metaphysical and the material, the infinite and finite, life and death. In the "Kindergarten Chats" (1901–2), all forms "stand for relationships between the immaterial and the material, between the subjective and the objective—between the Infinite Spirit and the finite mind" (Sullivan 1947:

45), independent of the function of the building. Sullivan's ideas were influenced by Leopold Eidlitz (*Nature and Function of Art*), Ralph Waldo Emerson, Walt Whitman, and Hegel. According to Eidlitz, the design of a building is the expression of a transcendental idea manifesting itself in form through nature. For Sullivan, the essence of a building is in its appearance, not its structural or functional requirements. The gridded façade of the Bayard Building (1899, Figure 5.2), for example, expresses the rhythms of life and death, Eros and Thanatos, growth and aspiration, as expressed in the *Leaves of Grass* of Walt Whitman. Sullivan was familiar with the Hegelian dialectic (*Philosophy of Mind*) through his friend John Edelmann, the dialectic of subjective and objective, particular and universal, organic and geometrical, which he incorporated in his architectural theory.

The dialectic of organic and geometrical, and form and structure, can also be found in the architecture of Victor Horta in Belgium (Tassel House, 1893; Maison du Peuple, 1899, demolished 1965; Maison et Atelier Victor Horta, 1900). Forms which appear to be structural are in fact non-structural, producing a double reading of the forms in the contradiction between form and function. In the Tassel House (1893, Figure 5.3), a filigree iron bracket only plays a role visually, to affirm the continuity of a line. Rivets and bolts are used as ornamentation, extending to beams with rivets which serve no structural purpose. In the Maison et Atelier Victor Horta, rue Américaine 25 (1900), non-structural plaster vaulting appears around the stairwell. Gilded metalwork under curved beams in the dining room appears to function as tie bars but does not, and a column at the entrance of the house appears to support a marble cantilevered ledge but does not. The fantastical architecture of Horta involves the dialectic of the human mind and nature, the transcendental idea and material forms, literal and figural, rationalist and poetic. The architecture suggests the Symbolist *chambre rêve*, involving the dissolution of the subject in space that would be described as psychasthenia by Roger Caillois ("Mimicry and Legendary Psychasthenia," *Minotaure*; *Le Myth et l'Homme*; *The Necessity of the Mind*), and the quality of *informe*, the dissolution of the boundaries of form. Horta's architecture evokes the Symbolist interior environment of artificiality celebrated in Joris-Karl Huysmans' *À Rebours*, and the Symbolist landscape of artificiality and death celebrated in Georges Rodenbach's *Bruges-la-Morte*.

The theories and works of the De Stijl movement in Holland (Theo van Doesburg, *Spatial Diagram*, 1924; Gerrit Rietveld, Schröder House, 1924; Piet Mondrian) were influenced by the Hegelian philosophies of Mathieu Schoenmaekers and Gerard Bolland. Schoenmaekers distinguished between *afbeelding* and *uitbeelding*, between representation in visual depiction and the visual representation of an inner reality beyond visual appearance, as in the *Vorstellung* and *Geist* of Hegel (*Introductory Lectures on Aesthetics*), the manifestation of *Geist* or spirit through *Vorstellung* or picture-thinking. The Absolute Spirit, beyond picture-thinking, can be invoked in the pure plastic work of art, according to Van Doesburg. Categories of thought defined by Van Doesburg in the perception of art, following Hegel, are based on Classical conceptions of thought (Plato, *Republic*; Aristotle, *Metaphysics*, *De anima*; Proclus, *Commentary on the First Book of Euclid's*

Elements) in the formation of a *Kunstreligion* toward a utopian society. The fixed panels on the exterior of the Schröder House (1924, Figure 5.4) have been called "trompe l'oeil" and "illusionistic": they are not the material they purport to be, they do not serve the function that they represent, and they mask the structure of the house. The form of the architecture contradicts the functional and structural requirements of the building, and the architecture can thus express the idea of the Absolute Spirit, the dialectic of the inner essence of being and the *Vorstellung*, representation in visual form and language.

The influence of De Stijl, and the contradiction between form and function, can be seen in the Barcelona Pavilion (1929, Figure 5.5) of Ludwig Mies van der Rohe, where there are no enclosing walls to provide shelter. The architecture can be seen as an architecture of text or signification in form, in the evocation of *Geist*, in the tradition of transcendental idealism. From Schelling (*The Philosophy of Art*), architecture must be a free imitation of itself; forms which are not functional must be functional in appearance, as in the I-columns on the façades of Mies' buildings in America. In the evocation of *Geist*, an absence is contained within the presence of the architecture, as in the false column of the Miesian Corner (IIT Classroom Building, 1946, Figure 5.6), wherein the form contradicts the structure. The trace of absence in presence corresponds to the instituted trace in language as described by Jacques Derrida in *Of Grammatology*. The trace or absence in language makes meaning and signification possible, according to Derrida. The absence at the core of presence in language can also be found in the *point de capiton* of Jacques Lacan, the connection between the signifier and signified which produces signification. Language for Derrida is *différance*, a play of differences which constantly defers meaning, revealing the absence at the core of presence. The false column also appears on Crown Hall (1956, Figure 5.7) on the IIT Campus. Crown Hall is suspended from hanger beams, creating an open interior space, and I-columns are attached to the curtain wall to give the appearance of structure.

The contradiction between form and structure can be found in the architecture of Frank Lloyd Wright (Robie House, 1909, Figure 5.8; Fallingwater, 1939) where hidden steel beams produce an organic Prairie Style aesthetic, and the architecture of Le Corbusier (Villa Savoye, 1929), where painted wood panels masquerade as machined forms according to the Purist aesthetic. At the Villa Stein at Garches (1927, Figure 5.9), overlays and intersections of grids create spaces which contradict the organization of the building. Colin Rowe and Robert Slutzky ("Transparency: Literal and Phenomenal," 1955–6, *Mathematics of the Ideal Villa*) compared the phenomenon to a Cubist painting, and contrasted literal transparency with "phenomenal transparency," or real space with formal space in a conceptual reading of a work, following Gyorgy Kepes in *Language of Vision*. There is a "continuous dialectic between fact and implication" (Rowe and Slutzky 1976: 169) in the architecture of Le Corbusier, according to Rowe and Slutzky, a dialectic of form and function. Le Corbusier said that architecture is a "product of the mind," and that it is "art in the highest sense, mathematical order, speculation, perfect harmony through the proportionality of all relationships" (Behne 1996 [1926]: 134), apart from the material presence of the building. At the Chapel of Notre Dame du Haut at Ronchamp (1955, Figure 5.10), Surrealist forms contradict the structural requirements of the building, in the same way that in the dreamwork of Sigmund Freud (*The Interpretation of Dreams*, *On Dreams*), dream images contradict dream thoughts, being transformed through condensation and displacement, mechanisms which are applied to Surrealist compositions.

The contradiction between form and function, between the irrational appearance of the façades and the rational organization of the buildings, in the architecture of Giuseppe Terragni in Como (Casa del Fascio, 1936, Figure 5.11; Casa Giuliani Frigerio, 1940, Figure 5.12), is attributable to the shifting and rotating of nine square grids in plan, and the overlapping of centripetal and centrifugal plan organizations, according to the analysis of Peter Eisenman ("From Object to Relationship II: Giuseppe Terragni, Casa Giuliani Frigerio," *Perspecta* 13). According to Eisenman, the architecture can be read within the framework of the "phenomenal transparency" of Colin Rowe, as a dialectic of surface structure (the appearance, material presence), and deep structure (the organization, geometry), borrowing the terms from the linguistics of Noam Chomsky (*Language and Mind*, *Cartesian Linguistics*), where surface structure is the phonetic symbol or syntax of a sentence, and the deep structure is the meaning produced or the idea communicated by language. The dialectic of surface structure and deep structure in the architecture, like the dialectic of Alberti's matter and lineament in the Renaissance, entails the contradiction of form and function. As Eisenman says in *The Formal Basis of Modern Architecture*, "the dictates of form are not always wholly reconcilable with the requirements of function" (Eisenman 2006: 27).

The visual experience of Terragni's buildings is fragmented, and is a composite of individual perceptions, in what can be called apperception, as described by Plotinus, Leibniz, and Kant. The experience of architecture as multiple perceptions, gathered together in a coherent conceptual totality, was also described by Paul Frankl in *Principles of Architectural History*, and Rudolf Arnheim in *The Dynamics of Architectural Form*. In the Casa Giuliani Frigerio, pictorial ambiguity is identified in the simultaneous occurrence of both an additive and a subtractive compositional process, and centripetal and centrifugal organizations of forms, and in the dialectics of planar/recession, solid/void, horizontal/vertical, and in the juxtaposition of forms generated by the superimposition and shifting of grids in plan. Pictorial ambiguity is seen as a compositional strategy in architecture to transform conceptual structures into formal structures, and to allow formal structures to be read as conceptual structures. Pictorial ambiguity enacts the dialectic of thought in perception and what is perceived, and the contradiction between form and function in perception, and the contradiction between form and function in architecture.

The oscillation between the fragmented and shifting appearance in the surface structure in Terragni's buildings, and the conceptual organization in the deep structure, which are connected by "transformational relations," corresponds to the fragmented and shifting play of words in the *différance* described by Derrida, which reveals the presence of absence in signification. It is only through the absences, the gaps and oscillations in language, that the unconscious can be known, according to Jacques Lacan (*Écrits: A Selection*), following the influence of Freud (*An Outline of Psycho-Analysis, The Ego and the Id*). A late project by Le Corbusier, the Villa Shodhan in Ahmadabad (1951, Figure 5.13), displays the same oscillation of readings and pictorial ambiguity as the buildings by Terragni, through manipulations of the nine-square grid rendered in *béton brute*.

Chapter 6, "Postmodernism: complexity and contradiction," begins with a discussion of a manifesto of Postmodernist architecture, Robert Venturi's *Complexity and Contradiction in Architecture*, which posits contradiction as an important aspect of architectural composition, as a reflection of human identity. In his design of the Vanna Venturi House in Chestnut Hill (1962, Figure 6.1), Venturi was inspired by the Casa del Girasole in Rome (1947, Figure 6.2), designed by the Italian neorationalist Luigi Moretti, which combines multiple historicist references to create an ambiguous, oscillating reading in relation to the program and organization of the building, a reading which can be found in works of art from Edouard Manet's *Le Déjeuner sur l'Herbe* to Robert Rauschenberg's *Buffalo II*. In early house compositions by Peter Eisenman (Barenholtz Pavilion or House I, 1968; Falk House or House II, 1970, Figure 6.3), and later projects (IBA Housing in Berlin, 1985; Wexner Center, 1989, Figure 6.4), the form contradicts the structure as a column does not support anything, or a column does not reach the floor, or a gridded façade does not correspond to the structure of the building, for the purpose of displaying the contradiction between the material presence of the building and the conceptual organization of the building, surface structure and deep structure, matter and idea.

In House I, beams clearly do not support anything; they in fact have "nothing to do with the structure of the building," as Eisenman explains in *House of Cards* (Eisenman 1987: 174). House II has two structural systems, of columns and walls, creating a "nonfunctional redundancy" in which "each system's function was to signify its own lack of function," in an architecture which is an "imitation of itself as the art of need" in the words of Schelling. A hole in the floor or a false entrance contradict the program and organization of the buildings. Columns "'intrude on' and 'disrupt' the living and dining areas" (p. 169), according to Eisenman. The syntax of the compositions is as the syntax of language, using rhetorical devices to produce signification and to challenge the logic of signification at the same time. Eisenman's compositional devices have historical precedent in the work of Alberti (Sant'Andrea in Mantua, Figure 3.2), Romano (Palazzo del Tè, Figure 3.4), and Borromini (San Carlo alle Quattro Fontane, Figure 3.6), for example. Eisenman borrows the syntactical structures of the architecture of Terragni, and the syntactical structures in the linguistics of Chomsky, to compose the trace or absence of presence in language, the void at the core of signification, in relation to the *différance* of Derrida (as described in *Positions*).

Form contradicts function in several icons of Postmodernist architecture, including the Pompidou Center in Paris (1979, Figure 6.5) by Renzo Piano and Richard Rogers, where the structural and functional elements of the interior of the building are placed on the exterior of the building, in excess of the functional requirements of the building, displaying the excess production of Late Capitalism. The architects were again inspired by an Italian neorationalist, Franco Albini, in a design for La Rinascente in Rome (1961). Works by Daniel Libeskind (Denver Art Museum, 2006) or Frank Gehry (Guggenheim Museum in Bilbao, 1996; Walt Disney Concert Hall, 2003; Pritzker Pavilion, 2004, Figure 6.6) also display a contradiction between form and structure in the excess use of materials, for aesthetic affect or appearance, in relation to the functional requirements of the buildings. The form of the Piazza d'Italia in New Orleans (1978) by Charles Moore functioned as a media icon in contradiction to the actual failed function of the structure, to provide a place to eat, resulting in a Postmodern ruin. The architecture displays the excess and artificiality of Late Capitalism in Western culture, as does the Gehry House (1978), the form of which is in contradiction to the function of the house, in structure and program, and to its own ideological basis, the constructivist vocabulary, which is a tenet of deconstructivist architecture.

Deconstructivist works by Zaha Hadid (Vitra Fire Station, 1993) or Coop Himmelblau (Rooftop Remodeling Project, Vienna, 1988) display a constructivist aesthetic in contradiction to both the historical origin of the aesthetic and the structure and function of the building, as do the follies of Bernard Tschumi at the Parc de la Villette in Paris (1998, Figure 6.7), whose goal was to relate the disjunction between form and function in architecture to the disjunction between the signifier and signified in language, as described in *Architecture and Disjunction*. The follies represent the point of escape from the orthogonal grid of rational thought and the logocentrism of the signifier, the irrational within the rational, absence within presence. The absence within presence is a *chôra*, as in the *Timaeus* of Plato, a place of becoming which is not a place, the "in between" between signifiers, the trace between presences. Architecture, according to Tschumi in *Architecture and Disjunction*, is a "thing of the mind" rather than a "pictorial or experiential art" (Tschumi 1994: 84), in which its vocabulary elements, "facades, arcades, squares" (p. 90), even architectural concepts, "place a veil between what is assumed to be reality and its participants," as does language itself. The form of the architecture veils the function. The form of the follies does not correspond to their program as parts of the park. The *chôra* was also the theme for a collaboration between Peter Eisenman and Jacques Derrida for the site in Paris, attempting to define the space of *différance*, and the void in signification, the gap in the definition of the Postmodern subject.

The final chapter, "Bioconstructivism: topological theory," discusses the development of a theoretical basis for bioconstructivism in architecture in the 1990s, focusing on concepts proposed by Sanford Kwinter ("Landscapes of Change: Boccioni's *Stati d'animo* as a General Theory of Models," *Assemblage* 19), such as topological theory, epigenesis, the epigenetic landscape, morphogenesis, catastrophe, and catastrophe theory. This development did not continue in the first decade of the twenty-first century, giving way to a "death of theory" in architecture, in deference to an overriding emphasis on material production, technological development, and consumerist novelty, as indicated in essays by Detlef Mertins ("Bioconstructivisms," *NOX: Machining Architecture*), for example, in which "self-generation" and "immanence" are seen to have replaced "predetermination" and "transcendence," and by Jane and Mark Burry (*The New Mathematics of Architecture*), which celebrates the complex geometries which computer systems are able to add to architecture, seen as dynamic in relation to the "dead geometries" and "rectilinear dogma" of Modernist architecture.

An experimental project by Amy Lewis in a Graduate Design Studio led by Andrew Thurlow at Roger Williams University (2011, Figure 7.1, Figure 7.2) enacts a theoretical basis for bioconstructivism in combination with a poetic expression, in the contradiction between form and function, in structure and program. The project combines the immanence and self-generation of biomimesis with the transcendence and predetermination of poetic expression, displaying the relation between the signifier and the signified in the contradiction between the form and the function, along with the topological, epigenetic landscape, and morphogenesis and catastrophe that the computer-designed form is capable of representing. The project combines the dynamism of computer-generated forms with a historicist approach in the treatment of typologies and formal relationships, continuing the development of theory-based architecture, or architecture as art.

Bioconstructivist projects that display a similar contradiction between form and function include the Cardiff Bay Opera House Competition project (1994) by Greg Lynn and the Oblique WTC project (2002) by Lars Spuybroek. The project by Amy Lewis recalls the dialectical relationships of Louis Sullivan, of organic and geometrical, horizontal and vertical, mind and nature, and life and death, in a poetic expression facilitated by the contradiction between form and function. The dialectical relation is based on the contradiction between the thesis and antithesis, from which a synthesis is drawn. The dialectical relation of form and function in architecture is an important element in architectural expression. Contemporary architecture sees an increasing neglect of the relation between form and function. Contemporary architects generate forms and justify them with function. In architecture, forms should be generated in relation to function, either as a response to it, or in contradiction to it.

In the neglect of theory, emphasis has been placed instead on the development of the technological means of architectural production, in particular computer programs, at the expense of the development of a theoretical or conceptual basis for architectural form-making. As Nikolaos-Ion Terzoglou writes, for example, "Architecture has concentrated mainly on technological means and instrumental procedures that, in certain cases, manage empty forms without conceptual content" (Terzoglou 2012: 172). The discipline of architecture has increased its dependence on other forms of technological production. Terzoglou continues: "This situation has marginalized architecture as a form of mental expression and spatial imagination. An almost exclusive and one-dimensional emphasis on material and technological means reduces the ontological complexity of architecture and often leads to results which lack mental depth and spiritual purposes" (p. 168). Theorizing a contradiction between form and function in architecture hopes to suggest an architecture of mental depth and ontological complexity, in the place of empty forms.

This book is part of a project to re-introduce the emphasis on the expression of ideas and on references to history in architecture. This is a major theme that runs throughout two recent books, *The Humanities in Architectural Design* and *The Cultural Role of Architecture*, the theme of the need to re-establish architecture as a form of human expression and as a humanistic discipline. This project hopes to "restore, or indeed, radically transform, the traditional dialogue between intellectual enquiry in the humanities and design creativity," to quote the Introduction to *The Humanities in Architectural Design* (Bandyopadhyay 2010: xix).

Chapter 1

Ancient and Classical: Egypt, Greece, and Rome

The symbolism of the pyramid

In the Egyptian pyramid, as in the Pyramids at Giza—Cheops, Chefren, and Mykerinos (Figure 1.1), from 2589 to 2504 BC—the massive structure of blocks is far in excess of the function of the structure as a tomb. The goal was to create a symbolic architecture in relation to the heavens and constellations, which contradicts the functional requirements of the buildings. Cheops means "region of light," Chefren means "the appearance of divine light," and Mykerinos means "the constant power of divine light" (Jacq 1998: 71). In the hypostyle hall, as in the Temple of Amon at Karnak, the forest of columns is far in excess of the requirement of supporting the roof. The goal was to create a symbolic architecture in relation to the Ennead and the passage to the other world, in contrast to the functional requirements of the building. Karnak means "heaven on earth," and the temple was intended to be a "city of light" (p. 111).

In the sarcophagus of the Pyramid of King Unas in North Saqqara, from around 2300 BC, false doors appear on the wall to represent the doors to the afterlife, between the visible and invisible, or occult, through which only the spirit can cross. The vocabulary element in the syntax of the visual form of the architecture, the door, is placed out of context to represent a metaphorical idea. The vault of the sarcophagus, as in many temples, is painted with five-pointed stars, representing the abode of the departed soul. The vault of the building doubles as the metaphorical vault of the heavens; the architecture is a catechism of a cosmology or structure of being. The hieroglyphs on the walls of the sarcophagus are called the Unas Funerary Texts or Texts of the Pyramids. The text of the hieroglyphs contains a description of a pyramid: "I have walked on your rays as if on a stair of light to ascend to the presence of Ra … heaven has made the rays of the sun solid so that I can elevate myself up to the eyes of Ra … they have built a staircase leading to the sky by which I can reach the sky" (Carpiceci 1997: 53). The pyramid is intended as a metaphorical stairway from earth to heaven and Ra,

Figure 1.1 **Pyramids at Giza, 2589–2504** BC

the god of light and the sun. The actual staircase in the architectural syntax doubles as a metaphorical staircase, a metaphysical concept, which the architecture is able to convey outside its functional requirements, because the actual staircase does not lead anywhere, and the form contradicts the function.

The apex of the pyramid represented the sun, as the unitary source from which all things emanate, what the Alexandrian Plotinus (204–70) would call "the One." The apex of the pyramid was gilded, to reflect the light of the sun and to appear as the sun. The base of the pyramid, a square in plan, represented the material world, as the material world is always represented by the number four—four corners, four seasons, four cardinal points, etc. The edges of the pyramid are the rays of light from the sun in the formation of the matter of the material world. Among the polyhedral atoms of the elements of Plato, the atom of earth was a cube, and the atom of fire was the tetrahedron (a three-sided pyramid). In cosmologies from the Classical world to the Renaissance, matter originates in an incorporeal and inaccessible light, and unfolds in a geometrical progression from point to line to surface to solid. The point is the closest thing to the immaterial in the material world.

As matter comes to being from an unknowable source, the soul exits the material world toward an unknowable destination through the door to the afterlife, in a *circuitus spiritualis*, or infinite cycle of being, as represented by the uroborus serpent eating its own tail, which can be found on the walls surrounding the necropolis at Saqqara. The *circuitus spiritualis* is enacted by the architectural vocabulary elements: entrance, exit, descent, and ascension are movements enacted by architectural space. It can be argued that the movements enacted by architectural space themselves are metaphors to begin with, in that architectural space is a metaphor. Architecture defines a certain space, but the space only exists as it is defined by the architecture. Even though a space is defined by architecture, space can still only be seen as indivisible, therefore its material existence can be questioned, and it is more easily understood as a concept projected onto the material world by the human mind, as Kant established. Architecture, space, and movement in architectural space therefore occur only metaphorically, as elements of architecture as a form of artistic expression, or an idea in the mind of the viewer.

Ra, the god of light, was one of the three primary gods of Egyptian cosmology, the other two being Amon, the "hidden one," representing that which is inaccessible, and Ptah, god of creation and the material world. The three gods were the three manifestations of a unitary principle, and appear to be a precursor to the Christian Trinity, where the Father is inaccessible, the Spirit is light, and the Son is the body, representing the same hypostases of being as the Egyptian pyramid. In the Book of the Dead, the hieroglyphic text of the Egyptian afterlife, the soul of the departed is weighed by Anubis, the guardian of the dead, and judged by Maat, the goddess of justice. If the soul is heavier than a feather, the body of the departed is eaten by Ammit, female demon and Devourer of the Dead; if the soul is lighter, the departed is escorted by Anubis to the throne of Osiris, who sits in judgment as lord of the underworld. The concept reappears in Christian iconography: while the Pantokrator Christ sits enthroned in judgment, the soul of the departed is weighed in purgatory by Michael and Mary. The weighing of the soul in the Book of the Dead is recorded by Thoth, or Hermes Trismegistus, inventor of writing, hieroglyphs, and philosophy. The passage though the underworld, or the *circuitus spiritualis*, enacted by architectural space, is connected to the origin of writing. The word, or logos, is the spiritual made physical; the emanation theory of light is connected to writing also. The origin of writing is thus connected to architectural space, as the formation of an immaterial idea in the mind made physical in the material world. The grouping of three into one is found throughout the architecture of the pyramids and temples in Egypt.

The three pyramids at Giza correspond in their configuration to three stars at the center of Orion's Belt, so that the pyramids would enact "Heaven on earth," as Egypt was thought to be. Orion's Belt was the celestial residence of the soul of Osiris, god of the underworld. The pyramids are a cosmology of the universe, and they connect earth and heaven, life and death, in the *circuitus spiritualis*, symbolized by Ra in a solar boat on Nun, the primordial ocean, rolling a sun disk, which is manifested in the material world by a black scarab beetle rolling a ball of its dung along the ground, from which eggs are hatched before the sun disk is received by Osiris in the underworld. The material world and nature are rationalized in relation to abstract concepts of space, and metaphors for the creation process, in order to be seen as part of a cosmology.

The pyramid later played a role in theories of creation and vision itself in the Renaissance. In the *Theologia Platonica*, written between 1469 and 1474, Marsilio Ficino proposed an intromission theory of vision in which rays of light projected by the sun emanate in the form of a cone or pyramid if they pass through a small hole on a plane (as it would be in a camera obscura). As rays of light from the sun pass through a hole in the pupil of the eye, they emanate in the same way in the form of a cone or pyramid into the soul, acting as a lens or pineal gland, or camera obscura, as a mirror to what is perceived. Leon Battista Alberti, in his treatise on painting, *De pictura*, in 1435, also proposed a theory of vision in which rays of light were arranged in a pyramid. Surfaces of material objects are defined and measured by rays of light, which translate visual matter into intelligible matter, giving it the qualities of proportion, arrangement, and measurement. Matter is understood through light, and at the same time light makes the intelligible material, in the process of creation from the originary light, as represented by the pyramid in Egypt.

In the *De anima*, Aristotle compared the active intellect, the cosmic intellect, that which actualizes human thought and perception, in an entelechy, to light itself, in relation to the potential or material intellect, the *nous hylikos*: "light makes potential colors actual" (3.5.430a10–25) (Davidson 1992: 19). The active intellect, as light, illuminates what is intelligible in the sensible world. Commentators on Aristotle, such as Abu Nasr Alfarabi (870–950), in his *Risala* (pp. 25–7), or *De intellectu*, in the tenth century, described the light of the sun, following Aristotle in *De anima* (2.7.418b9–10), as making the corporeal eye, or potential vision, transparent or illuminated, in the same way that active intellect illuminates potential intellect. Potential colors become actually visible, and potential vision becomes actual vision. Active intellect makes potential intellect transparent, as light is infused into the *oculus mentis*, and the transparency of light and color illuminates the intellect through vision. In the *Risala*, "as the sun is that which makes the eye sight in actuality and visible things visible in actuality, insofar as it gives illumination, so likewise the agent intellect is that which makes the intellect which is in poten- tiality an intellect in actuality insofar as it gives it of that principle" (Alfarabi 1967: 218–19).

According to Alberti, only certain rays of light define the outline, measure and dimension of surfaces, the "extrinsic rays." The extrinsic rays define the outline of the pyramid of light in vision. The pyramid is formed between the surface of the material object and the eye, which is also the source of an inner light, in extramission. As Alberti says, "The base of the pyramid is the surface seen [as the base of the Egyptian pyramid represents matter], and the sides are the visual rays we said are called extrinsic. The vertex of the pyramid resides within the eye [the light originating from the eye corresponds to the originary light in creation], where the angles of the quantities in the various triangles meet together" (Alberti 1972 [1435]: I.7). The pyramid of light encloses the "median ray," which is variable and absorbs light and color. The median ray extends between the vertex of the pyramid and the surface of the matter, and fills in the color and shadow found within the outline of the matter. The "centric ray" in the center of the pyramid is the strongest of the median rays, and forms a direct line from the vertex of the pyramid to the center of the surface, exactly perpendicular to the surface. The position of the centric ray, along with the distance of the ray from the vertex, determines the location of the outline of the surface.

Following Alberti, Piero della Francesca, in *De prospectiva pingendi*, in around 1480, described the extrinsic rays in the pyramid of vision as lines which emanate from the extremities of the material object and reach the eye, in between which the eye perceives the material object and transforms it into an intelligible object, as potential intellect and vision are activated by active intellect (Francesca 1942: 64). The border of the object is described by the rays of light of the eye, in extramission, in proportion and measure, that is, as an intelligible object. The borders of the material object, established through measure and proportion by the extrinsic rays from the eye, determine how things diminish in size in relation to the eye, corresponding to the sharpness of the angle in vision. It is thus necessary to understand the linear qualities of objects in a picture plane so that they can be represented in a painting, as copies of the patterns of intelligible objects. The pyramid is a necessary tool for Piero in the conception of a visual image, whether in the mind or reproduced on a painted surface. The pyramid is a primordial form in the architectonic, or architecture, of thought and perception.

Intersecting triangles (they were referred to as pyramids) were used as diagrams of processes of vision, and they were used as diagrams of the process of creation, in the coincidence of opposites, as vision and intellection were often seen in relation to creation, based in Hermetic, or Egyptian, philosophy. A diagram of intersecting pyramids or triangles was used by Nicolas Cusanus in his *De coniecturis*, or *On Conjecture*, begun in 1442. Cusanus described the intersecting pyramids as *figura paradigmatica*. The base of the pyramid of Cusanus is the darkness of primordial origin, the ocean of chaos (Nun), while the apex is the originary, unitary, incorporeal light, as in the Egyptian pyramid. In between the base and the apex is found all created matter, as in the theories of vision of Alberti and Piero. The intersecting pyramids of Cusanus are divided into the hypostases of being—the terrestrial, celestial, and supercelestial realms—as in the trinity of Egyptian gods, Ptah, Ra, and Amon, and the architecture of the pyramids in Egypt. As the pyramids of Cusanus intersect, unity is everywhere contained in alterity and alterity is everywhere contained in unity, in the *circuitus spiritualis* between the ineffable source and the material world, and a *coincidentia oppositorum*. Human knowledge, represented by geometrical forms, is a product of the emanation of light from the One, represented by unitary form, the point or apex, though knowledge of the One is impossible, as in Plotinus.

According to Cusanus, the human mind reproduces the mind of God, the active intellect, in the forming of conjectures, or concepts and judgments, in *nous poietikos*, as activated by active intellect. Conjecture should proceed from the human mind as the material world proceeds from divine intelligence (Cusanus 1972 [1443]: I.1.5), in the same way that the light from the human eye corresponds to the originary light, and the intelligible becomes material as the material becomes intelligible, in the action of the intersecting pyramids.

Athanasius Kircher began publishing in 1631, and arrived in Rome in 1634, the same year that Francesco Borromini began his design of San Carlo alle Quattro Fontane. Kircher was brought to Rome from Avignon at the recommendation of Cardinal Francesco Barberini to assume the Chair of the Mathematics Department at the Collegio Romano. Kircher's first significant publications were the *Primitiae Gnomicae Catoptricae* of 1633 and the *Prodromus Coptus Sive Aegyptiacus* of 1636. Kircher also wrote about such diverse subjects as magnetism, astronomy, perspectival construction, geology, and music. His most important works concern the philosophical and theological origins of Christianity and Neoplatonism in ancient Egypt, incorporating symbolic interpretations of hieroglyphs, published in conjunction with his collaboration with Gianlorenzo Bernini on the design of the obelisks erected in Piazza Navona and Piazza Minerva: *Obeliscus Pamphilius*, *Oedipus Aegyptiacus*, and *Obeliscus Aegyptiacus*.

The *De coniecturis* of Cusanus was well known to Athanasius Kircher in Rome, who copied passages from it in his own writing, and reproduced the intersecting pyramids, as paradoxical figures of light and dark, representing the progression from unity to alterity and alterity to unity. Intersecting pyramids also appear in the *Microcosmi Historia* of Robert Fludd, published in Oppenheim by Johannes Theodore de Bry in 1619. Fludd's *Microcosmi Historia* was also known to Kircher, who appropriated many of its ideas. Corresponding to the celestial hierarchies, the nine levels of angels that mediate between human intelligence and God, Fludd conceived of the universe as composed of three triangles or pyramids (body, soul, and spirit) divided into three parts each (terrestrial, celestial, and supercelestial), reiterating the hypostases of ancient Egypt. The pyramids proceed from the apex of the spirit, simplicity, and unity, to the base of matter, complexity, and alterity. The procession is created by light from the sun, which divides the world in substantial parts. In the diagram of intersecting pyramids, the base of the pyramid of light is the Trinity, represented as the sun, and the base of the pyramid of darkness is primordial unformed matter, the Aristotelian substrate, represented as the earth. Intersecting pyramids of light and darkness appear in Kircher's *Prodromus Coptus Sive Aegyptiacus* in 1636, and in his *Obeliscus Pamphilius* and *Musurgia universalis* in 1650.

The diagrams of intersecting pyramids in the manuscripts of Fludd and Kircher correspond to the creation myth of Pimander from the *Corpus Hermeticum*, compiled by Marsilio Ficino and translated into Latin in 1471, thought to be the writings of Hermes Trismegistus, the originator of philosophy in Egypt, though as it turned out the writings were done by later Platonic philosophers. Cosimo de' Medici commissioned Ficino to translate the Greek manuscript which had been brought to Florence in the Renaissance, which described the creation of the world and the ascension of the soul through the hypostases of being. Hermes Trismegistus was thought to be the most ancient source of wisdom in Ficino's *Theologia Platonica*. Ficino's translation of the *Corpus Hermeticum*, entitled the *Pimander* after the first of the Hermetic dialogues, had a widespread influence in Renaissance art and philosophy.

In the *Book of Asclepius* of *Hermes Trismegistus*, philosophy is seen as derived from an understanding of numbers and relationships drawn from astronomical observations. Much of the architecture of ancient Egypt was based on astronomical observations; for example, aerating channels from the funerary chamber through the north and south sides of the Pyramid of Cheops are directed exactly at the northern polar star and the southern star of Orion. The creation myth in the *Pimander* of *Hermes Trismegistus* describes the ascension of light and the descent of darkness in the formation of the four elements, as in the intersecting pyramids, and the *circuitus spiritualis* represented by the Egyptian pyramids. Matter itself has the power of self-generation, from light, through geometry. Light is the word of the inaccessible god which forms an ordered world perceptible only in thought, an intelligible world, revealing to the mind a necessary archetypal form prior to creation, the *exemplaria intelligibilis*. The sensible cosmos is a copy of the eternal cosmos as the pyramids at Giza mirror Orion's Belt. In the creation myth of Pimander, God is described as the indivisible unit of number, which is the source of all numbers, and contains every number within itself, but which is not contained by any number. God is apprehensible by thought, but cannot be known, and is motionless and complete, lacking the movement and becoming of the material world.

A diagram of intersecting pyramids inscribed in a circle in Kircher's *Prodromus Coptus Sive Aegyptiacus* is described as the *Sphaera Amoris* or *Sphere of Love*. It is composed of the Phi letter, a symbol of the material world; the letter V, showing love moving toward God; an upside-down V, showing love coming from God; and the letter O, expressing progression toward the material world. Love flows from unity to multiplicity, from the apex of the pyramid through the hypostases of the material world, and it connects the infinite with the finite, the spiritual and the physical, as Giovanni Pico della Mirandola described in the *Oration on the Dignity of Man* (1486). The description of love is taken from an ancient Egyptian tablet called the Bembina Tablet, according to Kircher, an element of Hermetic philosophy. In the *Oedipus Aegyptiacus*, Kircher describes the diagram of intersecting pyramids inscribed in an oval as the root of the thirteenth letter of the Egyptian alphabet, the name for which is love, through which the mechanisms of the universe are put into motion. The diagram represents a magical chain of love flowing through the universe.

The hypostyle temple

At the Temple of Amon in Karnak, from between 1295 and 1186 BC, a hypostyle hall with a forest of columns accommodates the passage from the material to the spiritual world, and follows the course of the sun, the passage of which represents the continuation of life in the underworld, or afterlife. A double row of six columns is flanked by seven rows of nine columns on either side. Nine is the number of the Ennead, representing the process of creation and self-reproduction, as nine reproduces itself when it is multiplied by a single-digit number and the resulting two digits are added together. Seven is the number of growth and change in the universe, combining three and four, the spiritual and physical. Seven is also contained in the pyramid, which has four triangular sides. The open papyrus capitals of the columns along the central aisle represent illumination by light, while the closed-bud capitals in the side aisles represent darkness. The columns of the hypostyle hall, like the pyramids, present an architecture in excess of any functional or structural requirements, for the purpose of communicating an idea, a catechism or *edificium* of the structure of the cosmos and of being, enacted through architectural forms. The forms of the structures contradict their physical functions in order to provide the architecture with a metaphysical function, as the physical and metaphysical, or the sensible and intelligible, are bound together in being.

The Classical temple

In the Classical Greek peripteral temple—for example, the Temple of Apollo at Delphi, the Temple of Zeus at Olympia, or the Parthenon on the Acropolis in Athens (Figure 1.2), built between 447 and 438 BC—the peripteral colonnade is excessive as well, and not structurally necessary to support the timber roof. The timber roof is, for the most part, supported by brick construction behind the marble façades of the temples. The colonnades on the front and back of the Parthenon do play a role in supporting the exterior entablatures and pediments, but not all the columns are needed for the support. The columns convey a false understanding of the structure of the building to the viewer. The columns might be seen as the shadows on the wall in the Allegory of the Cave in the *Republic* of Plato, which deceive the senses and are mistakenly taken for reality.

Figure 1.2 **Parthenon, 447–438** BC

In the Allegory of the Cave, prisoners in a cave cannot see themselves or other prisoners except as shadows cast on the wall. The source of light, a fire, projects the shadows from across a road, through a screen, a "luminous embroidered veil." The cave is the sensible world revealed by sight, as illuminated by the sun, represented by the fire. The screen is a curtain wall, which is "like the screen at puppet shows between the operators and their audience" (Plato 1955: 514b). The shadows represent perceived objects in the sensible world: what we see are false representations of a reality manifested by an archetypal intelligence. The objects that we perceive are formed and understood as intelligibles prior to their being perceived; they are only manifestations of a pre-formed reality, as if they are puppets dancing in a puppet show, manipulated by a higher, inaccessible form of intelligence, the active intellect, and the *nous poietikos* or higher form of intelligence in human thought which is able to go beyond immediate thought and perception, and is able to understand how sensible objects are formed and perceived.

The columns in the Parthenon are as the shadows on the wall of the cave, false manifestations of the intelligible structure of the building, which can be understood in a metaphysical sense as housing a connection between the material and spiritual, as it is a temple, like the pyramids in Egypt or the hypostyle halls. The columns are the projections of a puppet show, being manipulated by a cosmic intelligence in an intelligible reality, which involves the participation of the gods Athena, Zeus, etc. The purpose of the architecture is to display the relation between the world of the gods and the world of the human beings, in both their connection and disjunction, in the same way that the pyramid displays the relation between gods and humans, and between the material world and its inaccessible source, the physical and metaphysical. The Parthenon represents such a relationship in the contradiction between the form and function of the building, which corresponds to the contradiction between the metaphysical and physical. All form is metaphysical, because form only exists as understood in the mind. The contradiction between the form and function in the building reveals the metaphysicality of form.

Vocabulary elements of the architecture are further made deceptive to the senses through the use of the Golden Ratio and other numerical relations for proportioning, and through the use of entasis in the columns. In sculpture—for example, the *Spear Bearer* of Polykleitos—the human body can appear to be "naturalistic," or conform to nature, because it is proportioned according to the Golden Ratio, which is found in natural forms. Objects in nature are recognizable as such because they conform to certain proportioning systems; nature is only understood as based in purely abstract concepts in the human mind. "Nature" is a construct of the human mind, in the same way that Kant argued that space and time are constructs of the human mind.

As nature is only recognizable in relation to numerical relations, so "beauty" is also only recognizable in relation to numerical relations. A body is "beautiful" or "harmonious" insofar as it corresponds to the numerical proportions found in nature; in other words, insofar as the a priori concepts or intelligibles in the human mind are projected onto the sensible world. Nature and beauty are subjective judgments, not external facts. The sensible forms of nature and beauty are the shadows cast on the wall by their real existence as ideas or intelligibles. The numerical proportions used in the design of the Parthenon create a "visual harmony" or "beauty" which exists only in the mind and has no relation to the actual structure or material presence of the building. The building is just a pile of materials. The numerical proportions transform the building into "architecture," that is, they allow the building to be understood in the mind as it is perceived, and they allow the mind to perceive beauty and harmony, the *venustas* of the architecture, but a *venustas* that is disconnected from the material of the architecture.

The Parthenon is considered to be the most perfect building ever designed precisely because it is designed to be imperfect, to take into account the distortions of the physical world which occur through the processes of human perception in the science of optics, which demonstrates that the physical world as it is perceived by the senses is false. The columns of the Parthenon are bowed out, to take account for the fact that the human eye cannot perceive two parallel lines as straight. The entasis corrects the optical distortion, and the columns appear to be straight, to be contained within two parallel lines. The Greeks understood that as light projects an object into the retina of the human eye, the object is projected onto a convex surface and bends. A straight line in the physical world appears as a curved line. A curved line can appear as a straight line, as in the column of the Parthenon, or the base, which is also bowed. Such a sophisticated understanding of optics was lost in the Renaissance, where the *costruzione legittima* or mathe-matically based perspectival construction of Filippo Brunelleschi and Leon Battista Alberti attempted to transform the sensible world into a regular geometrical grid, not fully taking into account the disjunction between sensible and intelligible form. The Greeks understood that the shadows on the wall can be distorted versions of the archetypal forms, and so made adjustments, so that the archetypal forms could be seen, in contradiction to the limitations of the senses, and the limitations of human reason.

There is evidence that the Greek understanding of optics played a further role in architectural design. Vitruvius, in his treatise on architecture, *De architectura*, in the first century BC in Rome, defined the vanishing point in perspectival construction as the *centrum*, the center of a circle, and the point of the convergence of all lines (*ad circini centrum omnium linearum responsus*) (Vitruvius 1931 [27 BC]: I.2.2). It is conceivable that the *centrum*, the vanishing point in perspectival construction, was intended by Vitruvius to be in the eye. Vitruvius wrote, "Scenography [*scenographia*] also is the shading of the front and the retreating sides, and the correspondence of all lines to the vanishing point, which is the center of a circle." Vitruvius appears to have been referring to *scenographia* as the method of representing buildings perspectively on a surface, or more generally as the application of optical laws to the visual arts. *Circini centrum* can be translated as "center of a circle" and also "compass point"; the *centrum* is either a vanishing point within a picture or the eye of the viewer at the center of a circle of projection of visual rays from the center.

The circle of projection corresponds to the shape of the retina and the pupil; the visual rays converging on the compass point or center correspond to the lines of vision from the retina to the sphere of the physical universe, or from the surface of the object perceived to the sphere, in the diffusion of light. Erwin Panofsky argued, in *Perspective and Symbolic Form*, that this system of representation is manifest in the curvature of straight lines in architecture, adjusting them to the laws of optics: "In antique optics and art theory," and in philosophy, "we constantly encounter the observations that straight lines are seen as curved and curved lines as straight; that columns must be subjected to entasis (usually relatively weak, of course, in Classical times) in order not to appear bent; that epistyle and stylobate must be built curved in order to avoid the impression of sagging. And, indeed, the familiar curvatures of the Doric temple attest to the practical consequences of such findings" (Panofsky 1991 [1927]: 34). There may have been a philosophical understanding of the center of the circle as corresponding to the intelligible or archetypal, which emanates into the sensible world in multiplicity, as the pyramid of rays of light emanates from the apex.

For Plotinus in the third century in Rome, the center of the circle played a similar role to the apex of the pyramid in Egypt. Plotinus, in the *Enneads*, described the hypostatic structure of being as a series of concentric circles around a center. The circles are determined by radii projecting from the center. The center is identified with the One, the inaccessible source of being, which is isolated from the circles. Radii from the center point define the position of the circle, but the circle has no actual connection to the center point, in the same way that rays of light from the originary source of light define sensible objects, but sensible objects have no connection to the origin of light. The concentric circles represent different levels of intellect. Those closest to the One are defined as Intellectual Principle, which can be seen as active intellect and agent intellect in Aristotelian terms, *nous poietikos*. Concentric circles further out are defined as Reason Principle, which can be seen as potential or material intellect, discursive reason or *nous hylikos*. The further from the One or cosmic intellect, the less a level of intellect is able to understand archetypal or intelligible reality. In *Enneads* III.2.3, the heavens revolve in circular movement in the likeness of cosmic intellect.

In *Enneads* II.2.1, circular motion imitates Intellectual Principle, and is self-generated, as in the motion of the Same in the *Timaeus* of Plato. Deviation from circular motion indicates the complication and flux of the sensible world, in contrast to the intelligible or archetypal, which are immune to such complication and flux (II.1.8). The lower intelligences of Plotinus are interwoven with the sensible world and influenced by sensations, thus unable to see beyond the false representation of sensible objects. The center of the concentric circles is motionless in relation to the circles around it, as it is unaffected by change. The motion of the upper intelligences is self-caused, while the motion of the lower intelligences results from external causes. The lines radiating from the center point correspond to the multiplicity of being (VI.5.5). Multiple radii form a single surface in the circle, as sense perception and intelligence are formed by an underlying multiplicity of forces, and in nature, smooth surfaces on the earth are formed by a multiplicity of forces or vectors. The form of intelligence, and the form of nature, contradict the function in terms of structure.

In *Enneads* VI.4.7, the soul is described as a luminous center in a transparent sphere, as in *Timaeus* 34; the soul is placed in the center by the demiurge and is diffused throughout the body. The sphere of Plotinus is illuminated by the center, by a ubiquitous undivided light made up of multiple material entities (radii) while the center, or source, is transcendent and has no material presence. The center of the sphere corresponds to the apex of the pyramid, the location of the incorporeal light that is the source of the corporeal light which diffuses and defines the sensible world. Robert Grosseteste, in the thirteenth century, differentiated between the incorporeal light, *lux spiritualis*, and the corporeal light, *lumen spiritualis*. According to Plotinus, the light diffuses intelligence throughout the cosmos, as the active intellect of Aristotle diffuses intelligence through agent intellect, and the soul is diffused from the center and "partakes of reason and harmony" in the *Timaeus* (Plato 1965: 36).

Scenographia, defined variously as architecture, perspectival construction, scene design or stage design, played an important role in Roman architecture, and enjoyed a revival in Italian Renaissance architecture in the mixing of architecture and stage design through the *costruzione legittima*. The role of *scenographia* immediately suggests a disjunction or contradiction between form and function in Roman architecture, as the surfaces of buildings were treated as part of an urban stage set, and concealed the structures of the buildings. The Romans made great innovations in engineering, in the function and structure of buildings, but the *venustas* of the buildings, their appearance, was nothing more than an appliqué of Greek motifs, as the Romans covered up their cultural deficiencies by pretending to be descended from the Greeks, by way of Aeneas.

Natura naturans/natura naturata

According to Johann Joachim Winckelmann (1717–68) in *History of the Art of Antiquity* (2006 [1764]), architecture is more "ideal" than the other arts because it does not imitate objects in nature; its forms are rather derived from the rules and laws of proportion, which are abstract concepts. The principles of nature might be imitated in the derivation of the laws of proportion, but forms in architecture are the product of a *nous poietikos*, an intellection separated from sense perception, rather than being the direct imitation in mimesis of natural forms. Francesco Algarotti (1712–64), in *Saggio sopra l'architettura* (1784), explained that architecture "must raise itself up with intellect and must derive a system of imitation from ideas about things that are the most universal and farthest from what can be seen" (Lavin 1992: 107), that is, perceived by the senses. Thus "architecture is to the arts what metaphysics is to the sciences." Architecture is necessarily metaphysical, because its design is derived from systems which are not directly connected to sensible perception. Architecture is a product of the mind, as Le Corbusier would say in the twentieth century, and so the form of architecture is in contradiction to the function of architecture, to the extent that the mind is in contradiction to the physical world. While the basic functionings of mind in *nous pathetikos* are derived from sense perception, the higher functionings of intellect in *nous poietikos*, where abstractions and universals are formed from particulars, are disconnected from sense perception, and reveal the limitations and contradictions inherent therein.

In architecture, *natura naturans* is contrasted to *natura naturata*. While *natura naturata* is the direct mimesis of nature, *natura naturans* is an indirect or idealized form of mimesis, the imitation of the forming principles of nature rather than the forms of nature themselves. According to Plotinus in the *Enneads*, it is the purpose of all the arts to not just present a "bare reproduction of the thing seen," the *natura naturata*, but to "go back to the Ideas from which Nature itself derives" (Plotinus 1952: V.8.1), in the *natura naturans*, the ideal imitation of the forming principles of nature. Antoine Chrysostome Quatremère de Quincy (1755–1849), in his *Encyclopédie méthodique* (1788), described architecture as more ideal, more intellectual, and more metaphysical than the other arts, because architecture must transpose the qualities of the forms of nature into its own forms, and it must imitate the "spirit" of the forms of nature, in the universal idea, rather than a particular form (1:495). Architecture imitates natural forms analogically, or metaphorically, rather than literally. For Quatremère, architecture imitates the ideas from which nature derives rather than natural forms as given by sense perception. The perfect model for this type of imitation in abstraction was the primitive hut of Marc Antoine Laugier (1713–69), described in the *Essai sur l'architecture* (1775). While the cave is a model for architecture in the imitation of the forms of nature, and the tent is a model for architecture in the construction of forms disconnected from nature, the primitive hut is the perfect model for architecture in the construction of forms in the imitation of the principles of nature. In *De l'architecture égyptienne*, Quatremère described the primitive hut as the product of the perfection in the human intellect of the forming principles of nature, and it was that perfection which made the architecture of Classical Greece possible.

While Laugier saw the primitive hut as a purely natural model, Quatremère argued, in *Encyclopédie méthodique* (1:454), that the primitive hut was already an abstraction in human intellect, derived from the principles of nature. While for Laugier the primitive hut was a model that could be directly reproduced in architecture, for Quatremère it could only be indirectly reproduced, as the wood of the hut would have to be transformed into the stone and marble of Greek buildings, for example. Thus for Quatremère the primitive hut as model requires a double removal from or double contradiction of the natural forms of sense perception, recalling Plato's description of the arts as "thrice removed from reality." According to Quatremère, Classical Greek architecture was based on an underlying conceptual organization of abstracted forms and principles from nature, but it required in addition a dressing or costume that was completely disconnected from the forms of nature, and purely ideal. The result is that the "imitative system disguises the object imitated under a veil of invention and masks the truth with the appearance of fiction" (1:467) (Lavin 1992: 111). The imitation of imitation was necessary because of the transposition of the forms of the primitive hut from wood to stone. The material transformation mimics the transformation from the principles of nature in the forms of nature themselves to the principles of nature as understood in the human mind and executed in materials manipulated by human ingenuity. The transformation from the natural to the artificial reveals the presence of human reason in the imitation of the natural forms, and it reveals the contradiction between forms as a product of human reason and forms as a product of nature. The forms of Classical Greek architecture are the product of *natura naturans*, unnatural imitation; they are a product of the artificiality of human reason.

According to Quatremère, Greek architecture entailed the *natura naturans* while Egyptian architecture did not, because Egyptian architecture entails the direct imitation of stone by stone. It can be argued though that Egyptian architecture in certain places, which can be seen as precedents of Greek architecture, transforms the forms of nature in an artificial way and filters them through the analogical mechanisms of human reason so that they become disconnected from and contradictory to the natural forms. The transformation of wood to stone in Greek architecture, though, created an additional level of a contradiction between reality and illusion. The illusion inherent in the false imitation in Greek architecture is a source of intellectual pleasure for Quatremère, in *De l'architecture égyptienne*, because the viewer of the architecture is "fooled without being led into error" (Lavin 1992: 243). In fact, architecture requires that the imitation does not correspond to that which is imitated, in order that architecture be an expression of human reason or intellect and that it fulfills its identity as ideal, universal, and metaphysical. Architecture requires the contradiction between form and function. It is necessary that "for us to enjoy imitation we must perceive that the imitating object is only the image of the imitated object" (p. 206), as in René Magritte's "This is not a pipe." It is necessary to perceive the architectural forms, the colonnades and entablatures, as shadows on the wall in the cave, as false imitations of the principles of nature, in order to understand the relation between the human mind and nature, an understanding which architecture uniquely facilitates. It is necessary for the architect to avoid either complete conformity to the natural model, as in the example of the cave, or excessively disengaged *natura naturans*, as in the example of the tent, in order to achieve a successful architecture of imitation. Imitation of natural forms is successful in architecture if the imitation does not appear as imitation, if what is being imitated is not perceived as being imitated.

Architecture must perform a slight of hand in order to represent the relation between human reason and nature as perceived, because nature in perception is already illusory, as a false imitation. According to Quatremère, architecture has a moral responsibility to present the relation between human reason and nature as false, in the deliberate artificiality of its imitation. Abstraction in *natura naturans* in architecture is the manifestation of human reason in physical form, and conversely it is the manifestation of the metaphysical in the human mind. Imitation in the *natura naturans* gives the architectural form a metaphysical function, which contradicts the function of the building in relation to the form. Architecture is a "reasoned art" (p. 241) for Quatremère because it requires an abstracted and artificial imitation, and because it reveals the human mind as unnatural, in the spirit of Enlightenment Romanticism.

Roman architecture

On the façades of Roman buildings—for example, the Colosseum (72–80, Figure 1.3), or the early basilicas in the Roman Forum—the Greek columns combined with the Etruscan arches, in what is called the Tabularium Motif (because the combination first appeared on the Tabularium at the west end of the Roman Forum), do not support anything, they are just surface application. The columns and arches, forms associated with structural functions, do not function in a structural way, thus the form contradicts the function. In later structures, the columns which appear to support the cross vaults in the Roman basilica structure, as at the Baths of Caracalla or the Basilica of Maxentius in the Roman Forum, in fact do not. They are again for

Figure 1.3 **Colosseum, 72–80**

the most part surface application, to represent the false veneer of a culture. As the Roman Empire spread east, the column capitals were combined with impost blocks, a motif from Byzantine architecture.

The twenty-foot-thick wall of the rotunda of the Pantheon (Figure 1.4), designed by Hadrian (with help, but not from Apollodorus, between 125 and 128), appears to support the concrete saucer dome which sits on it, while the wall is in fact hollowed out and filled with a matrix of intersecting radial and circumferential arcades to disperse the downward load. What appears to be a spherical coffered dome on the interior of the Pantheon is created with plaster infill applied to the walls. The exterior dome is not the same as the interior dome. The interior dome is nothing more than a stage set, playing no structural or functional role, but creating a perfectly spherical interior, to allow the Pantheon to function as an horologium, and a model of the intelligible universe, with the sun shining through the oculus in the center of the circle or sphere, as described by Plotinus. At the back of the Pantheon, at the intersection of the circumference of the plan and the longitudinal axis (perpendicular to the entrance), the sun shines through the oculus onto the spot on only one day during the year, April 21, the birthday of the city of Rome. The mock architecture of the plaster dome allows the building to be a catechism of the relation between numbers and the sensible world, staging the relation between the intelligible and sensible through the contradiction between form and function.

Figure 1.4 **Pantheon, 125–8**

Chapter 2

Medieval: Byzantine, Islamic, Gothic

Elements of Classical architecture were absorbed into Christian and Byzantine architecture, while elements of Classical philosophy were absorbed into Christian theology (the fusion of Classical philosophy and Christian theology is usually referred to as Neoplatonism). Christian architecture continued the disjunction of the sensible and intelligible through the contradiction of form and function in the architecture, a disjunction which played an important role in the conception of the Christian God. The Christian Church rejected the idolatry of paganism, the worship of physical beauty, and as a result was dedicated to the destruction of pagan temples. Christian architecture and iconology nevertheless contain representations of the physical world, in relation to the spiritual world, though the beauty of the physical world is de-emphasized in relation to the beauty of the spiritual world. Christian iconography rejected the use of perspectival construction, until it was resurrected in the Renaissance, because it was seen as a false representation of the intelligible world, and a glorification of the sensible world, as containing the perfection of the intelligible world. For the Christian, only the Christian God can be perfection, and the human being suffers in imperfection, as a result of the Original Sin, until the Second Coming. Christianity glorifies the suffering of the human being and the material world in their imperfections, and the guilt which results from their condition, unable to partake of the perfection of God except as an escape from the physical world.

The Byzantine church and mosaic

In the pendentive dome at the Hagia Sophia (Figure 2.1) in Constantinople, now Istanbul, the dome is separated from the pendentives by a clerestory halo of light, and the dome is in fact supported by radiating conch shell domes. The Hagia Sophia was originally built by the Byzantine emperor Justinian as a Christian church between 532 and 537; it was later converted to a mosque, and then to a museum. The building was designed by a physicist and a mathematician, who supposedly had no knowledge of structures and designed a purely theoretical structure. The form of the Hagia Sophia is thus not based on a structural function, but rather a mathematical, or purely intelligible, function, so the form contradicts the function of the building. Amazingly, the structure has never failed. The floating saucer dome represents simultaneously the connection between earth and heaven, with the square below and the circle above, and human and divine intelligence, and the impossibility of such a connection, in the contradiction of form and function.

In the philosophy of Plotinus, for example, human intelligence aspires to the unity of the One, the ineffable source, but can never know it. In the *Enneads*, the building, like the universe, is "ensouled; it has a soul which does not belong to it, it is mastered, not the master, possessed, not possessor. The universe lies in soul which bears it up" (Plotinus 1952: IV.3.9) as soul bears up the dome of the Hagia Sophia. Soul is infused in all things, but remains apart from all things, as represented by the dome. The sensible world is mastered by soul as the shadows are mastered by an unseen puppeteer in the Allegory of the Cave, and the dome of the Hagia Sophia is supported by unseen buttresses.

Neoplatonic philosophy was prominent in the Constantinople of Justinian. Agapius, a student of Proclus (412–85) in fifth-century Athens, lectured in Constantinople, while the "Hellenes" of the east, knowledgeable in Classical philosophical traditions, were absorbed into the new Christianity of Justinian. Constantinople was seen as a "new Athens." Classical Greek literature was revived by Greek-speaking citizens and descendents of the ancient Greeks, and Plato's

Figure 2.1 **Hagia Sophia, 532–7**

writings in particular were found to be compatible with Christian doctrines. By 529, when Justinian closed the schools of ancient philosophy in Constantinople because they were not Christian, Neoplatonism played an important role in their curricula.

Classical optics also played a role in the Byzantine mosaic. Mosaic images such as those in San Vitale in Ravenna do not conform to the *costruzione legittima* of the Renaissance. There is no horizon line or vanishing point, figures are not organized in space on any lines or planes projected in a single direction. The figures seem to float in a space which has no dimensions or boundaries, but which seems to be projected on the inside of a concave surface. It is possible that the figures in the mosaics are organized according to a system of perspective where lines of projection connect a vanishing point at the center in front of the picture plane, in the eye of the viewer, to a circle or sphere beyond the picture plane, corresponding to a Classical model of perspective, in what is called "reverse perspective." It is possible that the figures in space are organized along lines projected from the eye of the viewer toward the picture plane, being the rays of vision projected onto the retina, so that the images in the mosaic are images of the intellect or vision of the viewer, hieratic or intelligible images, rather than objects which occupy a real space. The "beauty" of the images is an intellectual beauty, rather than a physical beauty, a beauty which is meant to communicate the intelligible world to the intellect, rather than the physical world to the senses, as true being. The Christian image rejects the material idolatry of pagan belief, but retains the distinction between the intelligible and sensible.

The hieratic figures would thus hover self-supported at the center of a sphere in the Byzantine mosaic in the same way that the soul of Plotinus occupies the center of the sphere of the universe. In the *Enneads* IV.5.3, Plotinus suggests a different kind of vision, not subject to perspectival construction, where the sensible object can be seen to occupy the center of a sphere, and can be seen to be identified with soul itself, in vision, as a projection of intellect, or the intelligible in vision. For Plotinus:

> the whole object is seen, and all those who are in the air see it, from the front and sideways, from far and near, and from the back, as long as their line of sight is not blocked; so that each part of the air contains the whole seen object, the face for instance; but this is not a bodily affection, but is brought about by higher necessities of the soul belonging to a single living being in sympathy with itself.

(Schroeder 2002: 66)

This intelligible or hieratic vision suggested by Plotinus can be used to describe the image of the Byzantine mosaic. It is given in Plotinus that the sensible image is a product of the intelligible image, thus the sensible image can be seen or constructed in the *oculus mentis* from multiple acts of perception, which are combined in apperception or understanding. The Plotinian model of vision takes into account the intelligible reality of the sensible world and rejects the limitations of a regularized geometrical construction of the sensible world in vision.

Corresponding to Plotinus' hypostatic model of the One surrounded by the concentric circles of intellect, the rays of vision dissolve into a totality like the radii of the circle, and vision loses its structural framework in the same way that the physical universe does. The circle of projection corresponds to the shape of the retina and the pupil; the visual rays converging on the center correspond to the lines of vision from the retina to the sphere of the physical universe. Lines in space, like the horizon line, are perceived as convex curves, as they are projected onto the convex surface of the retina in intromission, or, in extramission, onto the concave surface of the retina and the concave surface of space. Plotinus described the cosmos as constantly moving toward the soul, or the center, "not in the straight line, but in the curving course in which the moving body at every stage possesses the Soul that is attracting it and bestowing itself upon it" (Plotinus 1952: II.2.1). Classical perspective is distinguished from the *perspectiva artificialis* or *costruzione legittima* of the Renaissance, by being called *perspectiva naturalis*, which is based on an attempt to understand the laws of visual optics in the human eye.

The squinch dome in the Katholikon at Hosios Loukas (Figure 2.2) in the eleventh century, symbolic of the passage from the material to spiritual worlds, is in fact supported by radiating cells. In the squinch dome, the octagon mediates between the square and the circle, as Spirit mediates between the material world and the ineffable source, or between the body of Christ and God. The same hypostases of the Egyptian gods are represented—Ptah, Ra, and Amon. The Katholikon accommodates the ascension of the soul to heaven, and the ascension of intellect from material intellect to active intellect, facilitated by agent intellect, through the word (logos), provided by the Pantokrator Christ whose image is at the center of the dome. The word (logos, or language) is also represented by the screen in the Allegory of the Cave, through which intelligibles are projected into the material world, as sensible objects or false representations. The prisoners in the cave are prisoners of language, which is capable of representing active or divine intelligence through metaphors, but bars access to active intelligence in its connection to the material world. The metaphysical is contained within language, and thus cannot be accessed through language in discursive reason.

The iconostasis in the Byzantine church, as at Hosios Loukas, the screen with the icon on it that separates the altar from the worship space, can also be seen as a screen between the sensible and intelligible. The altar in the Catholic church is the location of the Eucharist and the Transubstantiation, the transformation from the material to the spiritual, represented in the architecture by the passage from the worship space to the altar. In the Byzantine church, the passage takes place through the iconostasis screen, in the same way that sensibles are understood as intelligibles when their projections are seen to have passed through the screen in the *Republic* of Plato. In the Western Latin Cross plan, as opposed to the Byzantine centralized Greek Cross plan, the passage from the sensible to intelligible is enacted by the *costruzione legittima*. In the *costruzione legittima*, the altar

Figure 2.2 **Katholikon, Hosios Loukas, 1012**

corresponds to the vanishing point, and the aisles of the nave correspond to the receding diagonal lines connected to the horizon line. The vanishing point, the point of the least materiality in the material world, represents the passage to the spiritual world, like the apex of the pyramid.

The Islamic mosque

The striped voussoir horseshoe arches in the hypostyle hall in the Great Mosque at Córdoba in the late eighth century, symbolically orienting the worshipper toward the qibla wall and Mecca, are far in excess of structural requirement. The geometrical patterns in the arches continue the proliferation of geometrical patterns found throughout the architecture, in stone carvings, faience tiles, and architectural ornamentation. The geometrical patterns take the place of icons, as

Islam is iconoclastic, in providing a medium for the worshipper to approach Allah. Sufism in Islam is very similar to Neoplatonism in Christianity; the origin of being is understood in relation to the geometrical constitution of matter. Contemplation of the geometry is contemplation of divine intelligence and the order of the universe. The horseshoe arches frame the view of the qibla wall and orient the worshipper in prayer. The niche or mihrab in the qibla wall has no function other than to represent the passage to the other world, as a portal from the material to spiritual worlds, like the false door in the Egyptian temple, the iconostasis, or the altar in the Latin Cross plan.

In the muqarnas dome (Figure 2.3) in the Hall of the Abencerrajes in the Palace of the Lions on the Alhambra Hill in Granada from the fourteenth century (1354–91), the structure of the dome is concealed, and the geometries of the architecture are so intricate that they appear to be organic forms, fusing the mind of man with nature or the mind of man with the mind of God. In order to overcome the distinction between the organic and inorganic in human identity, the form of the architecture contradicts the function. The dome floats above the space below as in the Hagia Sophia, and is illuminated from the light above. The dome is a catechism of the formation of matter and organic form through geometry from the originary light which becomes corporeal light. Like the sensible forms in nature, the organic

Figure 2.3 Alhambra, muqarnas dome, 1354–91

forms are the result of complex unseen geometrical matrices, as in the *Timaeus* of Plato, or the cosmologies of Robert Grosseteste in the thirteenth century, *De Luce*, or *On Light*, and *De Lineis, Angulis et Figuris*, or *On Lines, Angles and Figures*. The cosmological conceptions of Grosseteste were heavily influenced by the Arabic Commentators on Aristotle. The understanding of the sensible world in terms of light and geometry was intertwined with the role of light and geometry in vision and intellect, as enacted in the experience of the muqarnas dome in the Palace of the Lions in Granada.

Avicenna (980–1037)—in the *Liber Naturalis* (*al Tabi'iyyat*), for example—compared the relation between active intellect and material intellect to the relation between the sun and the sense of sight in illumination: "for just as the sun is actually seen through itself, and what before was not actually visible through its light, so also the disposition of the [active] intellect is in relation to our souls" (6.5.5) (Brentano 1977 [1874]: 6–8). The light of the muqarnas dome can be compared to active or cosmic intellect. Active intellect makes intelligibles, the concealed geometry and mathematics, visible to the *anima rationalis* or soul, if the *anima rationalis* is turned toward active intellect in actual intellect or acquired intellect, *intellectus accommodatus*, as the viewer is engaged by the muqarnas dome. The material intellect is able to see the intelligible form of the sensible object, the geometry in relation to the form of the muqarnas, in the *oculus mentis*, by the light of the active intellect, which proceeds or emanates from a first cause, and ineffable origin, and illuminates the intelligible form of the thing in the spiritual irradiation of the soul. In the *al-Madina al-Fadila* of Alfarabi in the tenth century, active intellect was compared to the sun, and light imprints the intelligible form of the sensible object in the material intellect, as in a seal on wax.

In the *Liber Naturalis*, "The rational faculty, illuminated in us by the light of the active intellect, considers the particulars that are in the imagination," and "in this way they are rendered free from matter and its appendages and are imprinted in the rational soul" (6.5.6), as in a seal on wax. The active intellect is that which illuminates, or the *ellampôn*, while potential intellect contains what is illuminated, or the *ellampomenoi*, and the multiple particulars which illuminate, or the *ellampontes*, represented by the muqarnas. The illumination of the particulars in the imagination or *phantasia* frees the particulars from their corporeal dependence, in that the incorporeality of light can participate in them, like the first cause or the One can participate in matter, and the illumination allows the particulars to be transposed into universals or intelligibles, or sensible forms into intelligible forms, as they "do not move by themselves from imagination toward our intellect," because they are products of the sensible world. The intelligible form is not possible without the illuminated particular form, but it is not the particular form which causes the intelligible form, nor is it the faculty of human intelligence, which alone cannot exceed its corporeal mechanisms. The movement from the sensible to the intelligible is the product of the illumination of the first cause, and the active intellect, which enters the mind of the viewer from the light in the dome, and allows the intellect of the viewer, in its activation, to see the sensible, organic forms of the dome in relation to the intelligible, geometric forms, and to understand matter in general and perceived sensible forms in relation to originary light, illumination, actualized intellect, and intelligible forms. In order for this to happen, the form of the architecture, the muqarnas dome, must contradict the function, the structure of the dome.

Because for Avicenna intelligibles cannot actually exist in human material or potential intellect, because they are incorporeal and properties of active intellect, as Platonic archetypes, only knowledge or representations of intelligibles can exist in human intellect, as in geometry and mathematics, so the illumination of active intellect is not of the intelligibles themselves, but of the faculty in the *anima rationalis* to know the intelligibles, the actual intellect. The illumination is of the mechanism of the *phantasia* or imagination, the mechanism of the *anima rationalis*, and not of the potential intelligibles in *phantasia*. The illumination is not of the intelligible form in the *oculus mentis*, but of the perception of the intelligible form in the *oculus mentis*, in actual or acquired intellect as active intellect participates in it through emanation or illumination, as facilitated by the muqarnas dome. The perceived form does not become an intelligible in its being transported from the compositive imagination, but rather in its being perceived by acquired intellect, which is so disposed because it is in conjunction with active intellect through the illumination, as described in the *Shifā: De anima* (235–6) of Avicenna. It is the *oculus mentis* rather than the form itself which is illuminated, the flashlight rather than the object which the flashlight makes visible. The muqarnas dome, in its intelligible form, is seen by the mind's eye, not the eye. Rather than stage the idolatry of physical beauty, the muqarnas dome stages the beauty of the mind.

In the *Shifā: De anima* (247), Avicenna compares the ability of intellect to achieve acquired intellection through the illumination of active intellect to the eye which has been made healthy in its vision through treatment, so it is able to see clearly. The architecture is an instrument in the clarification of vision, of both the sensible and the intelligible. The architecture is an instrument of the activation of material intellect by active intellect, through illumination and the process of forming intelligibles through the perception of sensible form. The architecture is an instrument of the ascension of human intellect toward divine intellect, and its particular forms are an instrument to motivate the will or desire of the viewer to ascend intellectually.

Gothic architecture and cosmology

Particular forms can be seen to play the same role in Gothic architecture. The diagonal ribs which were placed on the cross vaults in the choir of Durham Cathedral (1104, Figure 2.4), one of the initial acts of the Gothic, have no structural requirements, and appear to function more as a text interwoven into the architecture. According to Paul Frankl in *Gothic Architecture*, the Gothic style began when diagonal ribs were added to the Romanesque groin vault, the rib being defined as an arch added to the surface of the vault. The Gothic is thus defined as involving the articulation of structure, beyond structure itself. The rib can be seen as a signifier for structure, a linguistic element in architecture, which removes the reading of the architecture from the immediate presence of the architecture, in its structure or function, in the same way that language functions as a system of signifiers which is removed from that which it purports to signify.

Gothic architecture is architecture as a system of signification, resulting from the synthesis of theology and philosophy beginning in the eleventh century: the articulations of structure which are added to the structure correspond to the articulations of theological tenets in philosophical terms. The matter or material presence of the architecture is disjoined from its intelligible structure, which is formed by the added structural articulation of the rib. The rib was the first vocabulary element in what would become an extensive language of forms developed for the purpose of the articulation of the intelligible structure of Gothic architecture, that is, the structure of the architecture as it is understood, but not immediately perceived, in relation to scholasticism. The vocabulary elements would include the rib, ridge rib, pointed arch, tierceron rib, lierne rib, bundle column, conoid vault, umbrella vault, and syncopated arcading, which would define Gothic architecture throughout its development.

It may be that the rib was developed at Durham to provide extra support for the groin, but it has been shown that the ribs in the choir aisles at Durham provide no support. Some ribs in other places in Gothic buildings have been shown to provide extra support, while some have not. The groin, the intersection of the curved surfaces of the vault, is already the thickest and strongest point of the vault.

Figure 2.4 **Durham Cathedral choir, 1104**

The structure of the vault never fails along the groin, but rather in the cells tangent to the groin; thus cracks appear perpendicular to the groin rather than along it. The use of the rib to strengthen the sturdiest part of the vault may have allowed the masonry of the vault to be thinner, and to be placed on thinner supports, thus facilitating the "dematerialization" associated with the Gothic, but the earliest vaults with ribs are not thinner. The ribs did nothing to alleviate the downward pressure created by the vault on its supports, though they did make the vaults appear lighter.

The rib may have been seen as a logical continuation of the vertical articulation of the wall, the columns and shafts, in a visual signifying structure, but the earliest Gothic ribs are continuations of Romanesque wall articulations, with a discernable visual differentiation. So it is reasonable to assume that the rib was not introduced in relation to the wall articulation, or to make the vaults thinner, or to provide extra support for the vault, or to represent the structure of the architecture as a skeletal body. The rib can be seen not to have been developed for technical, aesthetic, or symbolic reasons. Since there is no precedent for its development in England or anywhere else, the rib cannot be seen to be related to an agenda of cultural identity. Thus the rib should be seen in relation to the agenda of signification, a textual presence outside the material requirements of the building, the development of an architectural language for the purpose of signifying the relations developing between theology and scientific philosophy in the eleventh and twelfth centuries. The rib can be seen to play a role in the representation of a cosmology, and in the mechanisms of the scholastic method, involving compartmentalization and subdivision for the purpose of clarifying the articles of faith in relation to reason.

Geometrical elements in architecture in excess of the structural requirements of the building have always been labeled "aesthetic" or "symbolic," but if architecture is seen as a language, as a signifying structure in itself, capable of being a catechism or *edificium* of knowledge, as the cathedral certainly was, then the language of architecture, its geometry, can be seen in certain cases as being neither aesthetic nor symbolic. Of course there are many cases in which the geometry in the architecture is aesthetic or symbolic, either in its structural function or in excess of its structural function, but it is the particular case of English Gothic architecture, especially in the Early English and Geometrical periods, that for the most part the geometry can be shown to be neither aesthetic nor symbolic. Geometry is aesthetic in architecture when it has no relation to structure, and it is symbolic when it refers to something other than itself. It is sometimes easy to read something as aesthetic or symbolic when it was not intended to be either, and it is easy to misread architectural intentions in those terms, because architecture in general now is no longer an instrument of philosophical understanding, it is no longer a text of knowledge, and it no longer has a didactic function.

At Canterbury Cathedral, the structural logic of the French elevation is turned upside down. The rebuilding of the eastern end of Canterbury was directed by William of Sens between 1174 and 1179. William of Sens' work consists of the choir; the presbytery, across three bays east of the crossing; and a final bay of the presbytery, containing the throne of St. Augustine, the first Archbishop of

Canterbury in the sixth century. William of Sens was able to replace the piers in the new French Gothic style, but he was limited to the original Norman plan. The resulting new building was much higher, with slenderer proportions, pointed arches, and a ribbed vault. The choir of William of Sens (Figure 2.5) is considered to be the earliest surviving Gothic building in England. The architecture is a compromise between the desire to build a new cathedral in the French style and existing local requirements.

The architecture is French in that it has a semicircular ambulatory, flying buttresses hidden under the aisle roofs, coupled columns, acanthus capitals, and two-bay sexpartite vaults. While the walls along the plan are thick Norman walls, with thick piers alternating between cylindrical and octagonal, a combination repeated in the sculpted capitals, the height of the arcade suggests the French cathedral; it comprises about 60 percent of the elevation, and the gallery and clerestory above look diminished in relation to it. Responds rising from the cylindrical columns support transverse ribs which transform a quadripartite vault into a sexpartite vault in the French style, but the continuity of the French system is interrupted by the alternating piers. A single shaft supports the extra transverse ribs, while tripartite bundled shafts support the diagonal ribs and the main transverse ribs, creating an alternation which expresses the hierarchy of supports.

The ribs of the vault rise from corbels with alternating square and canted abaci, corresponding to the alternating circular and octagonal piers at the bottom of the respective responds. The square abaci are placed on top of the single slender shafts, which support the extra transverse ribs which intersect with the diagonal ribs at a boss along the ridgeline of the vault, while the canted abaci are placed on the tripartite bundled shafts, which support the diagonal ribs and the

Figure 2.5 **Canterbury Cathedral choir, 1174–9**

main transverse ribs which delimit the bays of the vault. The corbels are placed at the bottom of the round arches of the gallery, at the same level of the abaci of the arches and sub-arches, so the springing of the vault is carried to below the base of the clerestory, in contradiction to French standards. At Durham, the corbels were placed about halfway between the sub-arches of the gallery and the base of the clerestory, in the spandrels between the main arches, but the spandrels are much reduced at Canterbury, given the height of the arcade and clerestory.

The diagonal ribs receive the most well-articulated support, as opposed to the nave of Durham, where the diagonal ribs rest on the corbels floating in the spandrels of the arcade. At Durham, the structural system is contradicted by the visual composition; at Canterbury, the visual composition represents a logical structural system, but it is a false one, an intelligible structure, as the vault is supported by the arcade wall and hidden buttresses. The responds rest on top of the abaci of the piers, propped up on their projecting ledges, as in contemporary French cathedrals, such as Notre Dame in Paris (similar arrangements can also be found at Ripon, Reims, Laon, Senlis, Sens, and Vézelay). At that point, the structural logic does not coincide with the visual composition, as it is impossible to imagine an entire vault being supported on the ledges of abaci of shafts. While the arcade is extended and the gallery is well articulated with arches set in arches and doubled Purbeck columns, the clerestory is pushed back behind Purbeck columns and almost hidden under the severies of the vault. The upper walls of the elevations at Canterbury are much thicker than in France; they are supported by transverse arches in the galleries and aisles, and an internal passage above in the clerestory. As happens often in English Gothic architecture, the elevations become thicker higher up, contradicting any structural logic.

From the eastern crossing, the first piers in the presbytery are encased in a number of thin Purbeck marble shafts with acanthus capitals, which continue through the arcade level. The second pier is a simple thick cylindrical pier with a Byzantine version of a composite Roman capital. The third pier is octagonal with widely spaced thin attached Purbeck shafts, then a pier consisting of coupled columns with attached marble shafts, then finally a pier which is octagonal at the floor but becomes circular halfway up. The eclectic and eccentric variety of designs in the presbytery of William of Sens exceeds any structural exigency, or structural logic, and appears to be a display of eclecticism, or syncretism, for syncretism's sake, where the form contradicts any structural or functional requirements. Such excessive eclecticism would be the defining characteristic of the architecture at Lincoln Cathedral of Geoffrey de Noyers, who worked at Canterbury prior to going to Lincoln, and it would become a defining characteristic in the development of English Gothic architecture.

The design of the aisle vaults of the presbytery of Canterbury is eccentric as well, with lopsided five-part vaults and distorted quadripartite vaults connecting the original Norman aisle wall with a new arcade. This eccentric vault can be seen as a precedent for the "crazy" vault of St. Hugh's Choir at Lincoln Cathedral, believed to have been designed by Geoffrey de Noyers. The vaults in the presbytery aisle at Canterbury connect two bays of the Norman aisle with one bay of the new arcade, so William set additional responds in the aisle wall and created a ribbed groin vault, as at Durham, with transverse ribs which are not parallel, and a fifth rib in each bay which is a transverse rib in the severy on the aisle wall side. The ribbed vault continues the precedent set at Durham, and elaborates the disjunction between the function of the building and the elaborate geometrical articulation.

William the Englishman succeeded William of Sens at Canterbury, and his architecture introduces more elaborate contradictions between form and function. The earliest work of William the Englishman, the eastern transept, disregards William of Sens' work entirely. In place of the French-based tripartite elevation, consisting of arcade, gallery, and clerestory, in measured proportions, William the Englishman inserted tiers of arcades, a blind arcade above a solid wall, with alternating light and dark shafts, then above that an arcade, with alternating round and pointed arches and a passage behind it, then above that, rather than a true clerestory, a tall arcade with a passage behind it. In chapels in the transept, almost Islamic-looking pointed arches, with shallow arcs and multiple archivolts, are supported by extremely thin shafts with round abaci and round bases, unlike anything produced by William of Sens. In appearance the shafts have no structural relation to the arches, as they do not in actuality.

The clerestory windows are not aligned with the existing windows in the chapels, but rather with the sexpartite vaulting above, in mathematical sequences, so that the vault and the clerestory do not match the elevation. The transverse ribs in the vault are "stilted," that is, the curvature is flattened out above the clerestory, as are the diagonal ribs, in order to let more light in through the clerestory. The proportions of the arches in the tier below are irregular, with long flat cycloid-like arches alternating with squeezed pointed arches, so that between the vault and the elevations the architecture looks very strange and disproportionate, nothing like logical French Gothic architecture. Again, it is not hard to make a leap from the architecture of William the Englishman at Canterbury to the original and eccentric architecture which would be produced shortly thereafter at Lincoln Cathedral by Geoffrey de Noyers, taking complete liberties with French precedents, and Norman precedents, in their structural logic and clarity, and with the expectation that the form of the architecture corresponds to its function.

In the dialectical process of scholasticism, initiated in part by Anselm, Archbishop of Canterbury (1093–1109), logic might be deliberately contradicted in order to illustrate the relation between reason and faith. Anselm and his predecessor Archbishop Lanfranc initiated the building of the Gothic cathedral at Canterbury. The architecture of William the Englishman is an example of Gothic dematerialization, and it is also an example of English Gothic compartmentalization, where the vocabulary of the architecture is elaborated and subdivided (as in the rib vault at Durham) in a way that corresponds to the organization of the scholastic *summa* (into *partes*, *membra*, *quaestiones*, *distinctiones*, and *articuli*) for the purpose of clarifying and articulating articles of faith in the *manifestatio*. The articles of faith can be clarified and articulated in excess because they do not need to be proven, as they are given to and products of the mystical and ineffable divine. This was reflected in the motto of Anselm of Canterbury, "faith seeking understanding" (*fides quaerens intellectum*), as expressed in his *Monologion*, in the goal of establishing a faith based in reason, a project which culminated in the *Summa Theologica* of Thomas Aquinas (1224–74), giving reason for Anselm, who succeeded Lanfranc as Archbishop of Canterbury, to sometimes be called the "Father of Scholasticism."

In the writings of Robert Grosseteste, Bishop of Lincoln 1235–53, sensible form, *species sensibilis*, contradicts intelligible form, *species apprehensibilis*, as also described in the Commentators on Aristotle. When we perceive an object, we are not aware that the object we are perceiving has been constructed in our mind as an intelligible form. In the architecture, the sensible form, the design of the elevation, contradicts the intelligible form, the structural logic of the building. In the dialectic, the intelligible can be represented in terms of vision, "by the progress of sight from shadows" (Plato 1955: 532), from the dark beyond human understanding, as described by Anselm in his *Oratio ad sanctum Nicolaum*, to beings and stars, or the articulated vocabulary of the architecture. The exercise of the dialectic is ultimately carried out by reason in the realm of faith without the aid of the senses and culminates in pure thought, *noesis*, the "summit of the intellectual realm." This is represented in the visual realm by the sun, or in the cathedral, the light of the stained glass window, in relation to the geometries of the tracery and vaulting, in a progression from the spiritual to material.

At Lincoln Cathedral, short ribs called tierceron and lierne ribs are introduced in the vaulting without any structural exigency. According to Nikolaus Pevsner in *An Outline of European Architecture*, "A bicycle shed is a building; Lincoln Cathedral is a piece of architecture" (Pevsner 1943: 15). Straying from Pevsner's reasoning, the cathedral is architecture, a form of art, because it expresses an idea separate from its material presence or function or structure, its physical requirements. All art is metaphysical, and the cathedral is metaphysical because its architectural forms contain a text which expresses an idea, and the text is legible because the forms contradict the function of the building.

The vaulting of St. Hugh's Choir (Figure 2.6) at Lincoln Cathedral was possibly designed by Geoffrey de Noyers at the turn of the century, or after the collapse of the crossing tower in 1237 or 1239, during the bishopric of Grosseteste. The vault began as a variation of a normal quadripartite vault. In each bay, two bosses were placed on the ridge pole, perhaps because of the short width of the bays, dividing it into three sections, perhaps to accommodate the three clerestory windows, and making a symmetrical vault impossible if it had diagonal ribs springing from the corners of the bays. The continuous ridge pole, the first of its kind in a Gothic cathedral, which Pevsner attributes to Geoffrey de Noyers, provides bracing for the bosses or keystones of the vaulting. The ridge pole is slightly arched between the bosses in an attempt to stabilize the vault longitudinally. Between the bays, four ribs spring toward the ridge pole from corbels placed between the arches of the triforium; the corbels are supported by shafts which run down the wall to a corbel between the main arches of the aisles. The shafts alternate between circular and hexagonal, making no sense in relation to the vault.

Figure 2.6 **Lincoln Cathedral, St. Hugh's Choir, 1200–39**

Because there are only two bosses in each bay, there is only room for three ribs to connect the corbels and bosses: two on one side and one on the other of each bay. The asymmetrical vaulting follows from the even number of bosses in each bay. The cone-shaped clusters of ribs springing from the corbels are asymmetrical: two on one side of the rib separating the bays, one on the other. As the asymmetrical staggering is repeated on the other side, this causes the vault to be asymmetrical, with two ribs connecting at a boss with one rib on the other side, and one rib with two, on both sides of the ridge rib. This is called a triradial vault, with three ribs emanating from each of the two bosses in each bay.

The single rib connecting the corbel with the boss on each side is called a tierceron rib, or "third" rib, and it is the first appearance of such a type of rib in the history of architecture. It has no structural function in the vault; it is just placed on top of the severy, and could easily have not been placed there, structurally, though it can be seen how it might strengthen the vault by increasing the mass of the skeleton and reducing the size of the cells between the ribs. But such potential structural function is minimal in relation to the presence of the rib. The third rib reinforces the triune grouping of elements in the vault, introduced by the three lancet windows in each bay of the clerestory. Pevsner calls the vault "the first rib-vault with purely decorative intentions" (Pevsner 1943: 207): the first non-structural geometries in the history of architecture. The intention is not for decoration, but rather for the creation of an architecture as *edificium*, a catechism of the structure of the cosmos through the use of non-structural geometries.

The effect of the vaulting is that the vault cannot be read as a series of distinct vaults or bays, as can any other vaulting system. As Pevsner puts it, the most significant result is that it "invalidates the bay division which to French architecture has been and was going to be for nearly two centuries the basic fact of Gothic composition." As in every other part of Lincoln Cathedral, the architecture challenges the very logic by which it is composed, challenges its own architectural forms as a scaffolding or representation of the sensible world in relation to human intellect. The vault can also not be read as corresponding to the bay divisions of the side walls, even in alternation, as in the nave. The reading of the vault as a continuous surface is reinforced by the continuous ridge pole. The non-converging cells of the vault can be seen as a counterpart to the syncopated arcading in the aisles, and the triradials of the vault correspond to the Y-tracery in the windows, in the spirit of the architecture as composed of variations on a consistent theme.

As with the vaulting of the nave, Pevsner compares the vaults of St. Hugh's Choir to "palm fronds," but instead of being in a symmetrical mirror image on each side of the ridge pole, the fronds are turned over in a reverse mirror image. The organic is represented by the inorganic in the architecture, as natural forms are represented by mathematical and geometrical forms, depending on the correspondence between mathematical logic in human reason and that logic perceived in nature. But in St. Hugh's Choir, the relation between mathematical reasoning and natural form, between the inorganic and organic, is disjointed, as the mirror image is reversed and the laws of physics, or in this case mathematics and geometry, are put to question in relation to nature. The form contradicts its own function.

Correspondingly, in the *Commentary on the Posterior Analytics* of Robert Grosseteste, reason or *ratio* is seen as a mirror reflecting the *virtus intellectiva*, the *nous* or intellectual in thought, that is, the non-discursive reason or the part of reason which participates in the divine or the organic. This can be found in the *Enneads* of Plotinus, I.1.8 and I.4.10. For Plotinus in *Enneads* I.1.8, intellect shines into matter and becomes present in it, as it does in reason. Light is the medium between spirit and matter in the cathedral. Bodies in matter become living beings, but intellect does not participate in matter or adapt to it in any way, nor is it affected by matter in any way, or by the operations of reason; it is only present in matter in "images or likenesses of itself like one face caught by many mirrors" (Plotinus 1991). The concept related to the image which is given to reason is a mirror image of the inaccessible concept in intellect or *nous*, and the source of the mirror image in reason is the inaccessible bridge between the image and concept in intellection.

Perception of form in matter can only be a product of reason, as the understanding of the world is constructed through mathematics and geometry, which entails the perception of the image as it is imprinted in the imagination as it is a product of the intellection. Modern optical theory has established that the image of the actual object perceived, the *eidos* or imprint of Plotinus, or *species* of Grosseteste, is reversed in the process of perception, and that in order to perceive something, it must be constructed in an intellective process. While the actual sensible object cannot be immediately perceived, a representation of it is perceived as a representation in the mind, what Sigmund Freud called the

Vorstellungsrepräsentanz, the representation of the representation, the residue of the imprint that is filtered into the thought process, as a distortion, in a contradiction between form and perception of form, or function in perception.

Conscious thinking occurs in between intellection and sense perception, and it has access to neither matter without form nor the intelligible without the discursive process. According to Plotinus, human thought is suspended in a play of mirror reflections, as it diffuses and multiplies, as matter diffuses and multiplies from light, and thinking does not have access to what is behind the mirrors on any side of it. The vaulting of St. Hugh's Choir appears to stage the relation between reason and faith, between human thought and nature, and between mathematics and organic form, in the process of intellection, as caught in the play of mirror reflections. The architecture corresponds to the concepts formulated by Bishop Grosseteste in his writings, which represent the methods of thinking about the natural world at the time, in their synthesis of Aristotelian natural philosophy and the importance of the senses, and Platonic and Neoplatonic concepts which correspond to Catholic theological concepts, in philosophies of intellect. The sensible experience of the architecture of the cathedral is staged to lead the intellect to the intelligibles, the manifestations of the divine in the material world, and the bridging of reason and faith. The dialectical but contradictory relation between the form and function in the architecture corresponds to the contradiction between sensible and intelligible, organic and inorganic, reason and faith in the human mind.

The geometries used in the architecture—bent and curved lines of varying lengths, conic sections, convex and concave surfaces—correspond to the geometries described by Grosseteste in his treatises on light and optics, *De Luce* and *De Lineis, Angulis et Figuris*. The geometries are described by Grosseteste for the purpose of explaining the functioning of natural phenomena, in particular the diffusion and rarefaction of light. Grosseteste's description of the functioning of natural phenomena in geometrical terms is a virtual architectural catechism of itself, which corresponds to the architecture of the cathedral, which was built for the purpose of representing the current understanding of the functionings of the natural world, as a cosmology, in relation to intellect and faith, and the processes of intellection.

Paul Frankl revived interest in Lincoln Cathedral in the 1950s, mostly by focusing his attention on the vault of St. Hugh's Choir, which he called the "crazy vault." Frankl described the vaulting as representing the intention to separate the form from its original meaning, then to use the form as such in a different way, while at the same time giving it a new sense (Frankl 1962: 76). In other words, the structural geometries are used non-structurally, for the first time in history, for the purpose of expressing an idea not related to the function of the building itself, thus allowing the architecture to function as art and as the *edificium* of scholastic thinking and the synthesis of reason and faith. Frankl invented a neologism, "akyrism," from the Greek word *akyros*, meaning "improper," to describe the approach to the design, as a conscious mannerist tendency, a departure from precedent.

In the nave (Figure 2.7), built during the episcopate of Robert Grosseteste between 1235 and 1245, from each springpoint dividing the bays of the elevations, seven ribs rise from a corbel to the ridge pole. The rib perpendicular to the wall elevations on both sides of the ridge pole marks the bays of the elevations, and three additional ribs rise on either side of it in each bay to the ridge pole. The perpendicular rib and the ribs on either side of it connect to the three bosses in each bay of the vault. The ribs to the outside of the central three in each bay connect to the bosses which divide the bays of the vault. The ribs to the outside of the central five in each bay connect to bosses placed between the ridge pole and the walls, about one third of the way toward the wall.

The visual effect is that from below the ribs of each bay of the vault look like four-pointed stars, and from an angle, because of concave surfaces between the ribs, the vaulting looks like a series of "palm fronds," as described by Nikolaus Pevsner. The visual effect of the vaults as autonomous organic forms contributes to the disjunction between the vaulting and the bay system in the elevations, in contradiction of the French model. The vaulting conceals the structural system of the nave; the form contradicts the function, in consistency with every other part of the cathedral. At many places in the cathedral, especially in the vaulting of the nave and choir, an irrational design appears to be the result of a rational process, or system of structural logic.

The vaulting at Lincoln led to non-structural vaulting in almost every English Gothic cathedral, in the form of tierceron and lierne vaults, net vaults, pendant vaults, and fan vaults. The vaulting is far in excess of any structural requirements, as in the scholastic summa the thesis in the dialectical process is taken to excess in order to demonstrate the presence of faith through reason. The

Figure 2.7 **Lincoln Cathedral nave, 1235–45**

architecture is intended as an *edificium*, a catechism or cosmology of the geometrical structure of matter, as described in the cosmologies of Robert Grosseteste, and the relation between human intelligence and divine intelligence, or between what Grosseteste called *virtus cogitativa*, the *nous hylikos* or discursive reason of Aristotle, and *virtus intellectiva*, the *nous poietikos* or higher form of intelligence which benefits from the participation of divine intelligence, *intelligentia*. The architecture is designed to facilitate the *solertia* of the worshipper, the will to ascend intellectually. The vaulting represents the gap between the signifier in discursive reason and the signified in *virtus intellectiva*, between the words and syntax of a language and what the language is capable of communicating.

Such a gap is displayed in the architecture at Lincoln Cathedral, at the service of the mysticism of Catholic theology and the relation between faith and reason. According to Pevsner, the presence of the irrational in the rational is an English characteristic, in the "distrust of the consistent and logical" (Pevsner 1943: 122). The "palm fronds" in the vaulting of the nave appear to be irrational, organic forms, but they are the product of a development of a rational sequence of geometries. It was understood that this is how nature produces forms. The task of the architect or artist, as Plotinus taught in the *Enneads*, is not just to copy the forms of nature but to copy the principles by which the forms of nature are created. The geometrical and mathematical basis of the generation of organic forms is described by Grosseteste in his *De natura locorum*. Lincoln Cathedral can be read as a series of rational geometrical sequences which are set up in composition, but in which kinks are inserted to throw the systems off, resulting in unique, seemingly irrational forms at every turn—in the nave vaulting and elevations, transepts, or choir vaulting—to produce an architecture which, while based on precedents, in its recombinations appears to be completely original and without precedent. The precedents are there, but they are hidden and manipulated in such a way as to be unrecognizable in the new original forms that are produced.

The vaulting in the nave achieves the effect of a continuous surface, with the ridge pole, as does the vaulting of St. Hugh's Choir, but at the same time each bay can be read individually, unlike St. Hugh's Choir. In relation to the vaulting of the choir and transepts, the vaulting of the nave constitutes a variation on a theme not only in terms of the formal articulation but also in terms of the visual effect. In the visual effect of the nave vaulting, the distinction between geometry and organic form is blurred, as it is so often in Gothic buildings. The blurring of the lines between geometry and natural forms is particularly relevant to the writings of Grosseteste, who, in *De natura locorum*, attempted to explain all of the natural forms of the earth's formation—valleys, mountains, clouds, etc.—in geometrical terms. The apotheosis of this development in vaulting occurs at Exeter Cathedral, where the proliferation of tiercerons takes the form of a skeletal, organic body.

According to Georg Wilhelm Friedrich Hegel, in the *Introductory Lectures on Aesthetics* in 1818, the function of architecture as art includes "manipulating external inorganic nature that it becomes cognate to mind" (Hegel 1993 [1886]: CIX). Architecture has the potential to realize the identity between the organic and inorganic, overcoming the duality between mind and nature, and making nature accessible through mathematics and geometry. The identity between organic and inorganic for Hegel is spirit, or *Geist*. Architectural forms, as they are based in mathematics and geometry, can only imitate or suggest the organic, like the ribs in the vault; they can never be organic, and can only ever be symbolic of the identity between the organic and inorganic, as a linguistic form. Architecture can thus not achieve pure spirit; it can only represent it. Architecture succeeds as art when it appears to synthesize the organic and inorganic in its form, but in fact does not. The form of the form contradicts the function of the form.

According to Friedrich Wilhelm Joseph von Schelling, in *The Philosophy of Art* in 1802, architecture can only be an allegory of the organic. It can never achieve an absolute identity between idea and matter, universal and particular, or inorganic and organic; in other words, the form must contradict the function. The only way that any identity can be achieved is when architecture imitates itself in its functional requirements as structure and metaphysical shelter, and contradicts them in its form, so that the identity of the inorganic and organic, or universal and particular, is unimpeded. The form of the architecture must imitate or mimic the function of the architecture while contradicting it. Architecture is only art when as form it is released from its functional requirements and allowed to represent spirit in the synthesis of human reason and the organic, or in scholastic terms, reason and faith. Pevsner's bicycle shed is not architecture because its form does not contradict its function in structure or shelter, which is not to say that that is not possible in a bicycle shed.

According to Schelling, "Architecture can appear as free and beautiful art only insofar as it becomes the expression of *ideas*, an image of the universe and of the absolute" (Schelling 1989 [1859]: §107), like the cathedral. Architecture cannot be organic form, so it must represent organic form in the idea. The symbolic is necessarily divorced from the organic as the human mind is divorced from nature, requiring faith. The symbolic is the self-realization of the artificial construction of meaning, the signification of the impossibility of meaning in language. The Great Synthesis of Scholasticism, in its philosophical basis and visual forms, contains such a self-realization, as represented in Gothic architecture. Philosophy is "symbolic science," as described by Schelling, as seen in scholasticism.

In *The Philosophy of Art* of Schelling, §111, "allegory of the organic is expressed through the anorganic." As the imitation of the organic in the inorganic, in mathematics and geometry, architecture as art is a "parody of the mechanical building arts," an imitation of the act of building in allegorical representation, as in the elevations and vaulting of the nave at Lincoln. The organic form which best serves architecture, which architecture is best suited to imitate in the inorganic, according to Schelling, is the plant form, as in the ribs of the vaulting as palm fronds, because the plant form is already seen only as an allegory of the organism of the animal or human body, which is the ultimate function of the architecture, as realized at Exeter Cathedral. The plant form is easily reducible to arithmetical and geometrical structures, symbolic structures which are translated into the inorganic forms of architecture. The plant form is the closest form in nature to the crystalline, mineral form; it is the most inorganic of organic forms. As the closest form to the inorganic, it is the closest form to the structures of reason, which is why plant forms are easily described in mathematical and geometrical terms, such as the Fibonacci Series and the Golden Ratio.

According to Schelling, proportions in architecture are primarily analogous to the proportions of the human body, and it is through the analogy of proportions to the human body that the inorganic forms of architecture can imitate the organic. Such an analogy depends, as always, on the symbolic mediation of language. The harmony of proportions exists only in the mind, as they are abstracted from the sensible world. Harmonic proportions in architecture are only allegorical, a poetic function of language, a mannerist trope. Through the allegorical, the temporal symbolic, or the narrativization of the symbolic, the universal is intuited through the particular, or the organic is intuited through the inorganic. Through the symbolic itself, the universal and particular are undifferentiated, and the symbolic is able to represent the synthesis of the inorganic and organic.

In the vaulting of the Lincoln nave, extra bosses are connected to the ridge pole by lierne ribs—non-structural ribs that do not reach the bottom of the vault. The severy bordered by the outside ribs forming the perimeter of each bay of the vault forms an indented concave surface which allows the light from the three clerestory windows in each bay of the wall to enter into the nave. The clusters of ribs between each concave severy are in the form of cones, spreading to the ridge pole. Each bay of the vault thus has seven ribs, four of which would be considered tiercerons, having no relation to the structure of the vault. In each bay, there is a pair of tiercerons in each transverse cell, and a pair of tiercerons in each longitudinal cell, creating the visual effect of the elongated star in plan.

As in the vault of St. Hugh's Choir, the autonomous, delineated bays of the French vault have disappeared, replaced by a vault which reads continuously, aided by the ridge pole. The reading oscillates between a set of diamonds formed by the tiercerons and diagonal ribs on either side of the transverse ribs, somewhat like the vaulting of the choir and the star pattern formed between the transverse ribs. The reading also oscillates between the boss at the top of each bay on the transverse rib as focal point and the springer which is shared by two successive bays, with the seven ribs rising from it. As in many places in the cathedral, there is an oscillation in readings, a lack of clarity in visual effects. The experience of the perception of the architecture is not fixed and definitive; the experience is better described as an apperception, a combination of multiple perceptions that make up a whole experience, as defined by Gottfried Wilhelm Leibniz, in what would be called a psychological flux.

The apperception of the architecture, as opposed to the perception of it, enacts the Classical relation between logic or discursive reason and *nous* or intellect, which corresponds to the modern concept of the unconscious, that is, thought processes which are not conscious, in the process of perception. The Classical *nous*, the inaccessible part of intellect, is a "deep structure," the underlying matrix of relationships and meaning created by the syntax of a language. The apperception of a building is a "transformational relation" that reveals the deep structure, the conceptual organization or intelligible structure of a building, in relation to the material presence of the building. Such a relation is similar to Leon Battista Alberti's conception in the Renaissance of architecture as composed of two things: the matter (the building stone) and the lineaments (the organizational lines in the mind of the architect or observer). Alberti's distinction is based on the distinction in the *De architectura* of Vitruvius between that which signifies and that which is signified in architecture. Such a concept reflects the Neoplatonic distinction between the physical world and the archetype or intelligible from Plato and Aristotle, and between logic in reason and *nous*, or intellect, that part of thinking which is inaccessible to itself.

The distinction is enacted at Lincoln Cathedral in the transformational relation created by the oscillation in visual readings, along with the structural contradictions, the irrational organic forms in relation to rational geometrical sequences, and the symbolically organic forms in relation to inorganic geometries. All of this depends on the function of language, in the function of architecture as a language, and the relation between the word in language (the logos) and the metaphysical (that which is inaccessible or unexplainable by language). The relation between the word in reason and the inaccessible in intellect itself is like that of an object and a mirror reflection; the material forms of nature are only reflections of the divine idea, the archetype or intelligible, as the material forms of the architecture are only a mirror reflection of the metaphysical idea which the architecture conveys.

In the *Enneads* IV.7.6, Plotinus distinguished between perception and what might be called apperception, or multiple perceptions. Actual perceptual experience is multiple and diversified; perceived objects have no necessary connections in size or position, and can be perceived in a variety of ways. In human perception all objects and acts of perception are unified to form a coherent whole which structures the world around us. When the fragmented and variable sensible objects of perception, like the variety of shapes in the vaulting, "reach the ruling principle they will become like partless thoughts" (Plotinus 1966); they are organized in a conceptual process through the mechanisms of language, with the forms of the architecture functioning symbolically, as words and syntax in a language. The forms in perception contradict their function, because it is impossible to be aware in conscious perception of the a priori processes of the *virtus intellectiva*, or unconscious thought, which predetermine forms as they are perceived.

In *Enneads* I.1.7, "the faculty of perception in the Soul [*anima rationalis*, lower intellect] cannot act by the immediate grasping of sensible objects, but only by the discerning of impressions printed upon the animate [intellect] by sensation: these perceptions are already Intelligibles" (Plotinus 1991). The architectural forms of the cathedral can be understood as intelligibles, as can sensible forms, as they are perceived. Perception involves the immediate grasping of the sensible object, while apperception involves the processing of the sensible objects into the coherent whole, but that can only be done when the sensible objects are already intelligibles, that is, already have a symbolic function, in the terms of Schelling. Architecture can only be understood as a coherent whole. The patterns in the vault of the cathedral are already intelligibles anyway: they are understood as constructs of reason, not just mute objects, and they are processed in the process of apperception as images, or imprints in perception, rather than material objects—as form rather than functional objects.

The discerning of impressions printed upon the intellect by sensation as images or patterns is the function of discursive reason in language, not immediate sense perception; in Plotinus, perception is a function of language. Sensible forms perceived as a coherent whole, as in architecture, are a function of language. Architecture only exists in its relation to language. The sensual impressions in visual perception are copies or derivatives of intelligible forms, mirror images, or shadows of archetypes, as in the Allegory of the Cave of Plato. The vaulting in Lincoln Cathedral, and architecture in general, stage processes of perception. Matter itself, the material of the architecture, cannot be an object of intellection. In *Enneads* V.9.5, ideas are only projected onto matter, and forms in matter are only derivatives and traces of an original which is a product of intellection. A building is only a pile of materials without the idea which is projected onto it, what Alberti called the lineament, as opposed to the matter. A work of art can only be a work of art when a metaphysical idea is projected onto a material substance. There is an inherent contradiction between form and function in architecture, as there is a function associated with the material presence of the architecture.

According to Plotinus, from Aristotle, the substratum of matter, the material substrate, is indeterminate and shapeless, while everything in intellection is determinate and has shape; thus matter cannot exist in the intellectual. In architecture, function cannot exist in form. Without the observer, the cathedral is just a mute pile of stone and marble. There is no necessity for matter in the intellectual or *virtus intellectiva* for Plotinus, because there are no elements or compounds there, no shifting or derivatives, as in matter. There are likewise no shifting or derivatives in visual form. Matter, unlike form, has no identity or permanence, and is in constant flux. Because it is already everything in the intellectual, patterns in reason and perception, in visual form, there is no possibility of flux or impermanence, as described in *Enneads* II.4.3. The form of a building provides a coherence and stability which the function does not.

In the cosmology of Robert Grosseteste, *De Lineis, Angulis et Figuris*, or *On Lines, Angles and Figures*, the *species*, or *eidos* (incorporeal virtue or likeness of matter, form or pattern), is transmitted by light in perception and is reflected and doubled, as in the imprint of Plotinus in the *Enneads*, in intellect, as are the architectural forms of the cathedral. In the *Commentary on the Posterior Analytics* of Grosseteste, as light emanates from the sun, intelligibles are illuminated in the mind in the *oculus interior*. The *intellectus* or *nous* in mind abstracts universal ideas or *principia* from the particulars of sense to form principles. *Species sensibilis*, sensible form, is apprehended without matter; *species apprehensibilis*, intelligible form, creates a likeness in understanding, as for Plotinus. The perceived form does not necessarily correspond to the sensible object, and the form may contradict the function in perception.

The vaulting in Lincoln Cathedral can be seen as the *species apprehensibilis* of matter, abstracted by the *intellectus* to form principles, in the process of perception, or apperception. For Grosseteste, from Aristotle's *De anima*, the cosmic or active intellect, *intelligentia*, makes forms intelligible to the human intellect, in the *virtus intellectiva*, or *nous*, as light makes forms visible through geometry. The architecture of the cathedral can be seen as an *edificium* of this process. The geometry of the architecture enacts the process of the discerning of sensible objects as intelligibles, and functions like light as a mediation between body and spirit, reason and faith. As an Aristotelian, Grosseteste stressed the importance of sense experience, in the perception of sensible objects, in the formation of the intelligibles which lead to higher knowledge. The experience of the cathedral by the observer relies on sense perception, as well as apperception, as the architecture acts as a device for enacting the formation of intelligibles in the development of the intellect. The architecture, as it is understood as intelligible in its forms, was designed to facilitate intellectual development, and to represent processes of intellection and perception, in contradiction of the structural and functional requirements of the building.

The excessive amount of ribs in the vaulting at Lincoln reduces the surface area in the severies of the vaults, and creates a form that looks like a skeletal structure, an organic form, though it does not function like one. The vault has no structural function in relation to the elevations anyway: it is not a roof, but is below the actual timber roof of the cathedral. The vault is an elaborate mock-up of a structure to suggest the vaulting of the body of the cosmos, as a cosmology or catechism, and the lack of intrinsic structural function of the forms of the vaulting is revealed in the visibly non-structural elements, though they mimic structural elements, as architecture is a form of art in its imitation of itself.

This approach to architecture can be called mannerist: not in the mannerism that Paul Frankl suggests at Lincoln Cathedral, in the purposeful idiosyncrasies of the designers, but in the linguistic play between the forms of the architecture and their functions. The tierceron ribs in the vault of the nave at Lincoln reveal the non-structural function of the structural form of the vault. They constitute a mannerist, self-referential game. Mannerism in architecture is carried out in reference to the language of architecture; it is a linguistic exercise. Mannerist architecture, in that it depends on tropic or figural language, is poetic architecture. In the vaulting at Lincoln, the vaulting is a metaphor for the vaulting of the cosmos; the ribs are a metonym for the skeleton of the body, as a symbol of the cosmos; the severies are a metonym for the skin of a body, making the vault a metonym for the body as well. The metaphorical and metonymical function of the vaulting links the structure of the cosmos to the structure of the human body, suggesting the human being as a microcosm of the cosmos, which can be found in the writings of Grosseteste, anticipating the humanism of the Renaissance. The lierne ribs in the vault are a synecdoche for a structural rib, a piece standing in for a whole, and the tiercerons are ironic in that they are structural forms that play no structural role. In fact the entire vault is a form of irony, as it is not the structural or functional roof of the cathedral. In this way, the architecture is fully tropic and poetic, following the *Rhetoric* of Aristotle, and self-referential and mannerist.

Between the bays of the clerestory and triforium, the springer ribs in the nave vaulting form the shape of a cone, and rest on clusters of three long vaulting shafts, on top of a corbel which is three-quarters up the triforium, just above the abacus of the clustered pier. The vaulting shafts demarcate a clear division between the bays. The triforium is divided in half vertically by the arches in the top half, with the three minor arches inside, and columns supporting the arches in the bottom half. The corbels for the springers are at the midpoint of the top half of the triforium. In the divisions of the architectural elements, the numbers three and four are constantly present in combination, representing the trivium and quadrivium of scholasticism, and the spiritual and material worlds—the Trinity and the logos of the four Evangelists, or the four elements in matter, for example—connected by the mathematics and geometry of light. The three long vaulting shafts which support the corbel for the springer vaults stretch down to foliated corbels placed just above the octagonal bundle piers of the nave, at the bottom of the spandrels of each bay which the long vaulting shafts separate and divide. The springers begin below the clerestory, as in the transepts, and rise above the clerestory to the top of the vault, allowing the maximum amount of light through the clerestory windows and into the nave.

All of this represents a skeletal, structural articulation that has nothing to do with the actual structure of the cathedral. It is often noticed that one of the strangest features of English Gothic cathedrals is that the walls are much thinner than the arcades or vaulting which they support, that the structural logic of the French Gothic cathedral is turned upside down. At Lincoln, the vaulting shafts attached to the nave wall obviously serve no structural purpose; they extend the springer ribs visually down the wall, and visually attach the webbed ribs of the vault to the wall, which connects the wall to the vault as a continuous enclosing envelope, but not as a coherent structural system. Architecture as structure is juxtaposed with architecture as enclosure. The design concept can be related to that of the Pantheon in Rome (Figure 1.4), where the shallow saucer dome sits on the thick rotunda, but on the interior the dome is hemispherical. The structure is hidden on the interior, and the saucer dome becomes a hemispherical dome by plastering in around the top of the drum and covering it with the coffering to form the hemisphere. Architecture as structure is similarly juxtaposed with architecture as enclosure and architecture as form, or metaphysical structure; there is a disjunction in both cases between the two basic metaphysical roles that architecture is supposed to play. The disjunction between the architecture as structure and the architecture as formal *edificium* or catechism of ideas is what allows the architecture to function as art—what allows Lincoln Cathedral to be architecture as distinct from a bicycle shed.

In the aisles of the nave of Lincoln Cathedral there are two lancet windows in each bay. The bays are divided by Purbeck shafts which support the vaulting of the aisles. Below the lancet windows is a continuous arcade of trefoil arches, five per bay. In the north aisle the ridge pole in the vault is continuous. Purbeck shafts are placed at the center of a trefoil arch in the arcade, contradicting the logic of compartmentalization; the subdivisions do not correspond directly with the larger components. There seems to be everywhere at Lincoln a desire to contradict the logic of scholastic organization while at the same time enacting it. The numerical and geometrical organization of the scaffolding of the material world is self-contradictory, as if to suggest that it is in fact scaffolding, as in mannerist architecture, a reflection of an organization that is hidden from view, inaccessible to sensible reality, as in a Platonic distinction between the physical world and its underlying reality, which is manifest in the inaccessible. In the south aisle of the nave, the arcade is not actually continuous; the vaulting shafts are placed in front of blank spaces of wall which divide the groups of five arches. The ridge pole in the vault of the south aisle is not continuous either. The wall in the south aisle is also more elaborately articulated, with a stringcourse above the capitals, tooth ornament, foliaged bosses in the spandrels, and an additional vaulting shaft in each bay between the two lancet windows on a corbel above the arcade.

The articulation of the stained glass windows in Lincoln Cathedral, in particular the rose windows, the Dean's Eye, and Bishop's Eye in the main transept, has in common with every other signature element associated with Grosseteste's period a geometrical basis not related to any structural exigency, but rather to a metaphysical model of the multiplication and rarefaction of matter from light as described in the *De Luce* and *De Lineis, Angulis et Figuris* of Grosseteste. In the *De Lineis*, the generation of light into matter, and of matter into three dimensions, is described in geometrical terms. The *species* or *eidos* of matter is projected by light in straight and in bent lines (as in the Y-tracery), over convex surfaces (as in the piers at Lincoln), concave surfaces (the vaults), in acute or obtuse angles (as formed by the tiercerons and liernes), and reflected off concave surfaces, so that it is diffused, refracted, and rarefacted, or multiplied, as in the arch tracery and syncopated arcades of the architecture, in what Erwin Panofsky would call the "principle of progressive divisibility" of the *manifestatio* of scholasticism.

The *virtus* or power of the *species* is amplified in shorter lines (as in the liernes), and projected in three dimensions in the form of cones (as in the conoid springer vaults in the nave, non-structural rib-cones in the chapels behind the west front, or the umbrella vault and springer vaults in the chapter house). The geometrical rarefaction can be seen in the reticulated patterns in the masonry, the syncopated vaulting of St. Hugh's Choir, the syncopated arcading in the aisles of the choir, the continuous ridge poles in the choir and nave, and the octagonal bundle shafts throughout the cathedral. All of these elements entail the application of geometry to the architecture, as a model of the structure of the physical world, a cosmology, in the form of structural architectural elements, which have no structural function. Lincoln Cathedral represents the first overt intention of a comprehensive disjunction between the form of the architecture, in non-structural geometries, and the structural function of the architecture of the entire building, in the history of architecture.

A disjunction between form and structure is usually taken to be an anathema in Gothic architecture, especially as it is interpreted by Gothic revivalists and structural rationalists like Viollet-le-Duc. While Lincoln can be seen as introducing all of the signature forms associated with English Gothic architecture, it is at the same time almost the opposite of Gothic in its principles of organization, as associated with the French cathedral. The fact that geometrical forms were introduced in a non-structural way for the first time in the history of architecture suggests that these forms were generated not in response to the structural or functional requirements of the architecture, but for the purpose of allowing the architecture to express an idea or ideas as a catechism or *edificium* of a structure of knowledge or a philosophical system, which, as is well established, was a fundamental purpose for the design of the Gothic cathedral. The non-structural geometrical forms in Lincoln correspond to the geometries and structures developed by Grosseteste in his writings, in the great revival in learning and scholarship which took place at the beginning of the thirteenth century, which can be seen to lead directly to Renaissance humanism.

Chapter 3

Renaissance and Baroque: architectural theory and form

Alberti and Vitruvius

In the Italian Renaissance, Filippo Brunelleschi's dome for the Church of Santa Maria del Fiore in Florence (1420–36) conceals a double shell filled with a trellis to disperse the load, as in the Pantheon. The façades designed by Leon Battista Alberti at the Palazzo Rucellai (1455, Figure 3.1) and Santa Maria Novella (1456–70) in Florence, and at Sant'Andrea in Mantua (1476, Figure 3.2), visually present a structural system which has no relation to the building behind it. Alberti, an active member of the Platonic Academy and a friend of Marsilio Ficino, distinguished between lineament, or the line in the mind of the architect, and matter in architecture, as described in his treatise on architecture, *De re aedificatoria*, or *On the Art of Building* (1443–52). For Alberti, architecture depends on a Platonic idea separate from and contradictory to sensual perception or physical presence. In the treatise, "It is quite possible to project whole forms in the mind without any recourse to the material" (Alberti 1988 [1452]: I.1). Architecture is the projection of the idea onto the material, as Ficino asks in his *De amore*, or *Commentary on Plato's Symposium on Love* (1484), "Who will deny that the house is a body and that it is very much like the architect's incorporeal Idea, in the likeness of which it was built?" (Ficino 1985 [1484]: V.5).

This disjunction between geometrical form and structural function would become a hallmark of Renaissance architecture, especially in Italy, where there was a deliberate desire to contrast the visual structure or scaffolding of visual reality with an underlying structure inaccessible to sensation, one of the core ideas of the Neoplatonism at the base of Renaissance expression, as seen in paintings as well as buildings. In paintings this can be seen in deliberate contradictions of natural elements, as in the *Mona Lisa* (1503–7) of Leonardo da Vinci or the *Tempest* (1506–8) of Giorgione da Castelfranco, where different elements of the landscape do not correspond to each other; or it can be seen in the distinction between the Platonic idea of beauty and physical beauty, as represented in the *Birth of Venus*

(1485) of Alessandro Botticelli, where the idea of beauty, represented by Venus emerging from the sea, is transformed into physical beauty when she arrives on shore and is clothed by Flora, the personification of Florence, in contemporary Florentine costume. The painting by Botticelli is seen as an allegory of the project of the Florentine Renaissance, to transform the idea of beauty from Classical philosophy into physical manifestations of beauty in the objects of the arts. Such a theme in the painting was probably dictated by Marsilio Ficino, director of the Platonic Academy, for the Medici family, for whom the *Birth of Venus* was painted.

In Renaissance buildings, the disjunction can be seen in the façades which have no relation to the pre-existing structures, such as the façades by Alberti. It can also be seen in the recurring disjunction between the design of interior elevations in Italian Renaissance architecture and the structure of the building. In the churches of Sant'Andrea in Mantua by Alberti (Figure 3.2), San Pietro in Rome by Carlo Maderno, around 1600, in the mannerist period, and San Carlo alle Quattro Fontane in Rome by Borromini (Figure 3.6), around 1640, in the Baroque period, for example, the vaults appear to be supported by the trabeated systems of the interior elevations, as they would be in Classical architecture. The interior elevations are only decorative though, pure geometry, while the structural work is being done by Gothic-style buttresses hidden in bays behind the walls. At Sant'Andrea in Mantua the visual structural system of the façade is continued in the elevations of the nave, which appear to support the coffered barrel vault, but the vault is in fact supported by the hidden buttresses. The scaffolding of the material world is inaccessible to the senses, as in the Platonic archetype, and the creation of the Christian God, in a perfect fusion of Renaissance Neoplatonism. The same system can be found in the nave of St. Peter's in Rome, designed by Carlo Maderno.

This device appears to be intended to correspond to the Platonic idea that the visual reality as given by perception is false, and that the world can only be understood by recognizing the intelligibles, those things that can be thought and understood but not perceived. The real structure of reality lies beneath the surface, in the archetypes or intelligibles, in the Golden Ratio or Pythagorean Harmonies, for example. For Plato, in the *Timaeus*, the real structure could only be found in an Idea which was separate from human intelligence, the archetypes; for Aristotle, in the *De anima*, the real structure could be found in the intelligibles in human thought itself. Both of these treatises were available to scholars in England at the beginning of the thirteenth century, as they were to scholars in Florence and Rome in the fifteenth, sixteenth, and seventeenth centuries. The *Timaeus* was partly translated into Latin by Calcidius in the fourth century. And many other circulating manuscripts incorporated these ideas, in the form of Neoplatonism: the *Liber de Causis* (1180), paraphrasing the *Elements of Theology* of Proclus, and the *Theology of Aristotle* (ninth century) paraphrasing the *Enneads* of Plotinus, for example.

The façade of the Palazzo Rucellai (Figure 3.1), designed for Giovanni Rucellai by Alberti around 1455, consists of seven vertical bays divided into three tiers, with two doors. The proportion of the door bays is 3:2; the proportion of the bays above the doors is 7:4; the proportion of the other bays is 5:3. The bays of

Figure 3.1 **Leon Battista Alberti, Palazzo Rucellai, 1455**

the façade are seen by Alberti as areas, each being a square which is proportionally enlarged according to a consistent ratio. Seen as extended squares, the bays on the façade of the Palazzo Rucellai are one plus a half, one plus two-thirds, and one plus three-quarters. These three ratios are the octave or *diapason* (1:2), fifth or *diapente* (2:3), and fourth or *diatessaron* (3:4) of the Pythagorean Harmonies. Alberti explained in his treatise on architecture, written around 1450, that in architectural design "an area may be either short, long or intermediate. The shortest of all is the quadrangle. … After this come the *sesquialtera* [*diapente*], and another short area is the *sesquitertia* [*diatesseron*]" (Alberti 1988 [1452]: IX.6). Alberti explained that "the musical numbers are 1, 2, 3, and 4. … Architects employ all these numbers in the most convenient manner possible" (IX.5), because "the numbers by means of which the agreement of sounds affects our ears with delight, are the very same which please our eyes and our minds." Marsilio Ficino, in his *Opera Omnia*, called Alberti a "Platonic mathematician." The belief was that if the architecture contained the same numerical ratios as harmonic music composed with the octave, fifth, and fourth, then the architecture would be insured a visual harmony, a *concinnitas* or delight. The harmony and *concinnitas* are in the lineament, the line in the mind of the architect or viewer, and not in the matter. The harmony is in the form of the architecture, rather than in the function or structure of the building.

To the typical tripartite division of the Florentine palazzo, Alberti added three orders of Classical columns: Doric on the ground level and Ionic/Composite on the *piano nobile* and mezzanine. This type of ornamentation on a building would have been identified as an imperial motif associated with the Roman Empire, as almost every important state building in Rome contained the same tripartite division and hierarchy of orders. Alberti's design is thus a historicist collage, combining two unrelated building types, and divorcing the form of the buildings from their functions. Alberti turned the Greek column into a pilaster and placed it under an arch, contradicting the relation between the form and function of the column, though only as a façade motif. Early Christian churches featured arches placed on columns, probably intended as a deliberate contradiction of the principles of pagan architecture. The façade of Sant'Andrea in Mantua (Figure 3.2) is similarly a historicist collage combining two unrelated building types—the Greek temple front and Roman triumphal arch—visually combined using underlying geometry and mathematics, resulting in a contradiction between the form of the façade (pagan Classical) and the function of the building (Catholic pilgrimage church).

Figure 3.2 Leon Battista Alberti, Sant'Andrea in Mantua, 1470–6

The placement of the pilasters in the façade of the Palazzo Rucellai, dividing the bays, is determined by the proportions of the Pythagorean Harmonies; the proportions of the pilasters are determined by the Harmonies as well, as they are related to the human body, as described by Vitruvius in the *De architectura*. But the proportions of the pilasters had to be adjusted, as Alberti explained in *De re aedificatoria*, in order to achieve *concinnitas*. Alberti defined *concinnitas* as "a harmony of all the parts ... fitted together with such proportion and connection that nothing could be added, diminished, or altered for the worse" (VI.2).

According to Vitruvius, proportion (or *analogia* or *eurythmia*), is one of six things of which architecture must consist, the others being order (or *ordinatione*), arrangement (or *dispositione*), symmetry, décor, and distribution (or *oeconomia*). Order is defined as the arrangement of the proportion, which results in symmetry, which consists of dimension, the organization of modules or units of measurement. Arrangement (the Greek *ideae*) is the assemblage of the modules to elegant effect; proportion gives grace to a work in the arrangement of the modules in their context. All of these are elements of the lineaments, which are projected onto the matter of the architecture, in the same relation between mind and the sensible object. Alberti followed Vitruvius in his definition of *concinnitas* or beauty in *De re aedificatoria*: "It is the task and aim of *concinnitas* to compose parts that are quite separate from each other by their nature, according to some precise rule, so that they correspond to one another in appearance" (VII.4). *Concinnitas*, like apperception, transforms disparate and unrelated sensible perceptions into a coherent whole, in a disjunction between perception and what is perceived, a contradiction between form and function.

Following Vitruvius, Alberti explained, "It is the function and duty of lineaments, then, to prescribe an appropriate place, exact numbers, a proper scale, and a graceful order for whole buildings and for each of their constituent parts" (I.1). Alberti described the building as "a form of body" (Prologue), but which consists of two things, "lineaments and matter, the one the product of thought, the other of Nature; the one requiring the mind and the power of reason, the other dependent on preparation and selection." Thought and nature, or the sensible world, are distinguished as irreconcilable entities. The material of the building is in nature, but the proportions of the building, and the five other categories described by Vitruvius, are in the mind. Alberti described lineament as a Platonic archetypal idea, existing separate from the specific material configuration of the architecture, and separate from any specific application:

> It is quite possible to project whole forms in the mind without any recourse to the material, by designating and determining a fixed orientation and conjunction for the various lines and angles. Since that is the case, let lineaments be the precise and correct outline, conceived in the mind, made up of lines and angles, and perfected in the learned intellect and imagination.

(I.1)

The distinction between intellect and material entails a contradiction between form and function, between thought and matter as it is perceived, which defines human existence.

The contradiction between the material and the idea in architecture is suggested by Vitruvius in the first chapter of the first book of *De architectura*, where he explained "Both in general and especially in architecture are these two things found; that which signifies and that which is signified. That which is signified is the thing proposed about which we speak; that which signifies is the demonstration unfolded in systems of precepts" (Vitruvius 1931 [27 BC]). In the seventeenth century, the Port-Royal School of linguistics defined that which signifies as the word, the physical or material aspect of language, organized in a syntactical structure to produce that which is signified, the meaning or set of conceptual relationships created by the language. That which signifies is the matter of architecture, in Alberti's terms, while that which is signified is the lineament of the architecture.

In the *Timaeus* of Plato, the creation of the material world is overseen by a demiurge in a process where lineaments or archetypes are transformed into matter, as architecture would proceed for Alberti. The children of the demiurge are described as welding individual portions of the elements together, according to arrangement and proportion, *concinnitas*, and creating material substance from an archetypal pattern, translated through geometrical and mathematical proportion, like architects. Matter was bound according to geometrical proportions, as "the best bond is one that effects the closest unity between itself and the terms it is combining; and this is done by a continued geometrical proportion" (Plato 1965: 31), as in the arrangement of Vitruvius and the lineament of Alberti.

The material world "must have been constructed on the pattern of what is apprehensible by reason and understanding and eternally unchanging" (29). "That which is and never becomes" (27), the archetypal idea, or lineament, is "apprehensible by intelligence with the aid of reasoning, being eternally the same" (28), the precise and correct outline of Alberti conceived in the mind and perfected in the learned intellect and imagination, while matter is "the object of opinion and irrational sensation, coming to be and ceasing to be, but never fully real," as in the preparation and selection of the material of the building in nature as described by Alberti, and the flux of the sensible world as given by perception. The archetypal idea, or *archê*, is the precise rule of Alberti's *concinnitas*, and the material world given by sight in apperception is the appearance of the correspondence of parts of *concinnitas*.

According to Plato, true understanding of the *cosmos* comes from knowledge perceived by the intellect rather than the senses, and geometrical forms are imperfect realizations of mathematical proportions. As Socrates expressed in the *Phaedrus*, "For there is no light of justice or temperance or any of the higher ideas which are precious to souls in the earthly copies of them: they are seen through a glass dimly" (Plato 1952: 250). The true revolutions of the cosmos are grasped by the mind and not by sight, as the true architecture, as a cosmology, is grasped by the mind and not by sight. Enquiry into the nature of the cosmos is enquiry into the nature of the mind: "God invented and gave us sight to the end that we might behold the courses of intelligence in the heaven, and apply them to the courses of our own intelligence which are akin to them." To the extent that architecture functions as a cosmology, a catechism of the structure of the universe, it also functions as a catechism of human intelligence, of perception and intellection, as communicated through the lineament.

The beauty and harmony given by *concinnitas* and lineament through vision in nature and building are governed by the same underlying proportional systems and archetypal rule as the beauty and harmony in music. In the *De re aedificatoria*, "The very same numbers that cause sounds to have that *concinnitas*, pleasing to the ears, can also fill the eyes and mind with wondrous delight" (Alberti 1988 [1452]: IX.5). This is demonstrated in the application of the proportions of the Pythagorean Harmonies to the façade of the Palazzo Rucellai—the octave (the ratio two to one, also called the *diapason*); the fifth (the ratio three to two, also called the *diapente*, or the *sesquialtera*, meaning one and a half); and the fourth (the ratio four to three, also called the *diatesseron*, or the *sesquitertia*, meaning one and a third). These ratios are described by Alberti in Book IX of *De re aedificatoria*. Mathematics derived from musical harmonies is translated into geometries in architecture, just like the children of the demiurge in the *Timaeus* translate the mathematical proportions of the archetypal idea into geometrical constructions.

The proportions of the Pythagorean Harmonies were also prescribed by Alberti in *De re aedificatoria* for the determination of plans of buildings, as "architects employ all these numbers in the most convenient manner possible" (IX.5). "When working in three dimensions, we should combine the universal dimensions, as it were, of the body with numbers naturally harmonic in themselves, or ones selected from elsewhere by some sure and true method" (IX.6). The human body is the universal body, or the body of the universe, in the same way that the human mind is the intelligence of the cosmos, composed of the same proportional solids that are translated from the mathematical proportions of the archetypal idea, the universal dimensions, in the creation of the universe.

The disjunction or contradiction between the archetypal idea, the lineament, and the matter of the sensible world can be found in the *Birth of Venus* of Botticelli, painted in 1485 as a *spalliera*, or wainscoting panel for the wedding chamber of Lorenzo di Pierfrancesco de' Medici, a second cousin of Lorenzo de' Medici, in a Medici house on Via Larga. The Venus is a *venus pudica*, or modest Venus, a copy of the Capitoline Venus, a Roman copy of a Greek original, a copy of which was owned by the Medici. Venus is shown standing on a seashell, being blown to shore from the ocean by Zephyr. Zephyr symbolizes passion and love, desire for the Good and love of universal beauty, *venere celeste*; in Ficino's terms, that which causes all motion, as in the motion of the seashell. Venus is a symbol of love itself, and as she comes to shore being blown by Zephyr, she is received by Flora, who prepares to dress her in a cloak covered with flowers. Flora is a symbol of Florence; the reception of Venus by Flora symbolizes the transformation of the heavenly Venus or beauty, *venere celeste*, into clothed earthly Venus, *venere vulgare* or material beauty, that is, the transformation of the lineament to the matter. *Venere vulgare* is as the shadows on the wall of the cave, a deceptive manifestation of the *venere celeste* in sensible form, which is made manifest in architecture in the contradiction of form and function. The façade of the Palazzo Rucellai is a veil, a copy thrice removed of divine intelligence, conveying celestial beauty through physical form.

In *De amore*, Marsilio Ficino proposed, "If anyone asked in what way the form of the body can be like the Form and Reason of the Soul and Mind, let him consider, I ask, the building of the architect" (Ficino 1985 [1484]: V.5). Ficino was referring to a section of the *Enneads* in which Plotinus addressed the question that he posed as to how the beauty of the divine intelligences may be revealed to contemplation, and used the example of the architect. Plotinus asked, "On what principle does the architect, when he finds the house standing before him corre-spondent with his inner ideal of a house, pronounce it beautiful?" (Plotinus 1991: I.6.3). The answer for Plotinus is that the inner idea, a copy of the divine intelli-gence, contains the same principle in indivisible unity that the matter of the building contains in diversity. So it is for the *concinnitas* of Alberti, which is a "harmony of all the parts," parts which are "quite separate from each other by their nature," which Ficino called into question in *De amore*.

So the artist for Plotinus, through the power of perception, "gathers into unity what still remains fragmentary, catches it up and carries it within, no longer a thing of parts, and presents it to the Ideal-Principle as something concordant and congenial," as the rule by which separate parts correspond to one another in Alberti's *concinnitas*. For Ficino in *De amore*:

> In the beginning the architect develops a Reason or Idea, as it were, of
> the building in his soul. Then he builds, as nearly as possible, the kind
> of house he has conceived. Who will deny that the house is a body and
> that it is very much like the architect's incorporeal Idea, in the likeness
> of which it was built?
>
> (Ficino 1985 [1484]: V.5)

The house is a body because the proportions and arrangement of the house correspond to the proportions and arrangement of the body, as a work of nature which is a copy of the divine idea. As it was for Vitruvius, for whom, "if Nature has planned the human body so that the members correspond in their proportions to its complete configuration, the ancients seem to have had reason in determining that in the execution of their works they should observe an exact adjustment of the several members to the general pattern of the plan" (Vitruvius 1931 [27 BC]: III.I.4).

Alberti also described the building as "a form of body" in the Prologue of *De re aedificatoria*, a body which consists of "lineaments and matter, the one the product of thought, the other of Nature" (Alberti 1988 [1452]). Alberti, like Plotinus, saw physical beauty, in particular the proportions of the body, as communicating universal, archetypal beauty, in that beauty involves the harmonious composition of the parts of a body, according to mathematics and geometry as determined by *concinnitas*, according to the principles by which nature forms its forms, as in the *natura naturans*. The proportions of the body correspond to the proportions of all forms of nature, including harmonic proportions, and the different sets of proportions should be combined in the architectural composition, by learned selection.

According to Ficino in *De amore*, the beauty of the body depends on three things: "Arrangement, Proportion, and Aspect. Arrangement means the distances between the parts, Proportion means quantity, and Aspect means shape and color. For in the first place it is necessary that all the parts of the body have their natural position" (Ficino 1985 [1484]: V.6). As was seen, Vitruvius named arrangement (*dispositione*) and proportion (*analogia* or *eurythmia*), as two of the six things of which architecture must consist, the others being order (*ordinatione*), symmetry, décor, and distribution (or *oeconomia*). Vitruvius defined order as the arrangement of the proportion, which results in symmetry, which consists in dimension, the organization of modules or units of measurement. Arrangement is the assemblage of the modules to elegant effect, while proportion gives grace to a work in the arrangement of the modules in their context. Ficino's formula for the beauty of the body is a condensed version of that of Vitruvius. If for Alberti in *De re aedificatoria*, beauty is "a form of sympathy and consonance of the parts within a body, according to definite number, outline, and position" (Alberti 1988 [1452]: IX.5), or "that reasoned harmony of all the parts within a body" (VI.2), then the lineaments are expected to prescribe the appropriate location, mathematical proportions, scaling, and composition for a building as a form of a body.

Plotinus, in the *Enneads*, used similar terms in defining physical beauty: "Almost everyone declares that the symmetry of the parts toward each other and toward a whole, with besides, a certain charm of color, constitutes the beauty recognized by the eye, that in visible things, as indeed in all else, universally, the beautiful thing is essentially symmetrical, patterned" (Plotinus 1991: I.6.1). Plotinus is more in agreement with Alberti's definition of *concinnitas*, and less in agreement with Ficino's formula, when he expressed: "Only a compound can be beautiful, never anything devoid of parts; and only a whole; the several parts will have beauty, not in themselves, but only as working together to give a comely total. Yet beauty in an aggregate demands beauty in details … its law must run throughout." Similarly, for Alberti, *concinnitas* involves the aggregate beauty which is derived from the combination of the individual parts, but not from the beauty of the individual parts. The aggregate of the *concinnitas* creates a connection between all the parts, and therein lies the beauty.

But of course, for Ficino in *De amore*, the qualities of arrangement, proportion, and aspect are not actually a part of the body, because they exist separately of an individual body, and thus belong to the lineament of the body, or the lines, in Alberti's terms, rather than the matter. Ficino asked "But who would call lines (which lack breadth and depth, which are necessary to the body) bodies?"

(Ficino 1985 [1484]: V.6). Arrangement entails spaces between parts rather than the parts themselves, and proportions are boundaries of quantities, which are "surfaces and lines and points," or points, lines, and planes, which Ficino defined as the qualities of essence, being, and virtue in the *Opera Omnia*. Thus, for Ficino in *De amore*, "From all these things it is clear that beauty is so alien to the mass of body that it never imparts itself to matter itself unless the matter has been prepared with the three incorporeal preparations which we have mentioned," which exist only in the mind of the artist or architect, as lineaments, in the terms of Alberti.

The aesthetics of Leon Battista Alberti, as they are manifest in his architecture and writing, and are infused with the concepts of Plato and Plotinus, play an important part in the humanist project of the Renaissance in Italy and the revival of the Classical standards in preference to Medieval standards. The humanist activity of the court of Nicholas V, Tommaso Parentucelli, in particular the writings of Nicolas Cusanus, and the translations of the manuscripts which were brought to Florence during the fall of the Byzantine empire, and carried out primarily by Marsilio Ficino for the Medici family at the Platonic Academy, including most of the works of Plato which had been previously unavailable in Latin, provided a textual basis for a theory of the arts which pervaded the production of the Renaissance. This theory of the arts, based principally on the writings of Plato, Plotinus, Proclus, Pseudo-Dionysius, Cusanus, Ficino and Pico, with evidence of it found in the work of Brunelleschi, Botticelli, Michelangelo, Bramante, and Raffaello, as well as Alberti, involved at its core the concept of a contradiction between visual form and function, based on the contradiction between the sensible world as given by the senses and the archetypal or intelligible world in the revival of Classical philosophy.

Mannerism

At the Church of San Satiro in Milan, the trompe l'oeil perspectival construction of Donato Bramante (1444–1514) creates an illusionistic space to fill in for the absent altar space, as Andrea Mantegna's trompe l'oeil perspective painting fills in for the oculus and balcony in the ceiling of the Camera Picta (1465–74) in the Palazzo Ducale in Mantua, and the painted walls in Leonardo da Vinci's *Last Supper* (1495–7) extend the architectural space of the refectory of Santa Maria delle Grazie in Milan behind the picture plane. In these examples, painted architectural space is a suitable substitute for real architectural space, as the real architectural space only exists as constructed by the lineaments in the mind to begin with, and the form is seen as contradicting the function. The systems of mathematically based perspectival construction, the *costruzione legittima*, which were designed as the scaffolding for a constructed and false representation of reality or real space, become the reality or real space itself, as the physical world constructed in the mind is permanently disjoined from the physical world as perceived as separate from the mind. In Renaissance humanism, the scaffolding of the world constructed in the mind is seen as related to the scaffolding of the real world in its structural architectonics; this relationship would come to an end with the death of humanism and the birth of the scientific revolution, the Enlightenment and the Age of Reason, and as a result, Romanticism.

Modern science tells us that the natural world is ultimately not completely accessible to the human mind, that it is impossible to see the limited functions of human reason as compatible with the complexities of the natural world. Galileo was the first to make this clear. The result was a perceived alienation of the human mind from the natural world, the basis of Romanticism, resulting in an even more profound contradiction between form and function in the arts. This contradiction is clearly present in Classical, Medieval, and Renaissance architecture, which lay a continuously developing groundwork for modern conceptions of human identity as they are manifest in the Enlightenment and beyond, with the contradiction between form and function in the visual arts as an underlying symptom. The mannerist and Baroque periods establish a more elaborate bridge between Renaissance and Enlightenment identity, furthering the contradictions between form and function in the visual arts. Paintings by Parmigianino and Bronzino present human bodies which are deliberately distorted to the point that they bear little relation to the real human body; the cultivated artificiality of the paintings severs any relationship between the body in nature and the body in the human mind. The form of the bodies in the paintings purposefully contradicts the natural function of the body, as the form of the trompe l'oeil compositions in the architecture contradicts the natural function of the building, in the mannerist prediction of further romantic alienation to come.

In the vestibule of the Laurentian Library (begun 1525) in Florence by Michelangelo, the structural logic of the Classical system is turned upside down and inside out, in a self-referential mannerist game where the rules of composition are purposefully broken and the form deliberately contradicts the function. Michelangelo deliberately and overtly broke the rules of Classical architecture. He was able to do so because of his fame and influence. Anyone else would have been scorned for breaking the rules in such a way. Beginning with Michelangelo, and the cult of personality in the arts, the breaking of the rules became an institution of creativity in the arts, in particular the breaking of the rules of representation, and the contradiction between form and function in representation. Mannerism was perhaps the result of increasing political and social instability on the Italian peninsula; the treatment of forms in art reflects the necessity of political and social change, in the turmoil of progress. The contradiction between form and function is a symptom of such treatment and instability, undermining the idea of art as a representation of a coherent, harmonious, or hegemonic social order. Form contradicts function in politics and society as well; a society perceived as harmonious from the exterior is often the most repressive, while a society perceived as chaotic from the exterior is often the most creative.

At Michelangelo's Porta Pia (1562, Figure 3.3) in Rome, elements of Classical trabeation are placed out of context and rendered nonsensical. Columns

Figure 3.3 **Michelangelo, Porta Pia, 1562**

are truncated, pediments are placed inside each other, and scrolls are turned on their side. The result is an anthropomorphization of the abstract architectural vocabulary elements, turning the architecture into sculpture, blurring the line between the abstract and figural, between the tectonic and representational. In the sculptural treatment of the architecture, vocabulary elements are also used as literary puns—the dish and towel, a symbol of the medical profession, for the "Medici," and the *palle* on the crenellation, a reference to the Medici family coat of arms. The Porta Pia was commissioned by the last Medici pope, Pius IV. The bricks of the Aurelian wall in which the gate is set are used in combination with travertine for the sculptural elements, but the entire gate is turned around, facing toward the city of Rome down the Via Venti Settembre, in contradiction to all Roman gates which face outward from the city. The entire gate is designed in a way that the form deliberately contradicts the function, in terms of the function of the building, and the function of architectural vocabulary elements in terms of sculpture and literary representation. Michelangelo's design for the Porta Pia is a perverted commentary on the nature of architectural and artistic representation. It would be inspirational in Robert Venturi's thesis in *Complexity and Contradiction in Architecture*.

At Giulio Romano's Palazzo del Tè in Mantua (1527, Figure 3.4), the mannerist masterpiece on axis with Alberti's Sant'Andrea, sections of the

Figure 3.4 **Giulio Romano, Palazzo del Tè, 1527**

Classical Greek entablature are cut out, and columns are taken out from under pediments, to reveal the contradiction between the structural form and the structural function. The trabeated Greek structural system which Alberti placed on the façade of Sant'Andrea, in contradiction to the actual structure of the building, is employed by Romano at the Palazzo del Tè, contradicting the structure of the building in the same way. But at the Palazzo del Tè the disingenuousness of the façade architecture, the contradiction between the form and function, is revealed in the architectural vocabulary of the façade itself, by slipping down pieces of the architrave, or removing columns from under pediments, to demonstrate that the representation of the structural system could not function in any way structurally, giving away the game played by Alberti down the street half a century earlier, revealing the contradiction between the form and function of the building by creating a contradiction between the form and function of the façade vocabulary. The architecture is an architecture of excess and contradiction; it is a self-referential mannerist game for the benefit of a well-educated humanist court. The architecture is a reference to itself, to the project of the revival of Classical architecture in Renaissance architecture, and the resulting contradictions between form and function in the attempt to paste the forms of one society onto the functions of another society in a historicist collage. The history of architecture is filled with such mismatched pastings, for the purpose of attempting to symbolize the identity of a society. Structural linguistics and deconstruction in the twentieth century have revealed the limitations of the role of the symbolic in language and art and architecture. As will be seen, with the obsolescence of the ornamental in twentieth-century architecture, syntax replaced symbolism as the primary operational element of architectural composition.

Mannerism in architecture is carried out in reference to the language of architecture; it is a linguistic exercise. The mannerist compositional devices of Michelangelo and Romano are based on the rules of figurative or tropic language taken from Aristotle's *Rhetoric*, a popular book in the humanist courts at the time. Tropes or figures of speech in poetic language, such as metaphor or synecdoche, contradict the ability of the language to make sense or convey meaning. In language or architecture, poetic expression requires the contradiction between form and function. Among the fourteen tropes described in the *Rhetoric*, the four main tropes are metaphor, metonymy, synecdoche, and irony. A metaphor is a comparison of two unrelated things for the purpose of describing one of the things: "the world is a stage," for example. The metaphor is a simple combination of two ideas, two signifiers to form a new signified, a condensation as Jacques Lacan would point out. The metaphor is poetic or figural language—it makes no literal sense, and requires a contradiction in terms in order to convey an idea. The form has to contradict the function. A metonym is a form of a metaphor, comparing two things in order to describe something, usually in reference to the human body: the "foot of a hill," the "mouth of a river," the "eye of a storm," the "leg of a table," etc.

The metonym is different from the metaphor in that a displacement takes place, where the part of the body becomes part of nature or an object. The displacement is seen in contradiction to the condensation, which are the two principal methods of Freudian dream construction, as pointed out by Lacan. Again, the metonym is poetic, figural language and makes no literal sense. Figural language is necessary in human expression and communication, especially poetic expression, or the expression of the human condition. The fact is that a great part of language is nonsensical. According to Giambattista Vico, metaphor was necessary for the ancient Greeks in mythology, to anthropomorphize nature in order to understand it or at least come to terms with it. According to Vico, metaphor was the dominant trope in the Greek language. Metonymy was the dominant trope in the Roman Latin language, because in Rome human beings were projected into god-like status and nature was not only understood but also dominated.

Synecdoche is the representation of a whole by a part: the "Crown of England," the "White House," etc. According to Vico, synecdoche was the dominant trope of the Enlightenment, because the whole was represented by the king in Enlightenment societies. Irony is the opposite of what would be expected: "this is as clear as mud." Irony is the dominant trope of the democratic (republican or representative) and capitalist society, where policy determined might be the opposite of the best policy—in issues such as gun control, freedom of speech, or budget decisions, for example, and the best-selling product might be the opposite of the best-quality product available, as in fast food or pop music. It is the basic law of capitalism that the most successful product is that which appeals to the lowest common denominator. The application of the tropes to historical periods by Vico was the subject of Hayden White's *Metahistory*.

At the Palazzo del Tè, the mannerist game in architecture depends on an understanding of the architectural forms as tropes in language. The column is a metaphor for a tree, connecting earth and heaven, or for the human body, which determined the proper proportions described by Vitruvius and Alberti. The base of the column is a metonym for the foot of the body, and the capital of the column is a metonym for the head. The scrolls of the Ionic column, for example, can be seen as buns in a woman's hair, as in the Hathor columns at the Mortuary Temple of Queen Hatshepsut in Egypt, seen as a precedent for the Greek Ionic order. At the Palazzo del Tè, the pediment left hanging with no columns below it is a synecdoche, the pediment standing in for the column/pediment system. The slipped piece of the architrave is a form of irony, the opposite of what is expected. The slipping of the piece of the architrave denies the entablature the structural role which it purports to represent in its form, as it had no structural role to begin with in Alberti's treatment at Sant'Andrea (Figure 3.2) fifty years earlier. Romano's architecture reveals the ruse of humanist architecture in the same way that Parmigianino's and Bronzino's paintings reveal the ruse of humanist painting. The form does not follow the function in the structure of the work, and in the mannerist treatment the form does not follow the function in the representational element of the work either.

Mannerist architecture, in that it depends on tropic language, is poetic architecture, expressing the human condition and human identity, in the contradiction between form and function. The disintegration of the structural form of the architecture is mirrored in the interior of the Palazzo del Tè in Romano's fresco of the *Fall of the Giants* in the Sala dei Giganti, where the walls come tumbling down in the battle between the gods and the giants. The battle is a Classical allegory of the battle between order and chaos, good and evil, or in this case between the Gonzaga family and their enemies. The chaotic, disruptive state of the architecture on both interior and exterior of the palazzo reflects the social instability of the time, and the precarious nature of the systems of humanist learning being perpetuated.

Baroque

In the architecture of Federico Zuccari for the Accademia di San Luca in Rome, or the Palazzo Zuccari (1592, Figure 3.5), the structural vocabulary of the façade is transformed into anthropomorphic sculpture, a direction suggested by Michelangelo's Porta Pia. Here the architectural vocabulary, although it is presumed, has disappeared, and been replaced by purely sculptural elements, leaving no relation between the form of the building and its function, except as a popular backdrop for photographs of tourists. The contradiction between form and function was inherent in the mannerist concept of the *bizzarro* at the arts academy in Rome, which, inspired by Michelangelo, was now seen to be an admired quality of a work of art or architecture, representing the creativity of the artist. In the humanist tradition,

Figure 3.5 **Federico Zuccari, Palazzo Zuccari, 1592**

based on the writings of Marsilio Ficino, the Accademia di San Luca distinguished between *disegno interno*, the design in the mind of the artist, and *disegno esterno*, the physical design, or between human imagination and physical form. The *disegno interno* was dependent on the *scintilla della divinità*, the participation of divine intelligence.

Zuccari was a product of the Accademia del Disegno in Florence, and continued the humanist tradition in Rome before the full force of the Counter Reformation was in effect. Architects such as Carlo Maderno, Pietro da Cortona, and Francesco Borromini attended the meetings of the Accademia di San Luca and were influenced by its theories in their architecture, which constituted a theoretical basis for Baroque architecture combined with the onset of the Counter Reformation. The ideas about art and architecture which were developed at the Accademia can be found in Romano Alberti's transcripts in the *Origine et Progresso dell'Academia del Disegno* published in 1604; the treatise on the arts by Federico Zuccari, *L'Idea de' pittori, scultori ed architetti*, published in 1607; and the treatise on painting and sculpture by Pietro da Cortona, *Trattato della Pittura e Scultura*, published in 1652, written with Domenico Ottonelli, using the pseudonyms Britio Prenetteri and Odomenigico Lelonotti.

Francesco Borromini, influenced by the Accademia di San Luca, incorporated contradictions between form and function in the design for the Church of San Carlo alle Quattro Fontane in Rome (Figure 3.6), his masterpiece and first independent commission, in the 1630s. The cupola of the church is supported by hidden buttresses, despite the fact that the architect goes to great length to show the structural forces on the false elevations in the worship space, in torqued arches under the cornice of the cupola and inverted volutes or scrolls in Composite

Figure 3.6 **Francesco Borromini, San Carlo alle Quattro Fontane, 1638**

column capitals under the straight sections of the entablature which are supposedly putting weight on the columns. In the loggia of the Palazzo dei Conservatori building (begun 1563) on the Campidoglio, Michelangelo twisted the volutes of the column capitals to align with the diagonals of the square bays. The mannerist play on the contradiction between form and function, influenced by the tropic treatment of architectural vocabulary elements by Giulio Romano, and the sculptural and tropic treatment of the forms by Michelangelo, is taken to its extreme by Borromini for the purpose of representing the mysticism of the Baroque.

In the mysticism of the Baroque, the human mind cannot understand the divine mind, despite its dependence on it, in the same way that the One of Plotinus is inaccessible, although it participates in everything. The geometry and mathematics of Renaissance humanism, though pushed to the limit in Borromini's architecture, fall short of a correspondence between human and divine intelligence, and human identity and creativity must rely on faith, in the Catholic propaganda of the Counter Reformation. The geometry and mathematics of the architecture construct a system, in hypostases and cosmologies, inspired by divine intelligence, which ultimately fails, in the spirit of mysticism, and in the contradiction of form and function. The apparently irrational geometries of the plan and elevations of the worship space of San Carlo are the product of rational systems of geometrical permutations, as discovered in Borromini's drawings; the rational appears to be irrational, as the form contradicts not only the function of the building, but itself as well. Borromini reveled in the *coincidentia oppositorum*, the coincidence of opposites, which was seen as a necessary factor in the process of creation.

The main geometric figure in the plan of the worship space is the oval, the preferred geometry in Baroque architecture. In the Renaissance armillary sphere, the archetypal model of the universe is in the form of a sphere, as designed by the Platonic demiurge according to geometry and mathematics—the Platonic solids, the polyhedral volumes of an atomic substructure of matter, and ratios and series such as the Golden Ratio, the Fibonacci Series, or the Platonic lambda, for example. A premise of Renaissance humanism was that the human mind could understand the divine mind, and the design of nature and the universe, through geometry and mathematics, and thus be able to see the universe as God designed it, in the form of the sphere. But the premise of Baroque mysticism in the Counter Reformation was that the divine mind and thus the design of the universe were ultimately inaccessible to the human mind, and the spherical forms of the demiurge, in their archetypal state, could not be seen. But if the archetypal sphere of the universe were illuminated, by angels, and cast a shadow on the ground, the form of the shadow would be an ellipse, which could be rounded off to form an oval. In the mysticism of the Baroque, only a shadow of the archetypal form is visible in the physical world by the human mind, as in the shadows on the wall of the prison in the Allegory of the Cave in the *Republic*, thus the preferred form was the oval. This was solidified by the discovery by Johannes Kepler that planets orbit in ellipses, rather than the circles represented in the Renaissance armillary spheres.

The plan of the worship space of San Carlo is the result of a series of permutations of geometries which Borromini enacts, as can be seen in drawings by Borromini in the Albertina Museum which survived his suicide. All of the geometries are standard Renaissance geometries, taken from treatises by Sebastiano Serlio (written between 1537 and 1551), for example, which Borromini uses to construct an unusual, undulating wall plan, which in appearance is a complete departure from any of the geometries used in its construction, and which is completely irrational in relation to the rational sequences of geometries which lead to it. The geometries include two tangent circles, the oval, two intersecting triangles, projected arcs, and sixteen columns located along the circumference of the plan, in reference to Bramante's Tempietto in San Pietro in Montorio in Rome. The resulting undulating plan is irrational in relation to the rational sequence of geometries from which it results, in the same way that the seemingly irrational forms of nature are seen to be the product of rational geometries and mathematics, similar to contemporary catastrophe theory for example, or theories in DNA cell reproduction.

As Leo Steinberg observed in his *Borromini's San Carlo alle Quattro Fontane: A Study in Multiple Form and Architectural Symbolism*, there are three operative geometries which are present in the plan, cupola, and lantern, that is, the three levels of the worship space. The geometries are the circle, cross, and octagon, representing the Father, Son, and Spirit in the Trinity (the church was built for the Trinitarians, a Spanish missionary order of the Catholic Church). The geometries are hidden in the design of the plan in the same way that the geometries are hidden in the design of nature. The geometries are organized in a pattern on the surface of the cupola in the same way that geometries are organized in patterns in the human mind. And the geometries are superimposed to form an emblem on the ceiling of the lantern in the same way that geometries are undifferentiated in the divine mind. The three levels of the three geometries corresponds to the three groupings of three angels in the Celestial Hierarchy, from Pseudo-Dionysius, the nine levels of angels which mediate between God and the mind of man, divided according to the Trinity. The same divisions appear on Michelangelo's Sistine ceiling.

Borromini's architecture is a catechism of the human mind in relation to the divine mind, and the limitations of human understanding of the universe through mathematics and geometry. The architecture is also a catechism of the hypostases of being: the physical world, the mind of man, and God, in relation to each other, as they are connected by emanation from the One, in the lantern, through a pyramid of light. The architecture enacts the humanist *circuitus spiritualis* which connects heaven and earth, and the humanist ideal of the human soul which connects heaven and earth, as described by Giovanni Pico della Mirandola in the *Oration on the Dignity of Man*. The oval inscribed in the rectangle in Borromini's plan can be seen as the Baroque version of the Vitruvian Man, representing the human being as that which connects heaven and earth. All of these symbols are hidden by Borromini in the architecture because, in the climate of the Counter Reformation and the Inquisition, he probably would have been executed for expressing such pagan, humanist ideas.

Borromini's logical geometrical progression disguised in an unrecognizable form is a reflection of the syncretic thought of the Renaissance, and a precursor to a quality of the Freudian construction of dream space in the twentieth century. In Freudian dream space, the manifest content of the dream, the pictorial content, appears as an irrational collage of images, while the underlying dream thoughts structure the dream in a syntactical manner analogous to linguistic structures, in a contradiction between form and function. According to Freud in *The Interpretation of Dreams* in 1900, "The dream thoughts are entirely rational and are constructed with an expenditure of all the psychical energy of which we are capable." While "little attention is paid to the logical relations between the thoughts, those relations are ultimately given a disguised representation in certain formal characteristics of dreams" (Freud 1965 [1900]: 544–5). In the plan of San Carlo, the relations between the three manifest geometrical shapes are given a disguised representation in the formal character of the plan. The plan is composed of a deep structure, an underlying conceptual or linguistic structure manifested geometrically, and a manifest content, its visual appearance.

Borromini incorporates a series of coincidences of opposites, as in the *coincidentia oppositorum* of Nicolas Cusanus, into a palimpsest of architectural forms, through the use of symbols and diagrams and geometrical transmutations which correspond to philosophical themes. Geometries in the plan are subjected by Borromini to fragmentation, juxtaposition, reversal, and distortion, as in images in dreams. As Freud describes, "Dreams feel themselves at liberty ... to represent any element by its wishful contrary; so that there is no way of deciding at a first glance whether any element that admits of a contrary is present in the dream-thoughts as a positive or as a negative" (p. 353). The form of the dream images contradicts the content of the dream thought. Such is the quality of the Baroque in the apparent proliferation of the signified or interpretation beyond the simplicity of the signifier or form, to represent the mind as a complex of interrelated significations, prefiguring the structuring of the unconscious through dreams by Freud in the twentieth century.

Freud defined psychical structures as a dynamic continuum of causal relationships in a palimpsest, as enacted in the plan drawings of San Carlo. According to Freud, dreams "are to be explained on a dynamic basis—by the strengthening and weakening of the various components of the interplay of forces, so many of whose effects are hidden from view while functions are normal" (p. 649). The psychical structure is to be explained in terms of the dynamic interplay of forces, but in an enigmatic representation, as the underlying rationale is unavailable to consciousness. Such is the nature of Baroque *stupefazione*, the inaccessibility of the unconscious as expressed by the unknowability of God in the structure of thought, as related by humanist *concinnitas* and the Neoplatonic *nous* in the higher level of the soul with access to the divine mind.

In the dreamwork of Freud, as a result of the complex network of psychical relationships which produce the dream images, and the mechanisms of condensation and displacement, dreams are composed of disconnected fragments of visual images, syntactical structures in language, and thoughts, the *Sachvorstellung* or thing presentation and the *Wortvorstellung* or word presentation, which are seen in a variety of logical relations to each other in a palimpsest of traces which is difficult to unravel, and which can appear to be irrational. The irrational appearance of a palimpsest of layers of rational relations between traces can be seen in Borromini's plan drawings. The palimpsest of dream images is seen by Freud as the condensation and displacement of figures and spatial relationships, such as foreground and background, and the coincidence of opposites, as in the *coincidentia oppositorum* of the triangles in the plan of San Carlo, pyramids of light and darkness which correspond to diagrams in texts by Nicolas Cusanus and Athanasius Kircher.

The network of logical relations which contribute to the composition of dream images is too complex to be unraveled in dream analysis, according to Freud. Displacement, condensation, fragmentation, substitution, and the *coincidentia oppositorum*, are products of the complex network of logical relations, or the mnemic residues of such, in the *Vorstellungsrepräsentanz* in dream thoughts, which is too complex to correspond to any logical structure. The *Vorstellungsrepräsentanz* is the dream image, which is a representation of a mnemic residue or memory trace of perception, which is itself a representation of the perceived object. The simple image itself is a palimpsest of traces which are processed to produce it. In the process of the dream formation, the logical links which hold the psychical material together are lost. It is the task of psychoanalysis to restore the logical connections which the dreamwork has destroyed, as dreams are seen as the royal road to a knowledge of the unconscious activities of the mind (but not part of the unconscious), as Freud wrote in *The Interpretation of Dreams*.

The relation between the dream image and the dream thought, or manifest content and latent content, the surface aspect and the deep aspect, can be seen in the relation of the thinking subject to language, and to forms in art, like the geometries in the plan of San Carlo. The dream image responds to the dream thought, the latent content, in the *Vorstellungsrepräsentanz*, as a form of psychical activity in response to perceptual activity. The content of the perception is anticipated and rearranged, as the subject is anticipated in language (in Lacanian terms); the word represents the image to another word as the signifier represents the subject to another signifier, and it is that series of relations which make both the dream and the language intelligible. The representation of the image by the word, of the subject by the signifier, is a tool for intelligibility in architectural composition.

Because the rational forms are concealed by the irrational forms, in the contradiction between form and function in both structure and representation, Borromini's architecture was misunderstood for three centuries. Colin Campbell, the great Scottish Neoclassical architect, wrote that Borromini's forms were so irrational ("odd and chimerical") that he was attempting to "debauch mankind" with his architecture (*Vitruvius Britannicus*, 1715). Borromini's architecture shows that the rational and irrational are intricately linked together in the human mind, as seen in dream formation in psychoanalysis, and that the separation between the two requires the contradiction between form and function, in the human mind and its products.

Chapter 4

Enlightenment and idealism

Schinkel

The Enlightenment was premised on the clarity of reason and a rejection of the mysticism of the Baroque, and Neoclassical architecture was premised on a return to the clarity of the rules of Classical architecture. As it can be found in Classical architecture, the contradiction between form and function can be found in Neoclassical architecture, especially in the popular concept of architecture as theater or stage set, the best example being the work of Karl Friedrich Schinkel (1781–1841). The early introduction of iron into masonry construction also created a contradiction between form and function, as in the iron reinforcement concealed in Jacques-Germain Soufflot's Panthéon (1756–97) in Paris. The trabeated façade of Karl Friedrich Schinkel's Schauspielhaus (1818–21, Figure 4.1) in Berlin has no relation to the structure of the building. The façade of the building is a stage set, and the form of the architecture contradicts the function of the architecture in relation to the structure of the building. As will be seen, the same contradiction can be found in the architecture of Ludwig Mies van der Rohe in the German tradition, and the necessity of the contradiction between form and function in architecture can be found in German idealist philosophy, in particular in the writings of Friedrich Wilhelm Joseph von Schelling (1775–1854) and Georg Wilhelm Friedrich Hegel (1770–1831).

The treatment of Schinkel's Schauspielhaus consists of a system of vertical pilasters and horizontal entablatures, forming bands of windows in a reticulated grid which turns the façade into a screen which unites the varied building masses behind it. The façade presents a harmonious ordered system which expresses the higher aspirations of the theater arts which take place inside the building rather than the architectural functions of the building. The design scheme is loosely based on a Classical precedent, perhaps illustrations of the choragic monument of Thryssalos in Athens in the *Antiquities of Athens*, but it is transformed into an original composition of harmonic relationships achieved in a tectonic order rather than through ornamentation. Schinkel himself wrote: "The beauty of a building does not lie primarily in the ornament employed, but rather first and foremost in the choice of relationships" (Bergdoll 1994: 64).

Figure 4.1 **Karl Friedrich Schinkel, Schauspielhaus, 1818–21**

Schinkel's approach to architecture was influenced in particular by two of his friends: Karl Wilhelm Ferdinand Solger (1780–1819) and Wilhelm von Humboldt (1767–1835). Solger introduced Schinkel to the writings of Johann Gottlieb Fichte (1762–1814) and Schelling. The two of them read Greek dramas together, which inspired Schinkel's stage designs. In his treatise on aesthetics, *Erwin*, published in 1815, based on lectures given at Berlin University in 1811 and 1812, Solger described the task of art as revealing the ideal (the transcendent idea, as in the *archê* or intelligible), through the manipulation of the phenomenal. This was an important basis of the aesthetics of Hegel, which were influenced by Solger's aesthetics. Like Kant, Schelling, and Hegel, Solger saw architecture as the most material of the arts, tied in unique ways to its structural and functional require- ments, but at the same time uniquely able to express the human condition and evoke the relation between the real and the ideal, between matter and thought. Solger saw this as possible through the metaphysical functions of architecture, in providing shelter and accommodating activities, and in expressing an idea.

Wilhelm von Humboldt was an influential friend of Schinkel's: Prussian Ambassador to Rome, Minister of Education in the Ministry of the Interior, and founder of Berlin University, with Fichte as its first rector in 1809–10. In a letter in 1817, Humboldt wrote, "To say that art derives from the imitation of nature is very incorrect. It is more correct to say that it derives from mathematics as the basic harmony of form and eurhythmics; it must penetrate through nature to this" (Bergdoll 1994: 65). As Plotinus established in the *Enneads*, the arts do more than just give a "bare reproduction of the thing seen," they "go back to the Reason- Principles from which Nature itself derives" (Plotinus 1991: V.8.1). The basis of architecture for Schinkel was the idea, in contradiction to the matter of the building, the form in contradiction to the function. For Humboldt, art and reality were contradictory, because art is capable of revealing the truth of reality, which reality itself is not, as "the character of reality never reveals itself in reality itself" (Bergdoll 1994: 65). Art has the capacity to provide access to the principles by which forms in reality are created, because art constitutes a representation of nature in conformity with our understanding of nature, or as Kant would say, in conformity with our a priori conceptions of nature in perception. For Humboldt, "art represents the character of nature not as it is in itself, but as it is comprehensible to our sense organs, harmoniously predisposed for them" (p. 68).

Schinkel saw art and architecture as capable of representing the underlying principles of nature and the true structure of reality, in contradiction to the play of the sensual forms of reality. Schinkel saw architecture as stage design, in contradiction to the functional requirements of a building, as the sensual play of forms in nature is in contradiction to the structural principles of nature. Nature is seen as transformed through human knowledge and perception and architecture unites the variable and multiple fragments of nature or reality, as given in perception, into an ideal, complete form, as what might be given in apperception. Thus in the terms of Schelling or Hegel, architecture is able to represent the ideal in relation to the real. Rather than imitate the Classics, the goal of the architect for Schinkel is to impose an original idea or set of principles, derived from an understanding of nature, onto the material form of the building, in order to allow the building to transcend its material requirements and express a comprehensive idea about the relationship between the human mind and the phenomenal world.

Schelling

In lectures delivered in Jena in 1802, collected in *The Philosophy of Art*, Schelling described the forms of architecture as inorganic, as would Hegel, and constructed according to geometry and mathematics, which make the forms schematic, and allow them to symbolize the particular through the universal. As with Hegel, only organic form can express spirit (*Geist*, the absolute), as the expression of the Idea, the archetype or intelligible. Reason is only indirectly related to the inorganic, and thus only indirectly related to architecture; it is only mediated through the schema or concept. In order to be an absolute art of the spirit, architecture must be in identity with reason, without mediation. In the organic, form and concept are identical, the subjective and the objective; there is no contradiction between form and function. Architecture can be beautiful (reflecting Hegel's definition of beauty in art as that which is born of spirit, in the identity of the real and ideal), but only when it becomes independent of purpose or need, as a mechanical art. Architecture, unlike the other arts, is necessarily tied to function and structure. Architecture must thus become independent of itself, and an imitation of itself in its form, in order to free itself from its functional requirements and operate as artistic or poetic expression.

Architecture is fine art only when it appears to be purposeful and symbolic, but in reality is not; only when its form contradicts its function.

According to Schelling, architecture can only be an idea or an allegory of the organic, or the correlation of form and function. Architecture can never achieve an absolute identity ("indifference" in spirit) between idea and matter, between form and function. The only way that architecture can achieve an identity of particular (form) and universal or absolute (Idea), an identity between subjective and objective, is when it imitates its own requirements of necessity, satisfying necessity and being independent of it at the same time. Only in this way can architecture express spirit, the identity of the universal and particular in the organic, toward the realization of the absolute, that which unifies and transcends both mind and matter, which is the object of philosophy. In *The Philosophy of Art*, §107, Schelling describes architecture as the "anorganic art form" (Schelling 1989 [1859]) within the plastic arts, and as necessarily based in geometry and mathematics, which involve functions of the relations of logic within the real, unable to represent the presence of unreason in reason, or the sublime. The presence of the absolute in the real is only possible in light and color in painting, the dematerialization of substance. Qualities of the real which contain the representation of the sublime, light, and vastness are possible in the perception and experience of architecture, as in the perception and experience of nature, but they are not possible in the architecture itself. A phenomenological interpretation of architecture, for example, is a subjective or poetic interpretation, based on the experience of architecture, that is, the presence of the architecture to the viewer, in contradiction to its actual existence.

Because architecture is composed of spatial relationships, arithmetic is necessarily manifest as geometry. Architecture is "solidified music," or "music in space," the spatial realization of proportional relations through geometry. None of the other visual arts are possible without the underlying role of arithmetical or geometrical relationships, as in the most substantial element of painting, drawing, and in especially the use of linear perspective. In order to become symbolic—that is, in order to express a relation between the real and ideal, between matter and thought—forms in both nature and art must cast off "the limitations of a merely finite regularity," which can only express the presence of the real in the ideal, in the realm of logic in reason. Forms in nature and art which go beyond the limitations of finite regularity display the "chaos within the absolute," the unreason within reason in the identity or indifference of the real and ideal which is Absolute Spirit in mind. The chaos within the absolute is the void within being, the aporetic gap between mind and its other in self-consciousness, as it symbolizes the real to itself. Chaos within the absolute is lack of form within form, that which exceeds reason in mind, the crisis of the symbol.

The highest form which architecture can take as an art is in the expression of an abstract idea in reason as an image or representation of absolute identity. "Architecture can appear as free and beautiful art only insofar as it becomes the expression of *ideas*, an image of the universe and of the absolute."

A true image of the absolute and an immediate expression of the Idea are only possible in organic form, which can only be achieved in the plastic arts. Unlike music, the conceptual counterpart of architecture, architecture cannot free itself from the representation of form in the real; it cannot free itself from matter and the insertion of thought as reason into matter, the ideal into the real, as geometric regularity. Architecture cannot represent the absolute in form alone; it can only represent the absolute in both form and essence simultaneously, that is, it must express an idea. The organic form in the plastic arts is an immediate representation of reason, because the organic form itself is "reason perceived in the real," reason's perception of itself in the real, the definition of beauty. The inorganic form is not an immediate representation of reason, because reason cannot perceive itself in the real in the inorganic form; the inorganic form is a product of reason, a product of the ideal. The relation between reason and architecture is thus an indirect one, and must be mediated by the organic, seen in relation to the organic, and as such mediated by the concept or the idea. Reason perceives itself directly in the real, in nature, in absolute identity, and in the organic form of the plastic arts; reason can only perceive itself indirectly in nature in the inorganic forms of architecture. Architecture thus stages the problematic relation between reason and nature, the inability of mind to perceive itself in the real, and the forms of architecture are the product of the struggle between mind and its self-perception in the real.

Architecture can only represent through the mediation of the concept, the idea, in reason. In order to exist within the realm of absolute identity, in the realm of spirit, architecture must achieve an absolute identity with reason itself, it must "in itself and without mediation be in identity with reason." An identity with reason cannot be achieved in materiality alone, in the realm of matter or the real, and in the concept of purpose associated with matter, the laws of cause and effect and necessity, as in the Principle of Sufficient Reason, or the structural and functional requirements of a building, as given by logic in the real. The concept cannot be found within the matter or emerge from it; it must be external to it, and superimposed onto it, as the lineament is applied to the matter in Albertian terms. In order to represent absolute identity, architecture must communicate an idea which is external to its material presence. It must enact the presence of an idea, or the possibility of an idea, in the Platonic sense of an *archê*, an idea which is not dependent on sensory perception, an idea which precedes its material manifestation, an idea of which its materiality is a manifestation, but which is external to its manifestation in the materiality, external to both nature and the identity of mind as perceived in nature or the real. In organic form in the plastic arts, the idea is not external to the material; the concept is infused into the material, creating a synthesis of the subjective and objective in mind, and thus a synthesis of the finite and infinite.

The organic form is thus an image of reason; the most ideal form of the organic is the human body, and the representation of the human body was seen in Classical art to be the most complete synthesis of the real and ideal in the plastic arts, and the synthesis of the real and the ideal in the anthropomorphized mythological figure. Architecture cannot achieve the synthesis of the subjective and objective and the finite and infinite in form; architectural form always displays the incompatibility of the real and the ideal within reason, to which it is bound. Architecture as art depends on its identity with reason in the realm of the ideal, and thus on the existence of the real within the ideal, and the presupposition of the ideal in the perception of the real, as in the a priori categories of Kant.

According to Schelling, architecture can only be beautiful, that is, it can only achieve a synthesis of the ideal and real, mind and matter, within the ideal, when it becomes independent of its purpose or function in its representational forms. In order to be beautiful, architecture must appear to be functional, but in fact must not be functional. Architectural forms must appear to obey the laws of cause and effect in the real, but at the same time be independent of those laws within the ideal. This in fact is the Hegelian definition of freedom, the independence in mind from the laws of necessity in the real, as given by self-consciousness. The Parthenon (Figure 1.2) is beautiful because the colonnade, entablature, and pediment appear to support the structure, but in fact do not. Those elements of the building assume only the form of structure, and not the purpose. The building communicates the discrepancy of the real and ideal, function and idea, within the ideal, within the concept which is communicated in connection to the material. In that way, the building assumes an identity with reason in relationship to nature; reason perceives itself in the forms of the building and judges it to be beautiful. The façades of the Palazzo Rucellai (Figure 3.1) and Sant'Andrea in Mantua (Figure 3.2) by Leon Battista Alberti are the epitome of architectural beauty in the Renaissance because the forms which are based in structural necessity do not function in any structural way. The same can be said of the Palazzo del Tè of Giulio Romano (Figure 3.4) or Borromini's San Carlo alle Quattro Fontane (Figure 3.6) in the late Renaissance, Schinkel's Schauspielhaus (Figure 4.1), or Ludwig Mies van der Rohe's Crown Hall (Figure 5.7), the Villa Stein of Le Corbusier (Figure 5.9), and the Wexner Center of Peter Eisenman (Figure 6.4) in the twentieth century. Peter Eisenman has in fact put forward this argument as a defense of compositional strategies in architecture.

For Schelling, "architecture is beautiful" (Schelling 1989 [1859]: §107), that is, represents the self-identity of the ideal within the real, only when it becomes "independent of need," as opposed to the other plastic arts, in which the organic form displays the identity of the real and ideal within the realm of necessity, the realm of the real. Organic form is taken as a symbol of the real, which contains within itself, the symbol, the possibility of the identity of the real and ideal. Architecture can never be completely independent of the real, of necessity and cause and effect, structural and functional requirements, thus in order to be beautiful it must be "simultaneously becoming independent *of itself.*" Architecture achieves its communicative potential when it becomes a "free imitation of itself." Architecture achieves freedom in mind, Absolute Spirit, in the same way that mind attains freedom as Absolute Spirit, in Hegelian terms: architecture becomes conscious of itself in its being-in-itself, its essential being in the real, and it becomes alienated from itself in its doubling of itself, its self-recognition as other to itself, and through its being-for-self becomes self-conscious in its return to itself, achieving a being-in-and-for-itself, which is freedom in mind as the absolute. In such a way, architecture mirrors the activity of mind in self-consciousness; it enacts the process of reason in imagination and understanding, and in that way is identical to reason itself, and can thus represent the absolute within the ideal.

According to Schelling, as soon as architecture "attains through appearance both actuality and utility without intending these *as* utility and as actuality," that is, as soon as it imitates itself in its forms, it "becomes free and independent art." Architecture imitating itself is as the real imitating itself in the ideal, or the laws of necessity and cause and effect imitating themselves in reason. In that way, reason in imagination is able to perceive the presence of the real, that which is external to it, within itself, and then to transcend the self-presence of the real in self-consciousness, to attain freedom from it, which is the purpose of philosophy, and the purpose of the development of mind in transcendental idealism. The object associated with the concept of purpose is transformed into an object of art devoid of purpose, or independent of the concept of purpose with which it was previously associated, as in the conceptual art of Marcel Duchamp. The concept of purpose itself becomes disassociated with purpose, and the presence of the ideal within the real is revealed, the perception of the real based in the presupposition of the ideal, the a priori categories. The concept of purpose itself becomes an artistic object, an idea which displays the synthesis of ideal and real within the ideal within the framework of the discrepancy of the ideal and the real, between thought and that which is external to it as given by thought in perception, in the doubling of mind in consciousness in being-for-self and the consequent self-alienation of mind.

In architecture, organic forms are displayed as preformed in the inorganic in the same way that the organic forms of life are understood to be preformed in the crystalline forms of the mineral, and the particular is seen to be preformed in the universal, as in the Platonic *archê*. It is necessary for architecture to present the organic as the result of the inorganic in order for architecture to appear to reason as reason, as the synthesis of the subjective and objective in the real. Architecture cannot represent reason alone in the organic because the forms of architecture cannot escape their necessity in matter, their structural and functional requirements, except as imitations of that necessity. The representation of reason in architecture requires both the organic and the inorganic; in other words, that which precedes necessity in logic in reason in the real, that is, the essential being-in-itself, unconscious being which precedes the conscious being, the dark ground of being which contains the chaos and formlessness of the absolute. As absolute formlessness is the equivalent of pure form in the ideal, as absolute chaos is the equivalent of absolute identity, so absolute formlessness is the equivalent of the abject crystalline forms of the inorganic, and as they are represented in the geometry and mathematics of logic in the real. The crystalline form of the inorganic in reason is the reduction to ground zero of form in being, the primordial state of form which has no prior, because it has no necessity. It is the crystalline inorganic form of geometry and mathematics which architecture imitates as itself in its representation of the identity of the infinite and finite within reason. The architectural form is a form which has no necessity of itself as geometry, but assumes necessity in the enactment of the geometry in function, then doubles and imitates the necessity as a form of expression, and separates itself from the necessity as art. This is the same process which mind follows from unconscious being, to consciousness and self-consciousness in absolute being, being-in-and-for-itself, the forms of which are equivalent to the forms of unconscious being.

Thus architecture as art must contain a representation of the relation between the organic and the inorganic, between reason in the real and the absence of reason in the real, between belonging in the world and alienation from it. Architecture as shelter establishes belonging in the world, but at the same time it establishes separation from the world, as both a physical barrier and a metaphysical function to express an idea which alienates human reason from the organic. In architecture, the organic can only be represented as preformed within the inorganic, belonging in the world as preformed within the alienation of reason from the world. As human beings build a place for themselves in the world, they construct the incompatibility between themselves and the world. In order for the organic to be present in architecture, in order for belonging in the world to be present, for reason to recognize itself in the real in the identity of the subjective and objective in architecture, the organic must be represented by the inorganic allegorically, as was seen in Gothic architecture in particular. The inorganic forms of architecture must signify the organic, as in the architecture of Frank Lloyd Wright; they must suggest their opposite or their other, the presence of reason in the real, as linguistic tropisms, and organize them in a temporal progression to represent the process of thought. Architecture as art is necessarily allegorical; it necessarily represents that which it is not, in order to participate in the absolute, in the indifference of the real and ideal.

In *The Philosophy of Art*, §111, "architecture, to be fine art, must be the potence or imitation of itself as the art of need" (Schelling 1989 [1859]). Architecture imitates itself allegorically. The inorganic form in itself cannot be symbolic, because it does not have a direct relation to reason; reason cannot see itself in the inorganic form, though the inorganic form is a product of logic in reason. Thus it is impossible for reason to see itself in a synthesis with matter in the inorganic form, and the inorganic form cannot be other than what it is to reason. It is only the organic form, that which is achieved in the plastic arts in the synthesis of the material and immaterial, the particular and universal, which can be symbolic to reason, which can suggest to reason the participation of reason in the real, and thus become to reason other than what it is. For Schelling, "the anorganic as such can have only an indirect relationship to reason and thus can never possess symbolic significance." The inorganic can only be symbolic in imitation of itself, as in architecture.

The pyramids (Figure 1.1), the primal form of architectural expression, are symbolic not in their materiality as necessity in the real, but as imitation of their materiality as necessity in the real, as enacted in the symbolic representation in language of the trope, in reason in understanding. The symbolic function or metaphysical expression of the pyramid, as the primordial mound, or the rays of light from the sun emanating to the four corners of the world, or a mirror to the stars in the heavens, is extraneous to the material function of the pyramid as an inorganic form. The inorganic form of the pyramid must double itself, through the symbolic in language, in metaphor and allegory, in order to symbolize something. In other words, the inorganic form, in the geometry and mathematics, is not symbolic in itself, but only in how it is perceived by reason, as it is extraneous to the perception of reason of itself in the real, because the inorganic form is always already reason in the real. The symbolic in language functions as a product of the inability of reason to see itself as itself in the real outside of its relation to the real, namely, that which it perceives through the senses and understanding. The symbolic is a product of the thrown-ness of reason from itself and from the real in self-consciousness, thus the symbolic becomes an instrument for the return of reason to itself. The same can be said for the allegorical, which is the narrativization of the symbolic. Architecture facilitates the return of reason to itself.

In architecture the organic form is only presented as an idea, as representation or imitation of itself, the representation of the real within the ideal. The organic is not present in architecture outside the framework of the inorganic, outside the framework of the inorganic as allegory of the organic, as in the "palm-fronds" of the Gothic cathedral, thus outside the framework of language. Thus the symbolic is only given in architecture as a product of language, in the idea projected onto the material. The identity between the idea or concept and the materiality of the architecture is an objective identity rather than a subjective identity, an identity which is facilitated by the relationship between thought and matter, rather than the indifference of thought and matter in both the real and the ideal, which is the absolute. The symbolic in architecture is the being-for-self of consciousness in Hegelian terms, a product of mind seeing itself as other, and attempting to return to itself. The symbolic in architecture thus signifies the self-alienation of mind in consciousness, and the inability of reason to see itself in the real, in that which it perceives. This is similar to Hegel's explanation for the symbolic character of architecture in Egypt as a reflection of the culture, in which it was impossible for human reason to identify itself in nature, in the real, and thus the synthesis of reason and nature, the ideal and the real, required a symbolic mediation, which made possible Absolute Spirit.

In that the symbolic in architectural form is a function of language, language itself is a symbolic mediation between the real and the ideal, between what is perceived and what is thought, in the impossibility of reason to identify itself in the real. Language is an allegorical construct of thought in imitation of the perception of the real in the ideal, or nature in relation to thought; language imitates nature as the symbolic imitates the organic in architectural form. In the hieroglyph, allegorical language, or alphabetical language, can be seen to be a product of symbolic language, or picture-thinking, reason as perception. In the symbolic element of the hieroglyph, the organic form is presented as an imitation of itself in the inorganic as the organic is present in the architecture. Symbolic architectural forms can be seen as hieroglyphics, in that their communicative function is based in the tropics of language.

The subjective indifference of the ideal and the real is not possible in the imitation of symbolic mediation in architectural forms, but it is possible in the organic forms of the plastic arts, which can directly symbolize the presence of reason in the real, according to Schelling. Architecture can only generate such an identity in its mechanisms, as is the case with language. The plastic arts of painting and sculpture are therefore seen as being able to communicate an identity between the ideal and the real which language cannot. Their ability to communicate the indifference of the ideal and the real within the real exceeds the possibility of such an indifference in language, as language is entirely within the realm of the ideal. The contemplation of the sublime as represented in a painting—for example, in the use of color and light—exceeds the symbolic mediation of language in the real, and represents the return of thought to itself in self-consciousness, to essential, unconscious being, the ground of being prior to language. Light and color are seen by Schelling as those elements in painting which contain the indifference of the ideal and the real most directly, because they signify the presence of the absolute in the real, outside the structure of the symbolic in language.

Hegel

As for Schelling, architecture is seen as a limited form of artistic expression, in the necessity of its material function, in the *Introductory Lectures on Aesthetics* of Hegel. The "material of architecture is matter itself in its immediate externality as a heavy mass subject to mechanical laws" (Hegel 1993 [1886]: CIX), and its forms are "merely set in order in conformity with relations of the abstract understanding" in mathematics and geometry. The forms of architecture can only be inorganic in relation to human reason. The Idea, the transcendent or spiritual, can only exist in architecture as an abstraction in the symbolic, through the mechanisms of language, or the syntax of architectural language. Architecture can thus only be a symbolic form of art, a representation to human reason of its inability to know the object of phenomena in its essence, in Kantian terms. The symbolic function of architecture, the metaphysical expression of an idea, requires the contradiction between form and function.

The beauty of art is beauty that is born "of the mind" (I, II), and because the mind is "higher" than the appearances of nature, in that the mind determines the appearances of nature, the beauty of art is higher than the beauty of nature, according to Hegel. The contradiction between mind and nature necessitates the contradiction between form and function. Beauty is defined as that which reinforces the understanding of mind. Beauty in architecture is that which reinforces the ordering of the sensible world by reason, and that which suggests the transcendent, the other than the material. Mind "comprehends in itself all that is" (I, III), so nature and its manifestations must be secondary. Beauty in nature is only a reflection of the beauty in mind, as the forms perceived in nature are made possible by mind. Beauty in architecture is likewise a reflection of beauty in mind. Beauty in nature, as in architecture, is imperfect and incomplete as a shadow of beauty in mind. Nature and architecture can only exist as completion in mind. Without apperception (the synthesis of the manifold), in Kantian terms, the disparate forms of the material world are fragmentary and incomplete. Because the forms of art are imperfect and incomplete in relation to mind, and because they cannot contain the beauty of the synthesis of the manifold, art achieves beauty by deception in appearance, as does nature. The deception in appearance entails the contradiction between form and function.

Mind is able to overcome the limitations of perception in relation to the phenomenal world, which is "erected as a beyond over against immediate consciousness and present sensation" (I, XIII); there is a schism or contradiction between mind and matter which mind is able to heal by investing ideas into sensuous forms in art. The work of art is the "middle term of reconciliation between pure thought and what is external, sensuous, and transitory, between nature with its finite actuality and the infinite freedom of reason that comprehends." Art is the mediation between mind and nature, between the ideal and the sensuous, as architecture is the mediation between mind and nature through geometry. While the forms of both art and nature are a deceptive semblance in relation to mind, the deceptive forms of art can lead to what is beyond them (the transcendent or metaphysical, the idea in relation to the form), in a way that the forms of nature cannot. In art and architecture, form contradicts function, because art and archi-tecture are a pure creation of mind disjoined from sensory experience. In nature, form follows function, because the forms of nature are the product of the under-standing in reason in relation to the necessity of cause and effect, and in relation to sensory experience.

The work of art or architecture is experienced as both sensuous object and idea communicated to mind. The form in nature is experienced only as sensuous object, though it cannot be known in itself in sensuous apprehension, but only as a representation given to understanding in mind. The representation of the form of the object in nature is nevertheless true to the object in sensual experience, while the representation of the form in art and architecture is false in relation to the sensual experience of the art or architecture, in the contradiction between form and function. While nature exists independently of the perception of it by human sensation and reason, art and architecture do not. Art and architecture only exist for the human mind. The sensuous only exists in a work of art as a semblance or surface, as a representation. Architecture cannot provide sensuous experience—it can organize space through geometry and mathematics, and the space which is a product of its organization can provide a sensuous experience. The form of the architecture in its geometrical organization contradicts the function of the archi-tecture in the space which is the product.

The semblance of the sensuous in art and architecture is a higher form of the immediate sensuous as perceived in nature in that the semblance of the sensuous can act as a mediator between the immediate sensuous and thought, which determines the form of the sensuous. The semblance of the sensuous is mere appearance, form in contradiction to the sensuous object. Art thus produces "no more than a shadow-world of shapes" (LVIII), in the form of a schemata, an organization which is a product of reason, in geometry and mathematics for example. But the schematic forms of the semblance of the sensuous in appearance in art "present themselves, not simply for their own sake and for that of their immediate structure, but with the purpose of affording in that shape satisfaction to higher spiritual interests." All art is metaphysical, and all architecture as art is metaphysical. The spiritual or transcendent is infused in sensuous shape, as it communicates to mind, in contradiction to the immediate structure. The idea infuses beauty into the sensuous shape in art; the universal is infused into the particular, to achieve a form of absolute (the Absolute Spirit), which is human identity.

Kant

Schelling's distinction between the real and the ideal, the sensible and intelligible, as it is applied to architecture, is derived from the a priori categories of Immanuel Kant (1724–1804). In the transcendental aesthetic of Kant in the *Critique of Pure Reason* (1781), what we perceive to be space and time do not actually exist outside of our thought. Geometry and mathematics are abstract representations of space and time which have no basis in the sensory world. As architecture is lineament, geometry, and mathematics, it can be inferred that it only exists in thought as a representation of space and time. It can be concluded that architecture itself is an a priori category, projected onto the material or the real, as are space and time.

In the *Critique of Pure Reason*, knowledge can only relate to sensible objects by means of intuition. "In whatsoever mode, or by whatsoever means, our knowledge may relate to objects, it is at least quite clear, that the only manner in which it immediately relates to them, is by means of an intuition" (Kant 1990 [1781]: 21). The object, or phenomenon, is the "undetermined object of an empirical intuition." The phenomenon consists of matter and form; the matter is that part of the phenomenon which corresponds to sensation, while the form is that part of the phenomenon which can be "arranged under certain relations." The matter of the phenomenon corresponds to the sensible form or *species sensibilis* of the Commentators on Aristotle, as opposed to the intelligible form, the *species apprehensibilis*, which corresponds to the form of the phenomenon for Kant. Both the matter and the form of the phenomenon are determined a priori; the a priori conception of the sensible form results in the perception of the form, while the a priori conception of the intelligible form results in the understanding of the phenomenon as part of a synthetic whole in the ordering of the phenomenal world.

Sensibility, the capacity for receiving representations, is the source of intuition, which allows sensible objects to be thought in understanding, from which arise conceptions. Objects and intuitions are given by sensibility; they are thought in the "understanding," from which arise conceptions. Thought is related to intuition and to sensibility by signs or symbols. For Kant, sensible objects can only be thought as representations. All material forms in architecture are representations, as are all words in a language. Sensations cannot arrange themselves or assume certain forms; forms must exist a priori in the mind, and be seen as separate from sensation. In the pure forms of sensuous intuition which exist in the mind a priori, "all the manifold content of the phenomenal world is arranged and viewed under certain relations" (p. 22). Architecture already involves the ordering of the phenomenal world by a priori sensuous intuition, and it should be understood as such so that it can facilitate intellectual development.

Kant distinguishes between the sensation and the intelligible, as the intelligible entails an arrangement of sensations, and the sensation assuming a form. The matter of phenomena is given a posteriori, following the form of phenomena in the mind; the a priori form must thus be seen as separate from sensation, and juxtaposed to it, in a contradiction. What is a priori in the mind is the transcendental, pure form of sensuous intuition, which arranges the manifold and varied content of the phenomenal world. The manifold content of the phenomenal world is arranged and viewed under a certain set of arrangements, which are determined by intuition and concept in understanding. Objects can only exist in perception insofar as they are in a certain relation to other objects; objects cannot exist in perception without a relation to other objects. In the transcendental concepts of time and space, a moment in time cannot exist without a relation to other moments in time, and a point in space cannot exist without a relation to other points in space. Time, space, and the manifold of phenomenal objects in perception thus can only exist in a conceptual continuity, a reality manufactured by human reason. Architecture, as the sequential organization of space, only exists as a manifold continuity manufactured by human reason. Architectural forms only exist in relation to other architectural forms. Architecture is a projection of an a priori intuition, a manufactured totality, onto the phenomenal world. It entails the coexistence of the ideal and the real, the intuitive and the sensible, which constitute a contradiction in understandings.

Kant defines the "Transcendental Aesthetic" as the "science of all the principles of sensibility à priori" (p. 22). There are two pure forms of sensuous intuition, which are principles of a priori knowledge: space and time. Space and time are not "real existences," but rather "merely relations or determinations of things" (p. 23). Space and time are not concepts which have been developed from outward or empirical experience in their entirety, but rather entail a dialectic between empirical experience and concept in understanding, manifest as intuition. Pure empirical experience does not exist. External or empirical experience is itself only possible as a result of a priori intuition, as sense experience is conditioned by what is understood in the mind. The perception of a sensible form is determined by an understanding of the corresponding intelligible form in the mind. A phenomenal object can only be perceived once it is understood in its relation to the totality or manifold of reality, as constructed in the mind. A form in architecture can only be perceived as it is understood a priori in relation to other forms in architecture, which constitute the totality or manifold of architecture. It is impossible to think of architecture without space, or time, thus space cannot be said to exist as a physical phenomenon. As a manifold totality constructed a priori in intuition, architecture cannot be said to exist as a physical phenomenon, but rather only as a concept.

The structural and functional requirements of architecture exist in the phenomenal world as products of the a priori concepts of space and time, in the relation of a posteriori perceived matter in relation to a priori conceptualized relations. The visual forms of architecture, when they are in direct relationship to the structural and functional requirements, are as the visual forms of matter, in relation to the manifold concepts of matter in a cause-and-effect relationship, as given by reason. If the visual forms of architecture contradict the structural and functional requirements, then the mechanisms by which architecture, and sensible reality, are understood in reason and perception are revealed; the contradiction between the sensible object as perceived matter and a priori transcendental intuition is revealed. Architecture thus functions as philosophy, to examine and reveal the mechanisms of reason and perception, in order to describe the relationship between the human mind and the phenomenal world.

Space is a necessary a priori representation, and it is the condition for the possibility of all phenomena. It is impossible to conceive of the non-existence of space; for that reason alone space cannot be seen as a phenomenal reality. It is also impossible to conceive of the non-existence of time, and all relationships are perceived in space and time. Modern physics tells us that the universe had a definite beginning and will have a definite end in both spatial and temporal terms, but it is impossible to conceive of anything prior to or posterior to space and time, just like it is impossible to conceive of experience after death, except as a mythology. Architecture is also a necessary a priori representation; it is impossible to conceive of the non-existence of architecture, thus architecture cannot be seen as a phenomenal reality. While space and time, and architecture, are manifest in discursive reason as containing relationships within a manifold totality, they themselves cannot be concepts of relationships, but rather pure intuitions, a priori concepts which are formed prior to sensory experience, much like the archetype or intelligible in Classical philosophy, in the active intellect or intellectual principle, *nous*, which is manifest in intelligible form in relation to sensible form, or the unconscious in psychoanalysis. Following the intuitions of space and time, geometry and mathematics are also products of a priori intuition, like architecture.

According to Kant, space is not a concept which is derived from outward experience, nor from relations between external phenomena. External experience is on the contrary only possible through the antecedent representation of space. Space is a necessary a priori representation; all conceptions of space are based on a priori intuition, as are the principles of geometry. Space is not a discursive concept, as it cannot be divided or multiplied. Architecture thus depends on a priori intuition in perception, rather than on sensory perception or discursive reason. It is impossible to think of architecture without space, thus space does not exist as a physical phenomenon, and it is reasonable to conclude that architecture does not exist as a physical phenomenon; architecture only exists as it is understood in the mind, as in the signified of Vitruvius or the lineament of Alberti.

Geometrical principles are apodictic, necessary truths. Rather than being based in the fragmented variability and malleability of the phenomenal world, they are a priori intuitions applied to reality. They cannot be varied to conform to sensible phenomena; rather, sensible phenomena must conform to them. The organization of a building must conform to a priori, universal rules of mathematics and geometry; the building is thus taken out of its phenomenal existence, and through architecture it enters into a transcendental existence. Mathematics and geometry, time and space, are not properties inherent to sensible objects which have an existence insofar as they are in conformance with a manifold set of rules and principles. Space is not a quality of an object, nor is it a quality of relations between objects; it has no relation to sensible objects other than as providing a field in which sensible objects can be perceived and understood. The mathematics and geometry in architecture which organize a building in time and space have no relation to the material forms of the architecture, other than as providing a field in which elements of a building can be organized as architecture. An element of a building is transformed into an architectural form when it is understood in relation to mathematics and geometry, that is, when it is transformed from a phenomenal object to a transcendental object of intuition and perception, from the real to the ideal, or the sensible to the intelligible, from any existence "in itself" to an existence determined a priori in intuition. The existence of the architectural form in intuition contradicts the existence of the matter of the building element in phenomena.

The experience of a building as architecture depends on the a priori intuition of time, as temporal succession and coexistence do not exist in the phenomenal world. A part of time cannot be understood outside of the manifold of time, as a part of space cannot be understood outside the manifold of space. Time and space are, rather than qualities of the phenomenal world, qualities of the intuition of the perceiving subject. Time and space determine the "relation of representations in our internal state" (p. 30), the representations of perceived phenomena. Time and space function as a syntax for the language of internal representation; they are the mechanism by which perceptions are organized and understood. Meaning is created in language through a relationship between signifiers, so time is a necessary a priori intuition for meaning in language, and the communication of meaning in the visual language of architecture, which also requires a syntax, an underlying matrix of rules of representation, which include mathematics and geometry, in order for meaning in representation to be communicated insofar as it participates in a manifold.

All communication in language requires a shared acceptance of a manifold, composed of syntactical rules based in the a priori intuitions of space and time. Space and time are constructed, artificial mechanisms through which all thought, language, communication, meaning and architecture are generated. If space and time do not exist other than as transcendental intuitions in the mind, then their grounding for all communication and meaning reveals a void within all communication and meaning, and within human identity. Meaning and communication have a metaphysical basis which is not to be found in phenomenal reality. Any meaning or communication which is achieved in a syntax in language, including the language of architectural forms, cannot be related to the phenomenal existence of the signifiers in the language, or the matter of the architectural elements. The metaphysical function of architecture certainly contradicts its material function.

Space and time, as internal a priori intuitions, can provide no form themselves, but can only be represented in forms, in formal analogies, such as cyclical or linear progression. The perception of a sensible object requires a dialectic between the sensible form of the object and the intelligible understanding of the object, as a relation in a manifold, which is given a sensible form in representation—what Sigmund Freud would call the *Vorstellungsrepräsentanz*. Space and time can only be represented through figural language, in linguistic tropes; they cannot be represented in literal language, because they do not exist in the phenomenal world. Architecture represents space and time through the tropic language of mathematics and geometry. Architecture can only be understood as existing within and determined by the manifold framework of space and time which it represents through the figural tropes of mathematics and geometry in its execution and experience. Architecture and human reason are thus defined by a metaphysical foundation which does not actually exist, but is represented by analogies in its non-existence. Communication and meaning in language and architecture, if they have resonance, incorporate the metaphysical void which is their basis.

It is impossible to perceive space or time; only relations within space and time can be perceived, as they have been determined in a priori intuition. It is thus impossible to perceive the epistemological basis of architecture; its basis is taken for granted as a transcendental a priori intuition, which is not a quality of the architecture or reality. The immediate condition of all internal, subjective phenomena, in perception and intellection, mediates all external phenomena in perception and intellection. Space and time are the modes of representation of the perceiving and thinking subject as object. In Hegelian terms, reason becomes aware of itself in consciousness, and objectifies itself, through the representations of space and time. Space and time are the conditions of the sensibility of the subject, the conditions of the subjective experience of reality, which is the necessary basis of reality. Space and time are the representations from which all "synthetical cognitions can be drawn" (p. 33), which include geometry and mathematics in discursive or cognitive thought, and thus the concept of architecture. Architecture is an expression of the human condition insofar as the human condition is a subjective representation, and not an external reality.

As for George Berkeley, empirical experience is necessary in the development of concepts from intuition, according to Kant; for example, the concept of change based in the intuition of time, as the succession of the determinations of an object. Empirical intuition is also a subjective experience, as relations between objects in space and time do not exist without the subjective constitution of the senses, or the perception of the subject. Objects are transformed into relations given by representations in intuition. It is impossible to know phenomenal objects outside of the subjective sensation of them, outside the subjective mode of perceiving them, which is a universal representation of a manifold. It is also impossible to know the mechanisms by which objects are represented in intuition in the framework of space and time; it is thus impossible to have complete knowledge of either the object or the subject in human perception. The human being is caught in a play of mirrors as it were, having access only to the subjective condition of human experience, with no accessible basis in either the phenomenal or cognitive worlds. Architecture is a product of the play of mirrors; it is a conceptual mediation between intuition and phenomena, neither of which are entirely accessible. Architecture remains eternally a labyrinth, the ur-architectural form which represented the identity of life and death, the temporal and eternal, and the infinitely confining and infinitely expansive in the human understanding of the human condition. It is impossible to know a building architecturally outside the intuition of architecture, which is inaccessible, and it is impossible to know a building outside the concept of architecture.

Cognition only consists of relations in discursive reason, as given by a priori intuitions. It is impossible to know a thing in itself in phenomena through its relations, to either other things or the perceiving subject. The relations of a thing are determined in the manifold of intuition; particular relations cannot be known or perceived outside the transcendental matrix of relations as given by intuition. All relations between phenomenal objects are representations of a priori relations in intuition; the reality of phenomena plays itself out only as it has been drawn up in the imagination. A building functions as architecture only to the extent that the architectural relations of the building, within the framework of space and time, mathematics and geometry, have been drawn up in the imagination, or in intuition. Phenomenal forms in reality are representations of forms in the imagination or intuition as they interact with the discursive functions of cognition.

The human mind represents itself to itself through those representational forms, not through the mechanisms of intuition, which are inaccessible. Thus the forms of human thought and perception cannot be corresponded to the functions of human thought and perception, and can be seen as contradictory, because the functions are inaccessible despite the reality of the representational forms. If the form in architecture contradicts the function, the architecture is true to the reality of the human mind, which attempts to have access to itself, and the phenomenal world, through formal representation, resulting from the interaction of intuition and sensibility, but in fact cannot, and is deluded into having such access by the reality of the forms in perception and cognition. Like the shadows on the wall of the prison in the Allegory of the Cave, the forms of sensible reality contradict both the function of sensible reality and the function of the perceiving subject. The object as it appears and is conceived in perception and cognition cannot be equated with the object as it exists as a thing in itself, and the object as a thing in itself cannot be seen within the framework of space and time, the a priori intuitions which transform the object into a perceived form.

Knowledge consists of the power of receiving representations and the power of cognizing by means of these representations, according to Kant. Sensible objects are received as representations by a priori intuition, as forms. The forms of architecture are perceived as representations in intuition. Sensible objects are cognized as forms of thought, transformed into signs and symbols, understood as abstracted universals, a posteriori. A priori cognition, insofar as it is dependent on understanding, is made possible by a synthesis or conjunction of a manifold of conceptions in relation to the "unity of apperception" (p. 86), the synthesis of multiple singular perceptions of sensible objects. The synthesis is "not merely transcendental, but also purely intellectual," and "the synthesis of the manifold of sensuous intuition, which is possible and necessary à priori, may be called figurative (*synthesis speciosa*)" (p. 87), as opposed to "conjunction of the understanding (*synthesis intellectualis*)," in cogitation, which is also a priori. The mechanisms of intuition are known by analogy, in tropic language, of the imagination. It can be said that the architecture of a building, as it entails a synthesis of the manifold material parts of the building, can be seen as a priori cognition or intuition, as a model or catechism of the processes of perception and intellection, in an expression of the human condition. As Kant says, "human reason is by nature architectonic" (p. 269), requiring an a priori unity, and accepting only principles which are part of a possible system.

Figurative synthesis is distinguished from intellectual synthesis: the intellectual synthesis occurs in discursive reason, in cogitation, while the figurative synthesis is related to the original synthetic unity of apperception and the transcendental unity which is the object of cogitation. Figurative synthesis is thus labeled "the transcendental synthesis of imagination" (p. 87), imagination being "the faculty of representing an object even without its presence in intuition," belonging to sensibility. Architecture, for example, exists in the imagination, as a transcendental synthesis, and that transcendental synthesis is projected onto the material form of a building. Intuition cannot be separated from sensibility, but at the same time intuition can only be known figuratively, through representations, as a product of language. Architecture, thus, is a product of language, figural or tropic language in particular. Architecture is a product of the imagination.

The productive imagination in intuition is distinguished from the "reproductive" imagination in discursive reason or cogitation, which depends on empirical laws of association, and can in no way explain a priori intuition or the transcendental synthesis. Reproductive, cogitative imagination depends on visual representation, as the visual sensible forms of objects, which have been received based on the principles of the a priori synthesis, and have been transformed into universals by those principles, in a dialectical relation. A geometrical line or a circle cannot be "cogitated" unless represented visually, by drawing in thought. Architecture thus cannot be thought unless it is represented visually, and figuratively, in the imagination. The dimensions of space cannot be thought without the representation of lines drawn perpendicular to each other. The representation of architecture is thus necessary in the representation of space; architecture, as a mediation between the human mind and the phenomenal world, also functions as a mediation between discursive reason and intuition. Architecture mediates between thought and both the external world and the internal world.

Time cannot be thought unless it is represented by drawing a straight line, which functions as an external figurative representation of an intuition, and leads to the synthesis of the manifold in intuition, in the internal world of the mind. The visual figurative representation allows time as the synthesis of the manifold to be cognized in unities and variabilities of dimensions, which must conform to the principles of the a priori synthesis, but which operate in the empirical laws of association in the reproductive imagination, which produces the visual figurative representation. The lines of architecture are visual, figurative representations, linguistic tropes, which function as analogies of the synthetic intuitions of space and time, which do not exist in the phenomenal world. Architecture is an intellectual diagramming of the representation by the mind of the phenomenal world to itself, as the lines of architecture are projected onto matter. At the same time, because architecture can only be representation, in relation to the phenomenal world and intuition, it prevents us from knowing either the external or the internal world, as does language. Architecture is a form of language, and both the phenomenal world and the inner workings of intuition are only known through representation in language; we can only know what is given by language, and anything outside of language is inaccessible.

The thinking self, the subject, can only be represented through representation in language to itself as well, so the self can only know itself as reified object in representation in consciousness, not as thinking subject. The self can only be cognized as an object of thought, as it appears in representation, rather than as it is. It is impossible to know oneself, except in external relations given by discursive reason, in the same way that objects are not knowable in themselves, and intuition is not knowable in cognition. Thus "we cognize our own subject only as phenomenon, and not as it is in itself" (p. 90). The a priori forms of internal and external sensuous intuition are represented in space and time, and the representations of space and time must always conform to the synthesis of the apprehension of the manifold in phenomena. The forms of representation are not possible without the synthesis, and the synthesis is not possible without the forms of representation. Intuition and sensibility are locked together in a dialectical relationship, in a transcendental idealism. The forms of representation, based on perceived sensible forms, are a product of the a priori intuition to begin with, through the construction of the intelligible form. As space and time are intuitions, a priori figurative representations of a manifold synthesis, and all cognition and perception must conform to the laws of space and time, intuition must be a priori to perception as well as cognition. It follows that architecture as representation, as both thought and perceived, must conform to the laws of the a priori intuition, although architecture can only be known through external relations in discursive reason.

Space is represented as a phenomenal object, in the necessity of its visual representation in geometry. The representation of space thus requires both the a priori synthesis of the manifold in intuition and a "form of sensibility" (the visual representation), which is the form of the intuition or a "formal intuition" itself. The synthesis of the manifold which makes perception possible (as representation) must conform to the mechanisms of discursive reason, as the mechanisms of discursive reason must conform to the a priori synthesis. Experience is defined as "cognition by means of conjoined perceptions" (p. 92), which can be called apperception. As apperception occurs according to the "categories" in discursive reason which are derived from intuition, the categories are thus "conditions of the possibility of experience." Perceptual experience is made possible by intuition by way of cognition or discursive reason. Perception is a form of thinking, as in the *Vorstellung* of Hegel or the *Vorstellungsrepräsentanz* of Freud.

As Kant writes, when "I make the empirical intuition of a house by apprehension of the manifold contained therein into a perception, the *necessary unity* of space and of my external sensuous intuition lies at the foundation of this act" (p. 92). Without the a priori intuition, apperception, cognition, and discursive reason would not be possible. The form of the house is drawn according to the synthetic unity of the manifold in space, which does not exist in phenomena, but rather only in the mind. Sensual perception and apprehension must conform to the synthesis of apperception, which is intellectual and a priori, and which is also spontaneous (and unconscious) in imagination and understanding. It is impossible to perceive or understand a form in architecture or phenomena without an under-standing of the synthetic unity or manifold, just as it is impossible to understand the meaning of a word outside a syntax. It is necessary to understand the mechanisms of thought and perception in order to understand architecture; the mechanisms of thought and perception are not completely accessible to thought itself, and must in part be ascribed to a priori intuition, or the mechanisms of unconscious thought. Architecture, if it is to accurately represent human thought and perception, should contain a metaphysical element that is not immediately accessible to sensory perception or discursive reason, but which can be understood through higher forms of intellection, in advanced forms of conceptual representation.

Thought is the condition for the possibility of architecture, as it is the condition for the possibility of experience. The subject draws "the form of the house conformably to this synthetical unity of the manifold in space," in geomet-rical representation. The synthetic unity is taken as a category of the a priori synthesis in intuition; the category exists in abstraction, in the visual representation of space in geometry, processed in discursive reason as a quantity, in a sequence of relationships, which conform to the manifold synthesis, as the manifold synthesis conforms to the categories. A perception must conform to the categories and the manifold synthesis, in the dialectic of sensibility and intuition which constitutes human thought for Kant. The synthesis of empirical apprehension must conform to the synthesis of intellectual apperception, in a spontaneous production which can be called both imagination and understanding. Neither the empirical apprehension nor the intellectual apperception is prior, as both depend on the synthesis of the intuition.

As phenomena are represented as quantities, as abstractions in relation to the a priori synthesis, in mathematics and geometry, for example, a phenomenon can only be understood as a quantity in relation to a whole, which is the a priori synthesis of the manifold in apperception. A line can only be represented in relation to the points which constitute it in a series of relationships, but drawing the line in thought does not require a reconstruction of all the relationships of the points; drawing the line in thought, as a visual representation, can be done by intuition. All phenomena are understood in intuition in extension, in successive synthesis in apprehension. All phenomena are thus aggregates, formed from "previously given parts" (p. 115), conforming to the synthesis of the manifold. No phenomenon can be apprehended outside of a relation to the a priori synthesis, and apperception in experience. It follows that architecture depends on the synthesis of the representation of parts in extension, as an aggregate. Through architecture, space can be represented as a phenomenon, in the aggregate of abstract geometrical representation. Geometry and mathematics are aggregates of extension based on the "successive synthesis of the productive imagination" (p. 116), as opposed to the reproductive imagination in discursive reason, in the generation of tropic figures. The aggregates of extension of geometry and mathematics compose the "schema of a pure conception of external intuition," in the categories of discursive reason in representation, in the conditions of the a priori intuition.

Mathematics is applied to experience according to the transcendental principle of a priori cognition. A concept is schematic, based on the principles of intuition. All phenomena can be seen as mathematical, insofar as they conform to the mathematical principles of cognition in the schema. Architecture, as mathematics and geometry, can also be seen to be applied to experience. The phenomenal world is experienced architecturally, insofar as it is experienced mathematically and geometrically. Thought is architectonic in Kant's system, and architecture mediates the experience of the phenomenal world, as Schinkel would have it. All objects of sense conform to the rules of construction in space, no matter what kind of construction that might be. Different philosophical systems propose different models of the construction of space, but space must be constructed in some way in any philosophical system. All apprehension and cognition depend on an architectural construction of space, which entails the aggregates of phenomena in extension in relationships of parts which conform to a synthetic whole, as represented by space and time. All perception, in apprehension, and all models of vision, depend on the architectonic construction of space.

Experience is defined by Kant as an "empirical cognition" (p. 122); a phenomenal object is determined by cognition through perception, in a temporal sequence, conforming to the a priori synthesis of the manifold, which constitutes "experience." Experience is thus apperception, a synthesis of perceptions, which is not contained in an individual perception, but which contains the synthetic a priori unity of the manifold of perception, as does intuition. The synthetic unity makes the perception and cognition of a phenomenal object possible, and it makes experience possible, but only through representation. It follows that architecture can be seen as a schematic or conceptual model for perception and experience, as they are represented in visual forms which conform to the synthetic a priori unity, and to the principles and mechanisms of cognition in relation to intuition. Individual perceptions, and phenomenal objects perceived individually, have no necessary relation to each other until they are submitted to the manifold of apperception, in spatial and temporal sequences, which, as representations of intuition, organize individual perceptions in experience so that they may be apprehended as part of a whole, as part of an all-encompassing allegory or narrative sequence of tropes or signs, which constitute the whole, which is given a priori.

Experience is only possible in the representation of the synthetic manifold, and "by means of a representation of the necessary connection of perception." Individual perceptions, which have no connection or relation to each other in themselves, any more than individual phenomenal objects have a connection to each other in themselves, must be seen to be necessary in their connections to each other for experience to be possible. The necessary connection between perceptions is only possible within the a priori synthesis in intuition. Without an intuition of the totality of experience, individual perceptions, like words in sentences, would make no sense in relation to each other, as in a condition of psychosis. The necessary connection between perceptions only exists in representation; they do not exist in experience, but rather experience is a product of the necessary connections in representation. It is impossible to know experience in the same way that it is impossible to know intuition, as experience can only be represented in spatial and temporal terms, through abstract visual forms, in the same way that the phenomenal objects of perception in experience are represented.

In architecture, the structural and functional requirements of a building are the product of necessary connections between perceptions in cognition, therefore they can only be known as representations conforming to the a priori synthesis of the whole which is "architecture." The different structural and functional requirements of a building, as relations or connections between phenomenal objects, exist independently but are apprehended in apperception to form the architectural whole. If the form of the architectural elements corresponds to the function, then the architecture can be apprehended as the phenomenal world is apprehended, as a necessary sequence of connections in apperception. But if the form of the architectural elements contradicts their function, the architectural elements as phenomenal objects can be seen as existing in themselves independent of the synthesis in apperception which is the a priori intuition. The contradiction between form and function in architecture pulls the veil away, as in the Allegory of the Cave, and reveals the scaffolding of perception and comprehension. Architectural elements are revealed as existing independently of the a priori synthesis of the manifold, or as existing in an a priori synthesis which is not given by the material forms of the architecture, but by the metaphysical, transcendental intuition which is applied to the materiality of the architecture, as the framework of human thought is projected onto experience in perception, and onto the phenomenal world.

The connection of perceptions in a temporal sequence, resulting in apperception, is a "product of a synthetical faculty of imagination" (p. 128), combining sensation and intuition, and determining an internal sense of time. Apperception, the comprehension of the phenomenal world as a totality of experience, is a product of imagination through representation; experience is a product of imagination. The architectonic framing of the phenomenal world in apperception, the architecture of reality, is imaginative, the product of figural representation in language. Space and time are not objects of perception, and the sequential relations between objects in space and time cannot be perceived, they can only be apprehended, based on the representation of the a priori intuition of the synthetic manifold. The experience of architecture is thus the product of imagination; it cannot be the product of direct perception. This is revealed in architecture in the contradiction between form and function, which reveals the contradiction between the apparent perception of spatial and temporal sequences, and the temporal and spatial sequences as representations. The connections between forms in architecture are only known through a priori intuitions preceding individual perceptions, in the same way that meaning in language is only generated through a priori intuition represented in the syntax of the language.

The connections between forms in the experience of architecture, like the connections between phenomenal objects in experience, are undetermined by perception. The connections between forms are only given as they are cogitated in discursive reason as necessary, in order to conform to the a priori manifold synthesis, though in external reality they do not exist. The conception of the necessity of relations is independent of perception and is the product of pure apprehension, which results in apperception. The conception is "of the relation of cause and effect" in the categories of discursive reason. Experience, the empirical cognition of phenomena, is possible only on the condition of the conception of cause and effect, as all phenomena are subject to the law of causality, in representation in imagination. All phenomena, conversely, are only possible because of the law of causality. The experience of architecture, for example, is dependent on the law of causality, which is not present in perception, thus the perception of the form of the architecture contradicts the sequential function of the architecture as an aggregate of phenomenal objects in matter.

The apprehension or comprehension of phenomena requires that each phenomenon have a specific position in relation to other phenomena in space and time, which is determined in a priori intuition. A perception becomes empirical experience only because what is perceived has been determined a priori as having a specific place in space and time. The perceived object can thus be placed in apperception according to a rule or schema which governs the apprehension of it in perception. In architecture, for example, a door (as it is understood as an architectural element within the schema of cause and effect in the law of causality) is perceived in relation to a room, or a space to which it provides access. The door is understood as a door in spatial and temporal sequences, but it is not perceived individually as such; it is rather comprehended as such in apperception. If the form of the door contradicts its function, then the door can be understood as a phenomenal object of perception which is submitted to the framework of apprehension in intuition through representation.

The manifold synthesis of phenomena is a transcendental idea. A transcendental idea is a pure conception of reason, and a necessary conception of reason, "to which no corresponding object can be discovered in the world of sense" (p. 205), like the Platonic archetype. Transcendental ideas are necessary products of reason which define empirical cognition as determined by a priori intuition in the synthesis of the manifold. The transcendental idea can never exist completely in phenomena, and phenomena can never be adequate to the synthesis of the transcendental idea. The totality of phenomena, which is given in perception through intuition, is only an idea, which cannot be completely represented, though it is adequately represented in sequences of forms and signs in space and time. The totality of phenomena, the basis of empirical experience, perception and apprehension, is thus "a *problem* incapable of solution" (p. 206). It is impossible to know the phenomenal world, or the mechanisms by which the phenomenal world is known in representation.

Human reason is "architectonic" in that all thoughts or cognitions conform to a possible system, in the same way that all phenomenal objects exist in sequences of relationships. A building, as a collection of phenomenal objects in sequences of relationships, can never be adequate to an architectural idea, the transcendental idea in intuition, because the pure idea can never be completely represented in the phenomenal world. Architecture, like all forms of human expression, is propelled by the fact that it can never be complete, just like the human being can never be complete, because the relation between the transcendental idea and concrete phenomena can never be resolved. The continuous quest for completion by the incomplete subject, in its reason and poetic expression (as in architecture), results in desire, as Freud or Lacan would have it, wholeness being the inaccessible object of desire. Thus is the desire of architecture, the impossibility of the representation of the void at the center of being, given by the impossibility of knowing either the self or the phenomenal world.

Kant defines transcendental idealism as the doctrine that empirical experience is only a form of representation in discursive reason, that phenomenal objects only exist in abstract sequences of cause and effect, in discursive reason, and that phenomenal objects have no existence in themselves outside of human thought. Transcendental idealism is also called formal idealism, to distinguish it from the material idealism associated with George Berkeley, according to which phenomenal objects do not exist at all. In transcendental idealism, space and time are representations which only exist in the mind. A priori intuition is also only known through representation, in space and time, as a phenomenon. It is not possible to know anything as real outside of empirical perception and the synthesis of apperception, which can only be understood as representations. Phenomena are only real in perception as representations, and perception is only real in empirical experience as a representation. Phenomenal objects do not exist outside of perception. Apperception, entailing the a priori synthesis of the manifold applied to phenomenal reality, is a false representation of the phenomenal world.

The contradiction between form and function in architecture reveals apperception to be a false representation of the phenomenal world, which does not exist or cannot be known outside of the false representation. Intuition known through representation is likewise a false representation of the self, the source of the architectonic system which is applied to phenomenal reality. The contradiction between form and function in architecture also reveals the false representation of the thinking subject to itself, the impossibility of knowing the mechanisms of cognition, the source of the architectonic, through representation, without contradiction. The architectonic and architecture are concepts which are necessary to experience what does not exist, which is a connection between mind and matter, thought and the phenomenal world, through intuition. Architecture, like the phenomenal world, is only possible because of thought, and the alienation of thought from itself in consciousness, a theme elaborated by Hegel.

Cognition by means of conceptions in reason is labeled "philosophical cognition" by Kant, based in a priori intuition (corresponding to *nous poietikos* in Aristotelian philosophy), in contrast to cognition by means of the construction of conceptions, which is "mathematical cognition" in discursive reason (corresponding to *nous pathetikos*). The construction of the conception in discursive reason requires the representation provided by the a priori intuition. This requires a non-empirical intuition, or an idea not connected to sensible reality, in transcendental idealism. A constructed conception or representation, such as architecture, for example, "must be seen to be universally valid for all the possible intuitions which rank under that conception" (p. 400) in the synthesis of the manifold in intuition and apperception. A triangle is constructed, for example, by imagination, in intuition or empirically, without reference to empirical experience, but based in the a priori synthesis. The components of the triangle, the length of the sides, etc., are irrelevant to the conception of the triangle as it exists as an a priori intuition. In the same way, the particular architectural forms in a building are irrelevant to the conception of architecture as an ordering principle of space and time in a priori intuition. The contradiction between the form and the function in the architecture makes this apparent.

Philosophical cognition apprehends the particular by way of the universal, working from a priori intuition to empirical experience, while mathematical cognition apprehends the universal by way of the particular, working from empirical experience to a priori intuition. As the design of a building entails mathematical cognition, the phenomenal elements (representations) of empirical experience are organized toward a "universal condition of construction," the a priori synthesis. As the apprehension of architecture entails philosophical cognition, transcendental concepts in the universal condition are organized toward the particulars of the construction of a building. Mathematical principles and demonstrations are derived from the construction of conceptions in discursive reason, rather than the conceptions of intuition, from the particular to the universal. Mathematics, thus architecture, entails a construction of symbols (representations), which are represented in intuition as signs (concepts), like signifiers in a language. Intuition operates according to the rules of language; as Lacan concluded that the unconscious is structured like a language, it can be concluded that Kantian intuition is structured like a language.

Berkeley

In *An Essay Toward a New Theory of Vision* in 1709, George Berkeley (1685–1753) asserted that the quality of distance, as in the qualities of space and time for Immanuel Kant, cannot be immediately perceived of itself, but must be a judgment which is learned through an accumulation of sense perceptions in relation to discursive thought. Judgment, according to Berkeley, or acquired understanding, is the product of experience rather than immediate sense perception; it is therefore necessarily the product of memory, of the mnemic residue in perception, the accumulation of which leads to the development of the imagination.

Berkeley wrote in the Fourth Dialogue of the *Alciphron*, "we perceive distance not immediately but by mediation of a sign, which has no likeness to it or necessary connection with it, but only suggests it from repeated experience, as words do things" (Berkeley 1963: §8). The sign is an abstraction from a particular, a product of discursive reason, which is itself a product of intelligibles. For Berkeley, in the same way that signs or signifiers, that is, words, in language immediately and unconsciously produce ideas or meanings, signs in the act of perception, such as distance relationships, immediately and unconsciously produce ideas and judgments about the perceived sensible world, in a process inaccessible to discursive reason, but which can be understood by discursive reason through the illumination of intuition. For Berkeley, perception functions as a language of signs.

The sign is constructed by reason in intellect, and has no necessary relation to the sense perception of the object, in a contradiction between form and function. As Berkeley explains in the *New Theory of Vision*, we are "exceedingly prone to imagine those things which are perceived only by the mediation of others to be themselves the immediate objects of sight" (Berkeley 1963: §66), just as in language we experience the immediate recognition of an idea, and not the mechanism by which the word conveys the idea. When we perceive an object, we are unaware that what we are perceiving is the sensible form of the object, which has no immediate connection to the object itself, and that the sensible form is formed in relation to the intelligible form, the idea of the form of the object, by the inaccessible *nous* or intuition. In the *Alciphron*, Berkeley asks, "may we not suppose that men, not resting in but overlooking the immediate and proper objects of sight as in their own nature of small moment, carry their attention onward to the very thing signified?" (Berkeley 1963: §12).

It is the idea of the object as given by intellect which is immediately grasped, the intelligible form, rather than the image itself of the object (the sensible form), which is imprinted on memory as a seal or sign. The objects themselves, according to Berkeley, "are not seen, but only suggested and apprehended by means of the proper objects of sight, which alone are seen." The proper object of sight is the seal or sign, the imprint or mnemic residue, the intelligible form, which are constructed in intellect and language, memory and imagination. In the *Alciphron*, the language of vision "is the same throughout the whole world, and not, like other languages, differing in different places," thus "it will not seem unaccountable that men should mistake the connection between the proper objects of sight and the things signified by them to be founded in necessary relation or likeness" (§11). It is thus "easy to conceive why men who do not think should confound in this language of vision the signs with the things signified"—the sensible form and the intelligible form (in this sense the thing signified)—in discursive reason which has not advanced to intellection, not been illuminated by intuition, which is the source of the essential principles which constitute the universals or intelligibles which formulate the universal language of vision.

In the *Critique of Pure Reason* of Kant, it is impossible to know an object outside its conception as an intelligible in intellect; perception in intellection ultimately transcends the experience of the sensible world in perception. In order to experience the world, reason by necessity must make itself inaccessible to the world, resulting in a contradiction. For Kant, the coherence and totality of the sensible world are necessary for perception, as perception is a basis for reason, but such totality is impossible in perception itself; thus reason exists on an impossible premise. As Kant wrote, "the absolute totality of all phenomena is only an idea, for as we never can present an adequate representation of it, it remains for us a *problem* incapable of solution" (p. 206). Reason is unrepresentable to itself, and requires the inaccessible *nous*, or intuition, in order for it to explain itself to itself. Imprints of sensible objects in perception "are mere representations, receiving from perceptions alone significance and relation to a real object, under the condition that this or that perception—indicating an object—is in complete connection with all others in accordance with the rules of the unity of experience" (p. 280). There is a disjunction in the relation between the sensible form as it is perceived and the sensible object, and between the sensible form and the intelligible form. "Reason never has an immediate relation to an object; it relates immediately to the understanding alone" (p. 360), the intellection of the object. The transcendental idea, then, is not just an idea of an object, but also a "conception of the complete unity of the conceptions of objects" (p. 361). The idea of an object is not possible outside the totality of the unity of objects: the sensible is not possible without the intelligible. The object is singular while the idea of it is synthetic, thus the idea of the object cannot possibly correspond to the object.

The distinction or contradiction between the sensible form and the intelligible form can be seen in relation to the distinction or contradiction between the signifier and the signified in language. The distinction between the signifier and the signified in language can be found in the writings of René Descartes in the seventeenth century, who anticipated Ferdinand de Saussure in the twentieth century by asserting that the signifier, the particular word, does not have an immediate relation with the signified, the idea that is associated with it. As Descartes stated in *The World, or a Treatise on Light and the Other Principal Objects of the Senses*, in 1664, "words do not in any way resemble the things they signify" (Descartes 2003: 85); the relationship between the signifier and the signified is arbitrary, and reveals a disjunction between thought and the sensible world, as does the relation between the sensible form and the intelligible form. As applied to architecture, the contradiction between thought and the sensible world, and between the signified and signifier, translate to a contradiction between form and function, the idea and the matter. Nevertheless, for Descartes "that does not prevent them from causing us to think about those things, often without us even noticing the sound of the words or their syllables"; the sensible form functions in discursive reason and perception without awareness of its connection to the intelligible form.

According to Descartes, the contradiction between signifier and signified is present in perception, which functions as a language of signs. Descartes asks:

> Now if words—which have meaning only as a result of a human convention—are enough to make us think about things that do not resemble them in any way, why is it not possible that nature may also have established a particular sign which would make us have the sensation of light, even though such a sign contains nothing in itself that resembles the sensation?

The sign is constructed by reason in intellect, and has no necessary relation to the sense perception of the object; it would correspond to the sensible form, which is a product of the intelligible form rather than the immediate perception of the sensible object.

In a revised edition of the *New Theory of Vision*, called *The Theory of Vision or Visual Language Vindicated and Explained*, published in 1733, Berkeley attempted to present a more scientific explanation for the disjunction or contradiction between the sensible object and the sign of it in perception, the signifier and the signified. The explanation is based on the phenomenon of the inversion of the projected image of the object onto the retina of the eye, which does not correspond to the object itself. The image is created by "pencils of rays issuing from any luminous object," which "after their passage through the pupil and their refraction by the crystalline, delineate inverted pictures in the retina" (Berkeley 1963: §49). These pictures, which are "supposed the immediate proper objects of sight," do not correspond in orientation to the object itself. In Classical optics, the sensible straight line appears to the eye as a curved line, as it is distorted by the retina. In both cases, the sensible form has been revised by the intelligible form, in order for the sensible world to be ordered.

Berkeley's explanation is that the image, the sensible form, and the mechanisms of inversion and refraction, cannot be taken as a true picture of an object, but must be taken as an image existing independently of the sensible object, the intelligible form. For Berkeley, "the retina, crystalline, pupil, rays crossing, refracted, and reunited in different images, correspondent and similar to the outward objects, are things altogether of a tangible nature," like words in a language which have no necessary relation to the ideas which they represent, as a kind of picture in the *oculus mentis*. For Berkeley the pictures on the retina are tangible objects themselves which are "so far from being the proper objects of sight that they are not at all perceived thereby" (§50), but "apprehended by the imagination alone."

It is necessary in the experience and perception of architecture that the sensible form, as it is perceived, contradicts both the phenomenal object of perception and the intelligible form of the phenomenal object, which precedes the sensible form and prevents it from corresponding to the phenomenal object. It is impossible to know a building in its phenomenal essence or existence as a "thing in itself," just like it is impossible to know phenomena in general, without the mediation of the concept or transcendental idea with what is perceived. This condition is present in the contradiction between form and function in the architecture of Karl Friedrich Schinkel, as it is throughout the history of Western architecture. The contradiction between the sensible form and intelligible form, between perception and understanding, between matter and mind, is present in the thought of Berkeley, Kant, Schelling, and Hegel, as it is throughout the history of Western philosophy.

Chapter 5

Modernism: structural rationalism to structural linguistics

Viollet-le-Duc

Eugène-Emmanuel Viollet-le-Duc (1814–79), in his *Dictionnaire raisonné de l'architecture* (1854–68), defined "style" in art as a "conception of the human mind" (p. 231), and "the manifestation of an ideal based on a principle" (p. 232), in the section "Style: The Manifestation of an Ideal Based on a Principle," Volume VIII (Viollet-le-Duc 1990). Style is defined as the universal principle in nature in the creation of natural forms. All crystals in nature, for example, although they are always different, result from identical principles of crystallization. In the creation of natural forms, nature itself never copies the outward appearance of a form, but generates forms from inner, universal principles. Architecture, likewise, is based on universal principles in human reason, and thus depends on reason as a universal rather than a set of particulars, as in the abstraction in *nous poietikos* as opposed to reason based on sense perception in *nous hylikos* or *nous pathetikos*. Unity in architecture is the result of the creation of form based on the principles of reason. It is reason alone which creates connections between the different parts and forms of a building, just as reason alone creates connections between objects in perception, resulting in apperception, the wholeness or totality of the sensible world which is a construct of the human mind, as described by Plotinus, Leibniz, or Kant, for example. It is the projection of the principles of reason onto the work of architecture which constitutes its "style." Imagination, the creation of form in the human mind, must thus follow reason, which plays the predominate role in the creation of form and the definition of style. Style is thus the product of universal principles rather than individual subjective sense experience, a concept which plays a pivotal role in Modernist movements in the twentieth century.

While the importance of universal principles of reason in design has played a role in conceptions of architecture since the Classical world, Viollet-le-Duc is the first to apply them to the new construction methods of modern architecture, resulting in "structural rationalism," that is, constructional determinism and structural expression made possible by the new construction techniques in iron and then steel, products of the Industrial Revolution. Viollet-le-Duc no longer needs to concern himself with the transformation of forms in nature to stone masonry, as Quatremère de Quincy did, or with the corresponding dressing or costuming of the building, which entailed a different kind of conception of "style." In Quatremère de Quincy's conception of style, the masonry dressing of a building created a kind of language or writing, in imitation of natural forms, which itself constituted a style. Architecture is no longer a form of language or writing for Viollet-le-Duc, because the essence of architecture can now be found in its structural forms alone, which are the pure product of human reason and crystallization in nature. Architecture is still based on imitation and abstraction, in line with Quatremère de Quincy, as expressed in Viollet-le-Duc's *Dictionnaire raisonné de l'architecture*, but for Viollet-le-Duc architecture can now bypass the aestheticization of form, in its dressing, which constitutes its writing or language, and express directly the relation between human reason and nature through structure. Style no longer involves the quotation, in the form of writing, of historical forms in the dressing of a building. Style can thus be purified of particulars with cultural associations, as it would be by the De Stijl group and the International Style architects.

Style is purified as an intellectual act, as extracted from previous architectures, in a formalistic solution to the problem of the structure of a building. Style has shifted from the visual associations connected to the writing of forms in cultural contexts to the universal principles of human reason in abstraction, which are shared by all human beings in the same way that the same principles are shared by all forms of nature. The principles of human reason and human creation are the same as the principles of nature and creation in nature. Style is not to be found in the finalized form of a building, but in the rational process which leads to the finalized form on the part of the designer. Style can in fact be found in nature itself, in its forming principles. In the mechanisms of reason or the intellect which constitute style as a forming principle, as it is constituted in nature, geometry pre-exists the creative process as an a priori, according to Viollet-le-Duc, as in the a priori intuitions of Kant, those products of the mind which determine all sensible reality.

On the frontispiece of the *Dictionnaire raisonné de l'architecture*, a Medieval mason accompanied by a member of the clergy and a member of the aristocracy traces a circle and an equilateral triangle in the ground with his compass. The circle and the equilateral triangle are irreducible a priori forms, like the Platonic solids, or the Pythagorean Harmonies in music, from which all forms are created as composites. The circle and the equilateral triangle are not creations or inventions, but are rather discovered as existing a priori in the process of making forms. They are discovered as well, logically, in the principles of nature in its form making. In the section on style in the *Dictionnaire raisonné de l'architecture*: "Nature is at work, her deductions follow one upon the other according to the order of invariable logic.

She traces a circle, and in this inscribes the only figure which can't be distorted, one in which the sides and the angles are all equal among themselves" (Bergdoll 1990: 24). The geometries are projected to three dimensions, as in the polyhedrons of the demiurge in the *Timaeus*: "She takes a sphere, and in this sphere, by induction, she inscribes a pyramid, whose four faces are each equilateral triangles, that is to say a solid that cannot be distorted and whose properties are the same no matter which one of the sides is used as the base."

The a priori geometries which underlie all forms of nature, from Classical philosophy, are the same a priori geometries which underlie human reason. Through geometry, architecture connects nature and the human mind. As all creation of human reason can be traced back to the circle and the equilateral triangle, the irreducible geometrical figures can be seen to persevere through all the variations and forms of human creativity, as the forming principles of nature persevere through the multiplicity of natural forms, and it is the persevering principles and a priori irreducible geometries which constitute style in both nature and human creation, according to Viollet-le-Duc. The drawing of the equilateral triangle in the circle by the Medieval mason is a form of triangulation, which was used as a system of measurement in Medieval buildings, and which symbolically represents the manifestation of the divine idea in the human mind and physical form, as the indivisibility of the circle corresponds to the indivisibility of God, and the triangle corresponds to the Trinity, as the manifestation of God in body and spirit. The a priori circle and triangle are the archetypal forms or intelligibles which underlie the forms of nature and the created forms of human reason; they are undetectable in sense perception, and are only known as intelligible forms in higher forms of intellect, *nous poietikos* or *virtus intellectiva*, as in the *natura naturans*.

The a priori geometrical principles of nature are, like the primitive hut according to Quatremère de Quincy, already abstracted and conceptualized models for architecture as derived from nature. The imitation of the a priori geometrical principles in form making in architecture, as for Quatremère, allows architecture to express its metaphysical function in its form as a representation of the relation between the human mind and nature. As the geometrical principles are already abstracted, there is a contradiction between the intellectual idea and nature itself. There is no contradiction between the form and function in the geometrical principles because the geometries are abstractions. As the resulting forms in architecture correspond to its metaphysical function, they contradict the actual functional requirements of a building, in order to constitute a form of poetic expression.

Sullivan

The terra cotta ornament designed by Louis Henry Sullivan (1856–1924) for the buildings of Adler and Sullivan—for example, the Wainwright Building in St. Louis

(1890, Figure 5.1) or the Guaranty Building in Buffalo (1894)—has no relation to the structure or function of the building, despite the supposed claim in "The Tall Office Building Artistically Considered" (1896) that "form ever follows function" (Sullivan 1947: 208), a claim repeated in the "Kindergarten Chats" (p. 170). Sullivan said that form should follow function in the creative process of the architect, and that "the essence of things is taking shape in the matter of things" (p. 208) in nature, but he did not say that the form of the building should follow the function of the building, its functional or structural requirements. For Sullivan, form follows function in the expression of life, in the process of birth and growth, and the dialectics of birth and death, organic and inorganic, physical and metaphysical. Form follows function in the emotional expression of life, which is how Sullivan defines a building, wherein "the same emotional impulse shall flow throughout harmoniously into its varied form of expression" (in "Ornament in Architecture," 1892) (p. 188). In the process of birth and growth, "the essence of things is taking shape in the matter of things" ("The Tall Office Building Artistically Considered") (p. 208); the form of things, the shape, follows the function of things, the essence. Form follows function in architecture insofar as the function of architecture is to express a metaphysical idea or a transcendental essence.

In the "Kindergarten Chats" (1901–2), all forms "stand for relationships between the immaterial and the material, between the subjective and the objective—between the Infinite Spirit and the finite mind" (Sullivan 1947: 45). Forms in nature and architecture are a means by which the human intellect can be connected to divine intellect, or active intellect in Aristotelian terms. The *nous hylikos*, material intellect of Aristotle, is distinguished from a universal, active intellect, a *nous poietikos* not connected to sense perception. According to Sullivan, "every function is a subdivision or phase of that energy which we have called the Infinite Creative Spirit" (p. 99) in the same way that the material elements of *nous pathetikos*, material intellect, as connected to sense perception, are subdivisions or phases of the universal active intellect. The word "function" is clearly not being used to refer to the functional or structural requirements of a building. Function is seen as an essence of the creative process of architecture, in that "the main function … will focus in the specific needs of those who wish to build, and that such needs are quite apt to be emotional as well as what is so generally called practical" (p. 170). Function is assimilated in order to express a creative impulse in truthful terms, satisfying beautiful forms.

In his thinking, Sullivan was influenced by the aesthetics of Leopold Eidlitz, the transcendentalism of Ralph Waldo Emerson and Walt Whitman, and the transcendental idealism of Georg Wilhelm Friedrich Hegel. Eidlitz (1823–1908) was born in Prague and moved to New York City in his twenties. He helped found the American Institute of Architects in 1857. In his *Nature and Function of Art* (1881), Eidlitz described the design of a building as the expression of a transcendental idea which manifests itself in form through nature. Architecture imitates nature insofar as nature forms itself by universal principles, as with Viollet-le-Duc. A work of art, "like a work of nature, is a realized idea" (Eidlitz 1977 [1881]: 57), and "must be

Figure 5.1 **Louis Henry Sullivan, Wainwright Building, 1890**

developed according to the methods of nature," or as Plotinus put it, "go back to the Ideas from which Nature itself derives" (Plotinus 1952: V.8.1). A building, as an organism, while it is developed according to the methods of nature, cannot be an imitation of any work of nature, as in the priority of the *natura naturans* of Quatremère de Quincy. Architecture is highest among the arts because the essence, the very definition and function of architecture, is the expression of an idea. Architecture can only be art if it expresses an idea, as Schelling established. Architecture is poetry, as poetry is "the expression of an idea in matter" (Eidlitz 1977 [1881]: 72), according to Eidlitz.

The essence of the function of a building is expressed in its form, in its outward appearance, according to Eidlitz. In the "Kindergarten Chats" of Sullivan, good architecture is the *image* of the function of the building: a "building, to be good architecture, must, first of all, clearly correspond with its function, must be its image" (Sullivan 1947: 46). In an article entitled "Style" in *Inland Architect* in May 1888, Sullivan proposed that architecture can only be art in the composition of the façade of a building and in the ornamentation of a building. The outward appearance of a building expresses its essence, the transcendental idea, in the same way that the essence of an organism in nature is expressed in its appearance. The essence of the building, its formulating principles expressed in its appearance, like the essence in nature, is defined by Sullivan as "style," seemingly following Viollet-le-Duc. In Sullivan's architecture, the influence of the structural rationalism of Viollet-le-Duc can be seen in the curved buttresses at the base of the Auditorium Building in Chicago (1886–90). The functional and structural requirements of a building play no role in the art of architecture for Sullivan, because they have no relationship with nature, but only with the technological progress and material development of society. The idea that the visual appearance of a natural organism best expresses the essence of nature can also be found in the essay "Thoughts on Art" (1841) of Ralph Waldo Emerson.

The essence of the building, the expression of the transcendental idea, the relationship between the human mind and nature, is expressed in the terra cotta ornament on the Wainwright and Guaranty buildings. The ornamental designs involve an interweaving of organic forms and constructed geometries, to represent the dialectic between a priori reason and sense experience. Sullivan also desired to represent the Hegelian dialectic between the objective, in the rational organization of the building, and the subjective, in the florid ornamentation. Sullivan also saw the dialectic between the objective and subjective in the contrast between Renaissance and Gothic architecture. Sullivan saw Renaissance architecture as purely rational, and Gothic architecture as purely emotional. The combination of the essence of Renaissance architecture with the essence of Gothic architecture would create a new, more advanced form of architecture, following the model of nature in creating new forms not by imitation but by forming principles, what Sullivan called "style." The combination of new American technology, the steel frame, with historicist references to European forms, would create a new, uniquely American architecture.

Sullivan's architecture is in the spirit of the American Renaissance, which looked to European precedents for inspiration. But Sullivan and the other members of the Chicago School did not want to just imitate European forms, as McKim, Mead, and White did for the Columbian Exposition in 1893, for example, but rather to interweave European forms with new technologies, and principles of structural rationalism, to create new forms of architecture, in a dialectical process. The organization of the Wainwright and Guaranty buildings, for example, is based on the tripartite division of the Florentine palazzo. The Gothic ornament of the terra cotta panels of the Wainwright Building were inspired by the horizontal and vertical panels, cusped niches, and naturalistic foliage ornamentation on the interior west wall of Reims Cathedral.

At the Marshall Field Warehouse, Henry Hobson Richardson interwove Roman arches with a steel frame, in the spirit of the conception of architecture as weaving promoted by Gottfried Semper with the Caribbean Hut in the Crystal Palace in London. Sullivan was inspired by the transcendentalist writers Emerson and Whitman, who had made the first significant and uniquely American contribution to world culture. Sullivan's transcendentalist architecture involved the dialectical method in multiple ways in his design process: subjective/objective, appearance/essence, rational/emotional, geometrical/organic, form/function. Form and function can more accurately be seen as dialectical opposites in Sullivan's design process.

The essence of the building is also expressed through the gridded façades of the Wainwright and Guaranty buildings, the horizontal and vertical panels, and in a more developed manner in the buildings in the 1890s, in particular the Bayard (Condict) Building in New York City (1899, Figure 5.2). Sullivan considered the Bayard Building to be his best skyscraper design. The grid of the façade enacts a dialectic of horizontal and vertical which expresses the dialectic of the material, in the weight of the downward pressure of the horizontal elements, and the spiritual, in the freedom from the pressure of the vertical elements. The composition visually interweaves the horizontal and vertical elements, and emphasizes the points of pressure and release, so that the dialectic is continuously present. The dialectic is between material intellect and active intellect, *nous hylikos* and *nous poietikos*, between the material and the transcendental idea.

The dialectic is also between what Sullivan called the "Rhythm of Life" and the "Rhythm of Death." In the "Kindergarten Chats," "It [the pier] is serene because within itself are balanced the two great forces, the simplest, elemental rhythms of Nature, to wit, the rhythm of growth, of aspiration, of that which would rise into the air: which impulse we shall call the Rhythm of Life" (Sullivan 1947: 121), and in the opposing force in the dialectic, "the counter-rhythm of decadence, of destruction, of that which would crush to the earth, of that which makes for a return to the elements of earth, the Rhythm of Death." It is as if the pier is Walt Whitman exclaiming "Through me the afflatus surging and surging, through me the current and index," in "Song of Myself" in *Leaves of Grass* (1855) (Fiero 2002: 19).

After finding *Leaves of Grass* in a bookstore, Sullivan was inspired to write a letter to Whitman, telling him that he was the greatest living poet. While the spirit or transcendental idea seeks its counterpart in form or the visual image, it involves itself in a dialectic of life and death. In the "Kindergarten Chats," spirit expresses itself both in "the very wedding-march and ceremonial that quickens into song the unison of form and function," and in "the dirge of their farewell" (Sullivan 1947: 45–6). The dialectic between life and death can also be seen as the dialectic of Eros and Thanatos. Eros corresponds to the upward movements, the detachment from the constraints of the material, while Thanatos corresponds to the horizontal confinement to the material. Sullivan interweaves the horizontal and vertical piers in such a way that neither has precedence over the other.

The dialectic in the visual form created by Sullivan can be seen as a precedent for the dialectic created by Giuseppe Terragni at the Casa Giuliani Frigerio in Como (1939–40, Figure 5.12), which involves an interweaving of centripetal and centrifugal plans, which creates a syntactical ambiguity which functions as a transformational relation between the "surface structure" (the visual forms) and

Figure 5.2 **Louis Henry Sullivan, Bayard (Condict) Building, 1899**

the "deep structure" (the conceptual organization of the building), as analyzed by Peter Eisenman for his dissertation research (this will be addressed later). Sullivan's grid can equally be seen as a transformational device, a mechanism for connecting the visual appearance of the building (the form) to the essence or "function" of the building (the transcendental idea that the building is designed to express).

    The dialectic of horizontal and vertical in the façade of the Bayard Building (Figure 5.2) also has an anthropomorphic element. The piers appear as if limbs of a human body, weighted to the ground while capable of surging upward. The arches at the top of the façade grid are tied to the piers while pulling them upward. The upward ascension is reiterated figuratively by sculpted winged female figures, representing the release from the material into the spiritual, or the transcendental idea. The winged figures are held in check by the cantilevered cornice. The upward pull of the façade grid in general is weighed down by the lintel of the ground floor. The interwoven suggested movements of gravity and ascension represent the dialectic of the rhythms of life and death, transcendental and physical, in the building, as they would be in the human body, and in the human being. As in the Schauspielhaus of Schinkel (Figure 4.1), the trabeation of the façade has no direct relation to the structure of the building, and the form of the building contradicts the function of the building.

In the *Nature and Function of Art*, Eidlitz saw the "mechanical work" done by the "human frame" as furnishing for the architect elements of artistic expression in structures (Eidlitz 1977 [1881]: 223). In the "Kindergarten Chats" of Sullivan, "The architecture *we seek* shall be as a man," generative, awake, attuned, "knowing and feeling the vibrancy of that ever-moving moment, with heart to draw it in and mind to put it out" (Sullivan 1947: 49). The dialectic of the building, like the dialectic of the human being, involves the understanding of the processes of nature and the ability to transfer those processes into visual form, establishing the rhythm of the relationship between the human being and nature. Sullivan's dialectic is a form of *Einfühlung*, or empathy, the act of inner imitation, *natura naturans*. The dialectic is also a form of gestalt, the projection of the human body and human mind onto the physical environment. The dynamism injected into the architectural vocabulary elements, the soaring of the vertical lines and the weight of the horizontal lines, projects the struggle between body and mind, material and spiritual, onto the building. The struggle is reminiscent of the figures of Michelangelo, struggling against the bodies in which their souls are imprisoned, like oysters in a shell as Plato put it. As a student at the École des Beaux Arts in Paris, Sullivan traveled to Rome and became obsessed with the figures of Michelangelo. A more literal anthropomorphism in architecture can be found in Michelangelo's Porta Pia (Figure 3.3).

It is clear that Sullivan was influenced by the writings of Hegel. Sullivan was probably introduced to Hegelian philosophy by John Edelmann in discussions at the Lotus Club in Chicago between 1874 and 1881. The relations between perception and language, and thought and nature, are explored by Hegel in the *Philosophy of Mind*, the third part of the *Encyclopedia of the Philosophical Sciences*, published in 1830. Mind (*Geist*) is a product of nature, but nature vanishes in the self-consciousness of mind, in the being-for-self of the idea in mind, in rational thought, *nous hylikos*. In self-consciousness the subject and object of the idea are the same, as in the *Einfühlung*, and the necessity of nature in the Principle of Sufficient Reason is no longer adequate or appropriate for the phenomenon of mind, as it sees itself in self-consciousness. The self-consciousness of mind necessitates the transcendental idea. The identity of subject and object in the idea, which does not occur in nature, is "absolute negativity" (Hegel 1971 [1830]: §381) because it does not consist of the externalization of essence, as in the visual form, which is necessary in nature as a function of material reproduction and the laws of necessity in reason. The *Einfühlung* thus involves the dialectic of the rhythm of life and death. The identity of subject and object is only possible outside of nature, and only possible in mind. Sullivan must have been aware of the impossibility of an identity between mind and nature in Hegel, resulting in the representation of the dialectical struggle, which is irresolvable. In nature, Idea is in a state of "asunderness" where subject and object are not unified in it; it is external to both itself and mind, and the essential nature of mind, in its self-conscious otherness which is not possible in nature because of the lack of the revelation of the absolute in nature, and because of the material necessity of the particular.

The "triumph over externality" of mind, in the transcendental idea, according to Hegel, is the "ideality of mind," the self-consciousness of mind in its opposition to causal necessity and to itself, as in the ideal of Schelling. The ideality of mind is itself a necessary product of the relation between mind and what is external to it, and the self-consciousness of mind in its relation to its externality, in its translation of its externality to its inner function, as philosophy entails primarily the translation of the particular to the universal. Mind defines itself in its translation of that which is external to it, as in the transposition of the essence or function of nature to visual form, and mind is thus set against nature. Language is a function in mind of the translation from the external to the subjective, and from the particular to the universal. The essence of nature is transposed to visual form metaphorically. The nature of the sign in language is that the particular becomes subject to the universal in the transition of the perceived object into the word, and the simultaneous transition of the word into the idea. The formulation of language is a process of the externalization of perception, of *Vorstellung*, into the particulars which mask the unified universality of existence and render existence fragmented and self-alienated, reversing the process of apperception described by Kant, in the same way that the instinct for self-preservation in the organic being renders the universal impossible in a nature composed of fragmented and self-alienated particulars. The dialectic of the particular and universal also plays an important role in Sullivan's architecture, on a metaphorical level, in the language of forms.

The word in language, and the visual form, abstract the universal from the particular; meaning is a product of the self-differentiation of the particular in language, the primordial dehiscence of the universal in nature. Any word in language given to designate a particular is automatically taken as a universal in abstract thought, thus in the transcendental idea. The universal is only given by the external manifestation of the particular in the word or visual image, and is thus necessarily a negation, a double negation, of consciousness in language in relation to externality, in the rhythm of life and death, the dialectical process. Self-conscious mind for Hegel "sets itself over against itself, makes itself its own object and returns from this difference, which is, of course, only abstract, not yet concrete, into unity with itself." Mind is thus necessarily given to itself in ideality, as a function of language. In its ideality, mind abstracts particulars into universals; it transforms the reality with which it is confronted, leaving it "poisoned and transfigured," transformed into a spiritual existence of the abstracted universal. The universality in abstract mind in fact prevents the material reality with which it is confronted to exist as independent of that universality and abstraction; mind is condemned to its own mechanisms in self-consciousness and self-differentiation. There is no possibility of mind overcoming itself, of knowing anything beyond itself, beyond its own premise of operations. In that mind sees itself as differentiated from nature, there is no possibility that mind can know nature beyond the premise of its self-differentiated relation to it, just as in the pre-scientific era mind could only know nature insofar as it could project itself into it, as in the *Einfühlung* and gestalt.

In the biological necessity of self-differentiation, the *Trieb*, mind can never be satisfied with its own limited activity in the abstraction of the particular to the universal, material reality in perception to the idea, in language and thought, and visual form. The product of this restlessness and dissatisfaction in philosophy is the desire for an absolute, the universal which is hidden by the externality of language in thought, the inner essence or function of nature which Sullivan seeks. Mind seeks the essence of the material in perception which is lost in language; philosophy and architecture are thus, like poetry and the other visual arts, a seeking beyond language, an attempt to rescue the essence and universal which has been lost by the activity of thought in its self-consciousness. The Idea is the perceived resurrection of the essence of being in reason, or finite thought, the re-entrance of the absolute into the self-differentiated and sundered structure of rational thought. In reason, ideality in self-consciousness develops toward the absolute in the dialectic, and is thus dependent on the self-differentiation and negation given by reason in perception, in the rhythm of death.

The transition from nature to mind, according to Hegel, is thus a "coming-to-itself of mind out of its self-externality in Nature." The transition from nature to spirit occurs in mind; it is not a natural transition, not governed by the Principle of Sufficient Reason in the real. Perception is constructed by reason, and spirit in mind is constructed by mind in self-consciousness. Though reason can be seen to be governed by necessity, in cause and effect, the scaffolding of reason, that is, language, which is an abstraction of perception in mind (a transition from "the singleness of sensation to the universality of thought"), comes to be seen more and more as a construct of mind in its development toward self-consciousness, and in the revelation of the absolute in mind. The revelation of the absolute in mind in fact dissolves the scaffolding of language in reason in mind, in the same way that light dissolves the material solidity of particular objects in the real, or the distinction between organic forms and geometrical forms is dissolved in the designs of Sullivan. Language, and the language of visual forms, come to be seen as elements in the mediating process of nature in mind, which begins to disappear in the development of self-consciousness. Mind reveals itself as the negative, the void, underneath the scaffolding of language in reason, and it is in that void that the absolute is revealed. This appears to have been Sullivan's goal.

Horta

The architecture of Victor Horta (1861–1947) in Belgium shares with the architecture of Louis Sullivan the dialectic of organic and geometrical forms, and the dialectic or contradiction between the visual appearance of the architectural forms and the functional and structural requirements of the building; in other words, the contradiction between form and function. The visual forms of Horta were inspired by nature but never imitated natural forms in mimesis. According to Horta, "Nature should not be seen through pictures but through the theories that can be derived from it" (Borsi and Portoghesi 1991: 14), as for Plotinus the purpose of the arts is not to present a reproduction of the perceived form, the *natura naturata*, but to return to the Idea from which nature derives its forms, in the *natura naturans*, the ideal imitation of the forming principles of nature. Horta saw the "theories of nature" as theories of living forms and mechanisms which are introduced into the human mind.

Like Sullivan, Horta was influenced by the structural rationalism of Viollet-le-Duc, the theory of a geometric origin of nature, consisting of circles and equilateral triangles as archetypal forms. Horta applied the use of equilateral triangles to the design of details of his buildings; for example, in soffits in the Maison du Peuple (1896–9, demolished 1965). But Horta did not want to imitate Gothic forms of triangulation any more than he wanted to imitate natural forms. Instead he wanted to apply the principles of triangulation to architecture, like the principles of the formation of nature, to create new forms in architecture. The use of triangulation in architectural proportions results in a "return to those immutable principles upon which gothic likeness are built" (Dernie and Carew-Cox 1995: 16), according to Horta. Geometries are visual symbols of the organic principles of nature, as understood in the human mind.

The "style" of Horta is as style defined by Viollet-le-Duc in the *Dictionnaire raisonné de l'architecture*, the "manifestation of an ideal based on a principle," exemplified by the Medieval mason who by tracing the geometries of the circle and equilateral triangle parallels the creativity of nature in its forming principles. As Viollet-le-Duc described, "Nature is at work, her deductions follow one upon the other according to the order of invariable logic. She traces a circle, and in this inscribes the only figure which can't be distorted, one in which the sides and the angles are all equal among themselves" (Bergdoll 1990: 24). In an address to the Académie Royale in 1925, Horta declared: "Since 1840 Viollet-le-Duc's theories bring back, by a tight, precise constructive analysis of each architectural element, the whole of architecture to its absolute origin: construction, out of which any art form derives, *ad aeternum*" (Dernie and Carew-Cox 1995: 16). The constructive logic of forms, in a dialectic of organic and geometrical shapes, appears throughout the architecture of Horta, but the constructive logic of the visual forms in the architecture rarely corresponds to the constructive logic of the building. As with the façades of Sullivan, the architectural forms of Horta are appliqué to the building, stage scenery as it were, creating poetic expression in the contradiction between form and function, not unlike the architecture of the Gothic cathedral.

Visual forms in the architecture of Horta appear to be structural, corresponding to the laws of the geometrical construction of structure as derived from nature, but the forms are in fact non-structural, introducing the same contradiction which can be found in every period of architectural history. In the Tassel House (1893, Figure 5.3), a filigree iron bracket only plays a role visually, to affirm the continuity of a line. Rivets and bolts are used as ornamentation, extending to beams with rivets which serve no structural purpose. In the Maison et Atelier Victor Horta, rue Américaine 25 (1898–1900), non-structural plaster vaulting appears

Figure 5.3 **Victor Horta, Tassel House, 1893**

around the stairwell. Gilded metalwork under curved beams in the dining room appears to function as tie bars but does not, and a column at the entrance of the house appears to support a marble cantilevered ledge but does not. This aspect of Horta's architecture was explained to David Dernie by Dalibor Vesely and Peter Carl at Cambridge, as Dernie explains in his book on Victor Horta. The aspect produces a double entendre and double reading of the architectural forms, which appear to be expressions of structural or constructivist principles, but serve no structural or constructional function.

As in the architecture of Sullivan, the constructivist forms derived from the structural rationalism of Viollet-le-Duc are disassociated from the structure and function of the building, for the purpose of expressing the dialectic of the human mind and nature, the transcendental idea and material forms, the spiritual and the physical. Horta's architecture consists of the overlay and dialectic of the literal and figural, the rationalist and poetic, the objective and subjective, evoking the Hegelian relation between mind and nature. The alienation of mind from nature is further evoked by the self-enclosed quality of the spaces. The play of ornamental designs is dissolved into a play of shadows and the light which filters in through the skylights of the buildings, further evoking the dialectic of the material and spiritual, in the dissolution of form into light, from whence it originated, as in the Medieval cosmology of Robert Grosseteste, for example, and the architecture of the Gothic cathedral.

The self-enclosed spaces and alienation of the mind from the physical world also evoke aspects of Symbolist prose and poetry. In the Tassel House, for example, the interior is closed off from the exterior with the use of thick "American" glass—chenille glass cast in small pieces, colored with pigments of gold and silver oxides, creating an iridescence that fills the interior space. The light filters through the matrix of slender columns, and is reflected off mirrored surfaces and refracted through translucent and transparent surfaces, creating a dreamy interior world, a *chambre rêve*, which corresponds to the introspection and transformation of reality in Symbolist work, the escape from the problems of the modern industrial world into self-absorbed imagination and fantasy. The play of light and shadows, ornamental forms and false structural forms, whiplash lines and reflective surfaces, encourage an ambiguity of depth and surface and a loss of spatial orientation, suggesting the Surrealist concept of psychasthenia as described by Roger Caillois in the essay "Mimicry and Legendary Psychasthenia" published in Paris in *Minotaure* (1937) and *Le Myth et l'Homme* (1938).

Caillois conceived of the dissolution of the subject in space. The dissolution begins with the questioning of the distinction between interior and exterior, as the mind's necessity coincides with that of the universe, as described by Hegel, in a fluctuation or dialectic rather than a separation. Distinctions in general are dissolved, "between the real and the imaginary, between waking and sleeping, between ignorance and knowledge" (Caillois 1993: 17), between dreams and reality. Boundaries dissolve between physical forms, as the forms dissolve in the iridescent light. Mimicry, the ability of an animal or insect to resemble its

surroundings or another species, in mimesis, is an "incantation fixed at its culmi-
nating point and having caught the sorcerer in his own trap" (p. 27), dissolving the
distinction between subject and space, the distinction between mind and nature.

The perception and representation of space and form are conceived as
complex phenomena, dynamic interplays of forces, of light and shape, structure
and ornament. As Caillois defined the perception of space as a fluctuating interaction of the mental and physical, of simultaneity and condensation, space is now
a "double dihedral changing at every moment in size and position" (p. 28). The
dihedral consists of intersecting vertical and horizontal planes; vertical planes are
the action of the perceiving subject and perceived object in space, while horizontal
planes are the action of the ground under the subject and the representation of the
ground under the object, negating perspectival orientation, as it is negated in dream
construction. The horizontal and vertical planes correspond to the (fixed) horizontal
and vertical forces in Sullivan's architectural theory. The dream space negates the
orientation in space given by perspectival construction or spatial coordinates;
the subject in the dream space, formed from the phantasmagoria of light and the
disjunction of forms from their functions, is thus "dispossessed of its privilege
and literally no longer knows where to place itself," being one point among many
without orientation, in the artificially constructed interior world.

Psychasthenia, the inability to resolve irrational uncertainties, results
from the loss of the self-identification of the subject as a particular point in space
in distinction from its surroundings. The subject is absorbed into the space, as in
dream construction, as the unconscious is absorbed into the universe. The dialectic
between the geometrical and organic, between the mind and the physical world,
which has been set up by the architecture, is dissolved. In *The Necessity of the
Mind* (1933), the main quality of space for Caillois is that it can be simultaneously
occupied by different representations, as in a mirror and what is behind it, and the
same form can have different representations, which are created by the repetitions of forms through reflections and refractions of light in the interior of the
Tassel House, for example. Perception gives a virtual image to which the imagination opposes a real content. The interior of the Tassel House is a virtual reality,
a projection of dream space in the imagination. Perceived objects in the sensible
world are often constructed the same way as dream images, as "imagination is
often defined as a virtual perception, and perception as a real imagination" (Caillois
1990 [1981]: 113), according to Caillois. The line between imagination and reality is
blurred in the architecture of Horta.

Perception itself is the product of unconscious construction, while
the imagination reconstructs certain aspects of perception. Freud showed that
perspectival construction, geometrical coordinates, and the presence of the subject
are absent from dream space; they do not exist in actual space because they are
not reconstituted by the unconscious. They are projected onto actual space by
the constructed logic of the viewer, and are absent from the psychophysiological
space of Caillois. Perspectival construction and geometrical coordinates impose
invariance onto a fluctuating world; implicit in perspectival construction for Caillois is

language as its signifying logic, distorting the perception of space. The architecture of Horta begins to offer an alternative form of space and experience, in its excess of materials and disjunction between form and function. The Art Nouveau movement was a Socialist movement designed to resist the effects of capitalism, of standardization and mass production, like the Arts and Crafts movement in England. In contrast to Chicago School architecture, which is designed to respond to the needs of capitalism (though Sullivan ultimately despised capitalism for its deleterious effects), Art Nouveau architecture, in particular the architecture of Horta, is designed to provide an escape from capitalism, and the other ills of the industrialized world.

Caillois saw a continuous fluctuation of phenomenal or noumenal transparency in spatial construction in human knowledge. In the Tassel House, there is ambiguity in the perception of spatial relationships; for example, what is behind something else. Certainty and invariance are impossible in a fluctuating world where there is "no appreciable difference between the known and the unknown," as he described in *The Necessity of the Mind* (Caillois 1990 [1981]: 87). As phenomenally perceived images fluctuate, so do consciousness and the unconscious. The known and unknown, the rhythms of life and death, fluctuate and dissolve into each other. Opposites coincide to transcend the boundaries of thought in *informe*, between forms. In Freudian dream construction, dreams represent themselves by their wishful contraries, so that there is no distinction between positive and negative in dream thoughts.

If unconscious mental construction is implicit in the perception of actual space, and consciousness is defined as a mirror reflecting the outside world, then for Caillois the mind is a microcosm of the exterior world. The necessity of the mind coincides with the necessity of the universe. "Fusing perfectly with the necessity of the universe, the mind's necessity would at the same time be absorbed in it" (p. 114). Exterior and interior are fused together and opposites dissolve. In the thought of Sigmund Freud, the reality of the unconscious was the same unknown as the reality of the physical world. As opposites dissolve and interior and exterior fuse, according to Caillois there is one barrier to the proper functioning of the unconscious in relation to the exterior world—the logic of language.

The "abstraction, generality, and permanence of the meaning of words" (p. 4) prevents proximity to an absolute identity of the subject. Identity is found instead in the "mobile nature of the realities of a consciousness," and in a "growing multiplicity of perceptions and sensations." Identity is achieved by a "lyrical language, which is experienced directly through dreams and reflexively through madness," as in the lyrical language of the architectural forms of Horta. Lyrical mechanisms express the inexhaustible complexity of the unconscious and external reality; the conventional use of words in terms of established definitions is discarded in favor of the dissolution of meaning in a pre-established signifying structure as representing an "ideal and abstract common denominator." The dissolution of the signifying structure of the subject would manifest itself in psychasthenia.

The self-enclosed, interior environment of artificiality is celebrated in the *À Rebours* (*Against Nature*, 1884) of Joris-Karl Huysmans (1848–1907). The protagonist, Des Esseintes, finds refuge from the world in the exotic excluded interior of his chateau in Fontenay-aux-Roses. The cure for the neurosis caused by industrial society was the protective retreat into the reality of dreams. "Travel, indeed, struck him as being a waste of time, since he believed that the imagination could provide a more-than-adequate substitute for the vulgar reality of actual experience," as Huysmans wrote in *À Rebours* (Huysmans 1959 [1884]: 35). In Symbolist literature, the world is seen in terms of absence; it is necessary to separate oneself from the world, in the self-indulgence of the subconscious, in order to come to terms with the world. In the *Bruges-la-Morte* (1892) of Georges Rodenbach (1855–98), the town is transformed in the perception of the protagonist to conform to thoughts of death, represented by decay, lifelessness, shifting patterns of light, dampness, fog, and cold still water. The interior condition is projected onto the physical world, as in a gestalt, or *Einfühlung*, increasing the sense of isolation in the solitude of an artificial world, as in the interior of the Tassel House. In *Bruges-la-Morte*, the isolation is aggravated by what the protagonist perceives as an exterior world of imposture and deception, in the sterility of the modern industrial world.

De Stijl

Theo van Doesburg (1883–1931) and the De Stijl movement sought to create a universal language in the visual arts and to eliminate "style," or to redefine style as the "manifestation of an ideal based on a principle" in the spirit of Viollet-le-Duc. De Stijl members saw themselves as social engineers, contributing to a utopian future which eliminates conflicts between interests, which are represented by styles. De Stijl imagery represents a tabula rasa for the human race, which can share universal elements of communication as it did before the Tower of Babel. The universal language in the visual arts entailed a purification and reduction of the vocabulary to primary colors and horizontal and vertical lines, as in the paintings by Piet Mondrian (1872–1944), and the Schröder House (1924, Figure 5.4) by Gerrit Rietveld (1888–1964). For Van Doesburg himself the diagonal line was still essential as well, because it, among other things, allowed for the axonometric representation of a house in the Spatial Diagrams. The axonometric was necessary to Van Doesburg to release architecture form the constraints of the traditional plan/elevation representation and to allow architecture to participate in the all-important new fourth dimension of the twentieth century—the dimension of time. The diagonal line and the axonometric represent a "plastic" space and a continuous uninterrupted sequence of spaces that corresponds to the presence of time.

The De Stijl aesthetic also sought the evocation of the "absolute" in the visual arts, the concept derived from the Absolute Spirit of Hegel. De Stijl theory was informed by two Hegelian philosophers and theosophists: Mathieu

Figure 5.4 **Gerrit Rietveld, Schröder House, 1924**

Schoenmaekers (1875–1944) and Gerard Bolland (1854–1922). Schoenmaekers distinguished between *afbeelding* and *uitbeelding*, two derivations of the Dutch word *beelding*, meaning "plasticism" or "representation." *Afbeelding* was used to signify representation in visual depiction, while *uitbeelding* was used to signify, in contrast, the visual representation of an inner reality beyond visual appearance, the making of the invisible visible. The consequence for Van Doesburg would be that the purpose of visual imagery was to evoke a transcendental idea. The ideas were also influential to Mondrian in Laren between 1915 and 1919. In an issue of the *De Stijl* journal in 1919, Van Doesburg wrote: "Pure modern art is *beelding* from innerness outwards. ... All Baroque arises from *beelding* from the outside, by means of imaging-off [*afbeelding*]. ... Style arises through *beelding* from the inside outwards, by means of imaging-out [*uitbeelding*]" (Padovan 2002: 38).

Van Doesburg used the "Baroque" as the antithesis of the goals of purified modern art and the representation of the inner reality and the transcendental idea. Ironically, the core theoretical basis of Baroque art at the Accademia di San Luca in Rome in the sixteenth century was the distinction between *disegno interno*, the design in the mind of the artist, or the inner reality beyond visual appearance, and *disegno esterno*, the representation in visual depiction. The theoretical bases of Baroque art and De Stijl, despite Van Doesburg's prejudices, are the same. *Uitbeelding* can also be seen as a form of *natura naturans*, the formation of the visual image based on ideas or principles, as opposed to the *natura naturata*, the physical mimesis of the visual image, which would correspond to the *afbeelding*. The word *beelding* can also be synonymous with *voorstelling*, or the German *Vorstellung*, meaning "representation."

In the *Phenomenology of Spirit* of Hegel, the formulation of language is a process of the externalization of perception, of *Vorstellung*, or the Idea. The identity of spirit and self-consciousness in the understanding is the identity of the universal and the particular in the art form, the relation between the *afbeelding* and the *uitbeelding*. The identity of spirit and self-consciousness is represented in the understanding as picture-thinking (*Vorstellung*), or reason in perception. From the beginning, picture-thinking and language are not manifestations of nature, of organic form, but rather of spirit in reason.

In the *Phenomenology of Spirit*, the form of spirit is the identity of the changing and the changeless, the outer substance (visual appearance) and inner essence of the form, the identity of self-consciousness and essence, which is manifest in the religion of art (*Kunstreligion*) (Hegel 1977 [1807]: 748). The religion of art is a part of the ethical spirit of a culture, where the individual self is submerged in the universal, communal spirit (750), as in the utopian aspirations of the De Stijl movement. The form of spirit in art is the externalization of the essence of the absolute, but it is enacted in the material forms of change, of "coming-to-be" (754). If the form of the coming-to-be is contained within itself, as an object of sensuous consciousness, then it is a "vanishing object" and aspires to "immediate unity with the universal self-consciousness." In that way the form of art is a part of the ethical spirit. If the form of art represents a world which is a universality and at the same time composed of the certainty of sensuous consciousness, then the form of art exists in the world "as existence raised into an ideational representation," corresponding to the idea of style as the manifestation of a principle, "the pattern of what is apprehensible by reason and understanding and eternally unchanging" (Plato 1965: 29), as described by Timaeus in the dialogue by Plato. The forms of art as a whole "constitute the periphery of shapes which stands impatiently expectant around the birthplace of Spirit as it becomes self-consciousness" (Hegel 1977 [1807]: 754), as the Idea or *Vorstellung* is identified with sensuous consciousness (*das Sinnliche Scheinen der Idee*), essence with substance, universal with the particular. At the center of the forms is the Absolute Idea, "the simplicity of the pure Notion," in which the forms are self-contained as archetypes or intelligibles, transcendental ideas.

As the transcendental idea or inner essence becomes visual form in the *uitbeelding*, so in the *Phenomenology of Spirit*, "remoteness in time and space is only the imperfect form in which the immediate mode is given a mediated or universal character; it is merely dipped superficially in the element of thought, is perceived in it as a sensuous mode, and not made one with the nature of thought itself." Thus "it is merely raised into the realm of picture-thinking (*Vorstellung*), for this is the synthetic combination of sensuous immediacy and its universality or thought" (764), the particular and universal. Form in matter is only a derivative or a copy of the idea of form; the nature of form does not correspond to the nature of thought. In order to participate in the universal, absolute form in matter must be perceived, must become a form of "picture-thinking," thus perception is the medium between the absolute and material, sensuous consciousness. It is in picture-thinking, in perception, that universality and sensuous immediacy are identified.

Reason for Hegel "does not require, as does finite activity, the condition of external materials"; it is self-generating and self-supporting, and it is only in the *image* (*Bild*) of reason, in picture-thinking, through perception, that forms in matter are possible. Thus forms in matter depend on the development of reason to form; the picture of reality given by perception is the realization of reason. Without reason there would be no picture of reality; all mental images are pre-generated by the reasoning process, through perception. As Plotinus explained in the *Enneads* (I.I.7):

> The faculty of perception in the Soul cannot act by the immediate grasping of sensible objects, but only by the discerning of impressions printed upon the Animate [soul] by sensation: these perceptions are already Intelligibles, while the outer sensation is a mere phantom of the other (of that in the Soul) which is nearer to Authentic-Existence as being an impassive reading of Ideal-Forms.

> (Plotinus 1991)

The discerning of impressions printed upon the soul by sensation is the function of reason, not perception, while perception is also a function of reason. Since the sensual impressions in perception are copies and derivatives of intelligible forms, perception itself is a copy and derivative of reason, which is closer to the intellectual, and thus the absolute.

According to Hegel in the *Phenomenology of Spirit*, it is through perception, or picture-thinking, that spirit becomes self-conscious, though perception itself is not the self-consciousness of spirit. Spirit cannot attain self-consciousness in perception because perception entails the separation of being and reason, of being and coming-to-be. The content of being (*Dasein*) becomes multiple and particular in perception; it is subject to time through sequence, and measurement through proportion. Perception, or picture-thinking, consists of moments of being "appearing as completely independent sides which are externally connected with each other" (Hegel 1977 [1807]: 765). The essence of being cannot be known by the level of consciousness as given by perception, but through perception self-consciousness of spirit can be attained, in perception as a function of reason toward the understanding of the intelligible form.

Perception or picture-thinking, *Vorstellung*, is the middle term between spirit and existence, the universal and particular. The self-consciousness of spirit is its descent into existence. Picture-thinking, as the middle term, is the synthetic connection of spirit and existence, the doubling of the self-consciousness of spirit, the "consciousness of passing into otherness" (767). Picture-thinking is a manifestation of spirit, as is the self-consciousness of the perceiving subject in the ascension through picture-thinking to spirit. These three manifestations of spirit correspond to Subjective Spirit (individual self-consciousness), Objective Spirit (collective picture-thinking), and Absolute Spirit. The "dissociation in picture-thinking" of spirit "consists in its existing in a specific or determinate mode," which is one moment among many in the diffusion of the nature of spirit throughout existence. Picture-thinking corresponds to Objective Spirit in that it is a collective activity, a shared consciousness. Perception plays a role in Objective Spirit as the laws and morals by which self-consciousness is manifest in society, the multiple determinates of individual subjectivity. In the objectivity of picture-thinking, spirit steps forward out of itself toward the absolute, where it is able to "become an actual Self, to reflect itself into itself" (766) in self-consciousness, through Objective Spirit as community, as collective picture-thinking.

In pure thought Absolute Spirit is "immediately simple and self-identical, eternal essence" (769). As an inner essence, Absolute Spirit is not a meaning or a signification, or even an existent, but being in its purest form. It is not the substance of picture-thinking or of reason, but rather the negative of thought, "the negativity of thought, or negativity as it is in itself in essence; i.e. simple essence is absolute difference from itself, or its pure othering of itself." The otherness of Absolute Spirit is Objective Spirit, as given by picture-thinking in its differentiation, but the self-differentiation retains a self-unity as it returns back to itself through Objective Spirit.

Absolute Spirit exceeds meaning and signification in language, and representation in picture-thinking. As essence in pure thought it exceeds reason, as thought in identity with the object of thought. For Hegel the absolute unfolds toward existence in three stages—essence, being-for-self as the other of essence, and being-for-self as self-consciousness in the other (770)—which correspond to Absolute Spirit, Objective Spirit, and Subjective Spirit. Being-for-self as the other of essence is an externalization, and the self-consciousness of essence itself, which is found in the collective, is the intersection of the universal and particular. Being-for-self as the other of essence is the word, signification in language, which "when uttered, leaves behind, externalized and emptied, him who uttered it, but which is as immediately heard, and only this hearing of its own self is the existence of the Word." The externalization of essence as other is the disjunction between thought and language, the alienation from essence or origin which constitutes thought in language.

The externalization of essence as other, and the self-consciousness of essence as other, in language, is picture-thinking (*Vorstellung*), or perception, given by reason in signification (in language). The externalization is self-consciousness degrading the content of its nature (essence) through misunderstanding, "into a historical pictorial idea." Thus only the external element is retained, and the inner essence vanishes. Essence itself, according to Hegel, is an other of Absolute Spirit, an abstraction in signification, a negation of the universal (772). Essence is the other of the self-contained and undivided of the absolute in existence, thus the originary self-consciousness. But the difference between the absolute and essence is immediately resolved in pure thought, or being, and is not differentiated as in reason or existence.

In the *Phenomenology of Spirit*, as the Absolute Spirit, "eternal or abstract spirit" (774), self-sufficient being, passes into the alterity of existence, when elements of pure essence "spontaneously part asunder and also place themselves over against each other" (773), the creation of the world of otherness is "picture-thinking" (*Vorstellung*), the self-consciousness of spirit that manifests itself in perception. Essence is posited as existence and universal elements of essence are posited as particulars in the "dissolution of their simple universality and the parting asunder of them into their own particularity" (774). Spirit retains its presence in all particularity; spirit is recognized in the particular when the individual self "has consciousness and distinguishes itself as 'other', or as world, from itself." The individual self must become an other to itself before it can recognize itself as spirit, as Absolute Spirit must become other to itself to enter into existence. The self-consciousness of spirit, and the individual self, as other, entails a withdrawal into itself, through self-consciousness. The individual self must become self-alienated, must see its existence as alien to being, in order to become conscious of its participation in spirit, or essence.

Thus, for Van Doesburg, "in the aesthetic emotion which the observer experiences in the presence of a pure plastic work of art," the pure product of the *uitbeelding*, "he immediately recovers … the absolute" (*De Stijl*, vol. 1, no. 4, February 1918, 47–8) (Padovan 2002), in the convergence of the universal and particular, the Absolute Spirit and the *Vorstellung*. According to Piet Mondrian, "The universal finds its purist, most direct expression in art only where there is a balanced relation between the individual and the universal," in the *Kunstreligion*, "for then through representation [*beelding, voorstelling*] the individual can receive the universal: in art it is possible for the universal to manifest itself as appearance without becoming bound to the individual, to individual existence" (*De Stijl*, vol. 1, no. 5, March 1918, 51) (Padovan 2002). This is achieved by eliminating the traditional elements of style, of particularities, nationalities, individual interests. The title De Stijl, "The Style," indicates that there is only one style, and because style is by definition multiple and variable, there can thus be no possibility of style.

The Schröder House in Utrecht (Figure 5.4) by Gerrit Rietveld was adopted as an icon of the De Stijl movement, although the carpenter Rietveld had no interest in the philosophical speculations of Van Doesburg or Mondrian, Schoenmaekers or Bolland. The architectural vocabulary of the Schröder House consists of the appropriate horizontal and vertical lines and planes, and the primary colors, used by Rietveld for psychological effect. For Van Doesburg the primary colors had philosophical or theosophical significance: red for the earth or the body of Christ, blue for the heavens, yellow for the light of the sun which is the origin of all matter, etc. The horizontal and vertical planes on the Schröder House are wood panels painted white in order to mimic machined panels. While the panels on the exterior are fixed, partitions in the interior can be moved to accommodate the lifestyle of the inhabitants; the house is thus a *machine à habiter*, to use the phrase associated with Le Corbusier, a machine for living.

The fixed panels on the exterior have thus been called "trompe l'oeil" and "illusionistic": they are not the material they purport to be, they do not serve the function that they represent, and they mask the structure of the house. The form of the architecture contradicts the functional and structural requirements of the building, and the architecture can thus express the idea of the Absolute Spirit, the dialectic of the inner essence of being and the *Vorstellung*, representation in visual form and language; and the architecture can communicate the utopian goals of the *Kunstreligion* of De Stijl, in the representation of the universal in the particular. The idea that all human beings can share a universal language, or share universally applicable characteristics, the utopian idea of the early twentieth century, became a basis for twentieth-century structuralism, in structural linguistics and structural anthropology, for example, which became an important theoretical basis for Modernist and International Style architecture.

Following Hegel, Van Doesburg defined three categories or levels of thought, and three corresponding phases of art. "Concrete thought" is thought based in sensory perception, the *nous hylikos* or *nous pathetikos* of Classical philosophy. "Deformative thought" is concrete thought transformed by conceptualization, as in the *nous poietikos* and *imaginatio* of Classical philosophy, or the a priori categories of intuition of Kant, the generative mechanisms of mind. "Pure abstract thought" is thought with no connection to sense perception or representation (*Vorstellung*), thought for which the only subject is itself, corresponding to the active intellect of Classical philosophy, and the self-consciousness of mind of Hegel. The subjects of pure abstract thought, rather than the objects of sense perception, are mathematics and geometry. Mathematics and geometry are the intelligibles in the *Republic* of Plato; they are the *principia essendi*, the principles of things. They are not objects of sense perception, not qualities of sensible reality. In Kant, they belong to the categories of a priori intuition as abstract representations of time and space, which are concepts, not qualities of phenomena.

In *A Commentary on the First Book of Euclid's Elements* by Proclus, for example, mathematics "occupies the middle ground between the partless realities—simple, incomposite, and indivisible—and divisible things characterized by every variety of composition and differentiation" (Proclus 1970: 3). Mathematics is the medium by which the pure forms in the intelligible world of Plato are transformed into the matter of the material world, as underlying mechanisms of the *Vorstellung*. For Proclus in the *Commentary* it is the "discursiveness of [mathematical] procedure, its dealing with its subjects as extended, and its setting up of different prior principles for different objects" (3) that establish mathematics as a being below the indivisible nature of the One, or the absolute. Mathematics is the most basic element in the unfolding of reason which arises from the absolute. Mathematics is a similitude of the Absolute Spirit formed in the mind, and it facilitates the extension of reason, and the extension of all matter in the universe.

According to Proclus, mathematics is an intermediate form of knowledge (4). Intellect corresponds to the indivisible realities, being free from matter, and superior to all other forms of knowledge. Opinion, as opposed to intellect, corresponds to the objects of sense perception, which are the lowest level of nature, and can only grasp truth obscurely. Between intellect and opinion there is understanding, which corresponds to the intermediates between the indivisible and divisible nature, and among the intermediates are the forms studied by mathematics and geometry. As in the *Republic* of Plato: "And I think that you call the habit of mind of geometers and the like reason but not intelligence, meaning by reason something midway between opinion and intelligence" (Plato 1955: 511). Opinion is concerned with the world of becoming, the transformations of material things, while intelligence is concerned with the world of reality, the stable and indivisible archetypal ideas.

Understanding (Van Doesburg's deformative thought) is superior to opinion (Van Doesburg's concrete thought) according to Proclus in the *Commentary* in its perfection, exactitude, and purity. It "traverses and unfolds the measureless content of Nous [Absolute Spirit for Hegel] by making articulate its concentrated intellectual insight, and then gathers together again the things it has distinguished and refers them back to Nous" (Proclus 1970: 4). In the *Republic* of Plato, the mind is unable to go beyond the assumptions of a first principle and rise to the intelligible, but it can make use of the images in the sensible world as illustrations, an example of these images being geometrical figures (Plato 1955: 511). Through the process of dialectic, assumptions can be used as starting points in the ascent to a first principle, though the assumptions themselves partake of no principle. From the ascent to a first principle, in the process of the dialectic, a conclusion can be reached. Assumptions must be abandoned for any understanding to take place; if not, the mathematicians and geometers can only dream about reality, and can "never wake and look at it as it is" (533). Dialectic is "the only procedure which proceeds by the destruction of assumptions to the very first principle," as in the deformative thought of Van Doesburg.

While the reasoning of mathematics is in an intermediary position between intelligence and opinion, the objects of mathematics have an intermediary position between the objects of intellect and the objects of sense perception, according to Proclus. The objects of mathematics are superior to the objects of sense perception because they are more precise and are devoid of matter, but they are inferior to the objects of the intellect because they are divisible and more complex. They are a clearer reflection of intelligible reality than are perceptible things, but they are still only images, or reflections and shadows for Plato, which are imitations of indivisible being and the uniform patterns of being. They contain in the imitative patterns the unity and constancy of the indivisible, as well as the particularity and compositeness of the divisible in matter. In that the forms of mathematics copy the principles of the intelligible, the principles of mathematics are to be found in the absolute being, Absolute Spirit, and "all-pervading principles that generate everything from themselves," in both the finite and the infinite.

The forms of mathematics and geometry as described by Proclus in *A Commentary on the First Book of Euclid's Elements* are derived from material forms in nature, in numbers and geometrical shapes, but their exactness and certainty in their proportions and ratios, divisions and compositions, are derived from intelligible principles. Proclus defined mathematical and geometrical thought as dianoetic, being composed of dialectical and discursive processes. Dianoetic thinking is different from thinking associated with *nous*, which is "perfect and self-sufficing, ever converging upon itself" (Proclus 1970: 18), apart from the dialectical and discursive. Mathematics does not have the quality of *nous* as being "filled from itself," thus being the "unmoved mover," nor does it have the quality of sense perception as being satisfied by external objects (19). Mathematics and geometry are the means by which the motion of bodies can be applied toward the dialectical movement of understanding toward *nous*.

Mathematical understanding moves in two possible directions, either from the infinite to the finite—that is, from unity to plurality, or the reverse, from multiples back to unities—or from conclusions back to hypotheses, seeking the originary principles of *nous*. As Proclus explained:

> Consequently it is only natural that the cognitive powers operating in the general science that deals with these objects should appear as twofold, some aiming at the unification and collection of the manifold for us, others at dividing the simple into the diverse, the more general into the particular, and the primary ideas into secondary and remoter consequences of the principles.

> (19)

The dianoetic process of mathematical understanding operates in both directions, in dialectical and discursive thinking. "The range of this thinking extends from on high all the way down to conclusions in the sense world"; from *nous* to the objects of sense perception, encompassing all of being.

In their binary dialectical movement, from unity to plurality and plurality to unity, mathematics and geometry are able to force the mind out of sense perception and into contemplation of the intelligibles of a higher reality, the Absolute Spirit, as would Van Doesburg's pure abstract art. As Proclus put it in the *Commentary*:

> the beauty and order of mathematical discourse, and the abiding and steadfast character of this science, bring us into contact with the intelligible world itself and establish us firmly in the company of things that are always fixed, always resplendent with divine beauty, and ever in the same relationships to one another.

> (20)

Geometry for Plato is a kind of knowledge the objects of which are "eternal and not liable to change and decay" (Plato 1955: 527). As a result it will "tend to draw the mind to the truth and direct the philosophers' reason upwards, instead of downwards, as we wrongly direct it at present," and geometry is thus a necessary subject for citizens of the ideal republic. Among other things, knowledge of geometry can provide an important disciplinary framework for the pursuit of all other subjects, as "there is a certain facility for learning all other subjects in which we know that those who have studied geometry lead the field." Similarly, the geometry of pure abstract art serves the *Kunstreligion* of Van Doesburg toward a utopian society, a universally shared knowledge of the absolute.

According to Proclus, mathematics is necessary in order to gain intellectual understanding, to awaken to "genuine being and truth" (Proclus 1970: 21), and to become familiar with immaterial nature, as the discursive process of reasoning leads from particulars to universals. "When he uses this as a model," the philosopher "can be led to the practice of dialectic and to the contemplation of being in general." Mathematics is necessary for all branches of philosophy, according to Proclus, and above all, theology, because the discipline of mathematics is necessary for the "intellectual apprehension" (22) of the truths about the gods. Numbers, because they participate in the abstract, immaterial laws of *nous*, "reflect the properties of being above being." Mathematics is necessary for the understanding of physical science as well, as it "reveals the orderliness of the ratios according to which the universe is constructed and the proportion that binds things together in the cosmos." Mathematics is also necessary for the understanding of the beauty of things, as for Aristotle in the *Metaphysics*, "those who assert that the mathematical sciences say nothing of the beautiful or the good are in error" (Aristotle 1952a: 1077). Beauty according to Aristotle is composed of order, symmetry, and definiteness, "which the mathematical sciences demonstrate in a special degree" (1078). Mathematics leads the understanding to beauty in the same way that it leads the understanding to philosophy and theology, in that its elements in number and proportion contain the principles abstracted from the absolute in its manifestation of the material world.

In *A Commentary on the First Book of Euclid's Elements*, Proclus differentiated between three modes of being in the relation between the universal and the particular, or between the absolute and material form, which correspond to Van Doesburg's categories of thought. The absolute or One assumes three forms of being in relation to particulars: it "exists prior to the Many and produces plurality by offering its appearances to the many instances" (Proclus 1970: 50), so that it is shared in by the particulars; it "appears in the particulars and has its existence in them and is inseparable from them"; and it "is formed from particulars by reflection and has existence as an after-effect" (51), so that it is a predicate or a supplement to them, and can be known by intellect. Matter shares in the universal according to Proclus through both sense perception and the imagination, the two lower categories of thought for Van Doesburg; thus universals are both perceptible and imaginary.

Matter shares in the universal because of the nature of intelligible objects in the imagination, that they necessarily have "divisible extension and shape," that is, they are subject to the laws of form governed by mathematics and geometry, as categories of the a priori intuition of Kant. As Aristotle described it in the *De anima*, mind participates in both the becoming of things (in the particulars of matter) and the making of things (that is, being prior to them, in a priori intuition). In this sense, mind is "separable, impassible, unmixed" (Aristotle 1952b: 430), like the universal. Knowledge in mind is in one way "identical with its object" and not supplementary to it. In the imagination, "what thinks and what is thought are identical; for speculative knowledge and its object are identical," in the approach to the Absolute Spirit.

In the *Introductory Lectures on Aesthetics* of Hegel (*The Introduction to Hegel's Philosophy of Fine Art*, 1886), the purification of thought from the object to the idea is the revealing of the Absolute Spirit which is present in the particulars of the *Vorstellung*. Pure abstract thought is the "free thought" of Absolute Spirit, to which art aspires. In art, for Hegel, the categories of reason, those by which reason is seen in nature, can be transcended. The categories of reason are manifest in the "shadowland of the idea" (Hegel 1993 [1886]: VII), the reflections and forms which are given by reason in perception. Art, in that it functions through perception, is precisely the means to represent that which perception itself cannot, that is, the absolute, the identity of mind and form. Thus "in the forms of art we seek for repose and animation in place of the austerity of the reign of law and the somber self-concentration of thought" (VII); repose and animation in intellect are given by understanding of the absolute, of reconciliation, of reassurance in being which has been lost in reason. The human being desires to both transcend the laws and limitations of reason through reason itself, in the dialectic, or in science, which gives reason a higher purpose and dispels the responsibility of reason to itself, or to transcend the laws and limitations of reason in non-reason, intuition, the imagination, and the mystical experience of the absolute, or the divine. Art provides for the repose of reason and the self-concentration of thought in relation to the sensory world within being.

For Hegel, the forms created by the artist are infinite in comparison to the forms created by nature, because mind is infinite, while the organic in nature is not. Organic forms in nature can only be finite representations of the infinite possibilities of the absolute in nature, while in art the infinite can be represented as itself, as the absolute, in both content and form. In content, the infinity of art corresponds to the infinite creativity of the mind of the artist, as ideas in the intellect, in the *nous poietikos*, are unrestricted by their material counterparts. In form, the infinite can be represented symbolically in all forms of art, and schematically in the forms of art least restricted by their material condition, namely painting and poetry. The combination of the infinite, that is, freedom, and the absolute, with the finite, the sensible form, creates beauty in art. In that nature, the sensible world, is given by mind, nature is a finite category of mind; obviously, to imitate natural forms in art, in mimesis or *natura naturata*, is to not do justice to the infinite quality, the freedom, of mind, as a function of the absolute, the reconciliation of mind and nature, for which the *natura naturans* is necessary.

Art, if treated on a purely intellectual level, as in pure abstraction, reduces its possibilities to a "simplicity devoid of reality" and a "shadowy abstractness." Art must transcend reason in order to reveal the absolute. Art, as a mechanism of philosophy, must transcend the intellectual in order that both it and philosophy accomplish what science does not, as science does not transcend the intellectual, which is to pose the question of the being of the intellectual itself, in relation to the phenomenal world. Art is a form of thought which is able to transcend certain limitations of thought in reason. Art is the principal means, along with philosophy and religion, of the self-understanding of a culture; art is the purest expression of the *Geist* of the culture. In that art represents the ideal in the real, thought in matter, it represents a "supra-sensuous world, which is thus, to begin with, erected as a *beyond* over against immediate consciousness and present sensation" (XIII); the world given by sensible perception is represented within consciousness and sensation. Such representation is parallel to the revelation of the absolute. Consciousness and sensation are the "*here*, that consists in the actuality and finiteness of sense"; the means by which the beyond is accessed is that element of thought in reason which is free, not governed by the necessity of cause and effect. Art is a reconciliation between the here and beyond, between necessity and freedom, the particular and universal; it is a mechanism of the dialectical process of reason.

Universals can only exist as abstractions of particulars, and particulars only exist as manifestations of universals. Particulars are only meaningful if they reveal the universal; universals are only meaningful if they provide a basis for particulars. It is impossible to have a complete conception of existence, given the interaction of thought and sensation, or the idea and the sensible world, if particulars are not taken in relation to universals, and vice versa, and engaged in the dialectical process. Sensible form in appearance is a particular that can only be understood in relation to a universal; if it is not, then it is a distraction from the whole of existence. "Genuine reality is only to be found beyond the immediacy of feeling and of external objects" (XIV), but it can only be known in relation to that sensible world, like the categories of a priori intuition of Kant.

That which is "genuinely real," which combines the idea and the sensible so that it is not a distraction from the essence of existence, is that which preserves the universal in the particular, that which preserves its "self-centered being" in the sensible world. Art for Hegel is potentially that which is genuinely real in that it has the capacity to reveal the universal in the particular. The universal which art is capable of revealing in the thought of Hegel is an ethical universal, a universal of ethical relationships which creates community, like the universal language of art promoted by the De Stijl movement. The universal values of a community are manifest in its individual members in the same way that universal ideas are manifest as particular forms in artistic representation. Art can serve as a heuristic device for the role of the individual in relation to the state, for the identity of the individual in relation to the ethics of the state.

Art for Hegel has the capacity to identify ways in which the particular may be related to the universal, which sensory perception and logic in reason do not, because art inserts the intelligible into the sensory world, and thus reveals the relation between the universal and the particular. The sensory world is given by perception as "a chaos of accidental matters, encumbered by the immediateness of sensuous presentation, and by arbitrary states, events, characters, etc." (XIV). The sensory world is a "fleeting world" of semblance and deception, while art "liberates the real import of appearances from the semblance and deception of this bad and fleeting world, and imparts to phenomenal semblances a higher reality, born of mind" (XIV). This would have been the intention of the pure abstraction of Van Doesburg. The reality of forms of art is higher than the reality of objects of perception in the sensible world, because the forms of art define and identify sensible forms of matter in relation to the universal, the Idea, of which they are manifestations, in the definition of thought and perception, in the interaction between mind and matter, and between intellect and the absolute.

The sensuous forms of art (*das sinnliche Scheinen*), in their representation or embodiment of the absolute, are more genuine in relation to the absolute than the forms of matter and the forms that constitute historical narrative, but less genuine than the intelligible forms of philosophy and religion. Historical narrative is a purely intellectual construct, extracted from the particulars of memory; the historical dialectic is insubstantial in relation to the dialectic of art in revealing the relation between the finite and infinite—thus historical narrative is eliminated from art, as by De Stijl. Hegel asserts that the art form "refers us away from itself to something spiritual which it is meant to bring before the mind's eye" (XV). The ideal is not represented in the real in perception, that is, it is not possible to see the absolute; the ideal is represented in the ideal in thought, which constructs the mechanisms of perception, then seeks to intuit that which is beyond its limitations. Sensual form in matter does not appear to be deceptive to perception, but it appears as deceptive to thought in the ideal. Sensual form in art does appear to be deceptive to perception, but does not appear to be deceptive to thought. Art inverts thought and perception in relation to each other; that which is given by perception is the dialectical antithesis of that which is given by thought.

In modern culture, according to Hegel, "we subject the content and the means of representation of the work of art and the suitability or unsuitability of the two to our intellectual consideration" (XVIII), as art becomes a medium of philosophical development. "Therefore, the *science* of art is a much more pressing need in our day," that is, the theory of art, the formulation of the principles of art and architecture as philosophical expression. Art and architecture are no longer perceived in a mythological, religious, or sensuous framework; they are perceived in a philosophical framework, and the theory of art concerns itself with the relation of art to the philosophical structures of the culture. All architecture in the modern world is accompanied by a theoretical apology, a philosophical scaffolding which gives the architecture its significance in relation to the culture; the philosophical scaffolding is unrelated to, and often in contradiction of, the functional and structural requirements of the building. In past cultures the existence of a universal standard in art was sufficient to allow for a direct, unmediated experience of it; in the modern world, the absence of the embodiment of the universal in architecture requires that it correspond to a particular tenet of a philosophical structure in relation to the epistemology of its culture, and that tenet cannot be fully understood in the immediate perception of the architecture alone; it requires a philosophical scaffolding, in contradiction to the phenomenal presence of the building. Such is the nature of the culture of freedom and self-consciousness; immediate experience itself is devalued, as it becomes the subject of a fully developed self-consciousness which reflects to the perceiving subject both the intellectual scaffolding of his or her perception and the necessary self-alienation of the subject given by the nature of that perception.

Art is the philosophical expression of the absolute in the real, and a complete understanding of the absolute in philosophy is impossible without art, as the ideal can only be understood in relation to the real. Philosophy cannot be disassociated from experience in perception, and art is to experience in perception as philosophy is to mind. Art is not possible without philosophy, and philosophy is not possible without art. Through art, the individual subject participates in the Absolute Spirit which is the Absolute Spirit as manifest in mind (*Geist*) and history (*Zeitgeist*). Beauty in nature, especially beauty of the body, arouses a desire for absolute beauty, but it does not reveal the absolute, as does beauty in art. The desire for the absolute is the desire for self-knowledge, and the desire for the reconciliation of the self-alienated mind in self-consciousness. Beauty in art is a product of mind, thus it is the absolute made known to mind through mind, through reason and intuition. Beauty in art is the sensuous representation of the idea (*das sinnliche Scheiner der Idee*) in the identity of the real and ideal, the idea being the intuition of the absolute in the intellectual, the participation of reason in the absolute. The finitude of reason is a function of the infinity of the absolute in the Idea. Spirit (*Geist*) as intelligence, is as absolute in the real as in the ideal for Hegel, which allows it to be revealed in the sensuous forms of art. Art is the first manifestation of the absolute, in sensuous form, which leads to the manifestation of the absolute in the ideal, thus art is an instrument of philosophy. Beauty in art is the absolute in philosophy in sensuous form; through art, consciousness perceives the absolute within itself as beauty. The absolute is not completely revealed in art, as sensuous form is limited to the real, but it is through the revelation of the absolute in sensuous form that the absolute is revealed in mind.

As instruments of philosophy, but no longer catalysts for philosophy in the development of self-consciousness, art and architecture can only express self-consciousness and freedom in terms borrowed from philosophy, and mirror the *Zeitgeist*, the manifestation of the absolute, the universal spirit, in the culture. The visual arts can thus continue to play a secondary role in cultural expression, according to Hegel, but a role which is important for the individual subject in the self-identity of the subject in relation to his or her culture, in the understanding of the relation of the philosophical development of the individual in relation to the philosophical development of the culture, of the relation of the experience of thought and perception in the individual subject, the individual thinking mind, and the universal self-consciousness of the culture as a manifestation of the same spirit of the absolute.

Such were the themes adopted by De Stijl as utopian social engineers. The goal of the *uitbeelding* was to represent a universal, abstract reality in order to define, in philosophical terms, the role of the individual in society, in the *Zeitgeist*, and the freedom and self-consciousness of the individual thinking mind, through purified abstraction toward the absolute. In De Stijl painting, there is a contradiction between the form of the painting and the function of painting as either mimesis, *natura naturata*, or the enactment of the principles of nature, *natura naturans*, in the desire to represent the absolute as transcendent of the physical world. In De Stijl architecture, there is a contradiction between the form of the architecture and the function of the building for the purpose of representing the same disjunction between matter and the absolute, in order to reaffirm the participation of the individual consciousness in the *Zeitgeist* of a utopian society.

Mies van der Rohe

The influence of De Stijl can be seen in the Barcelona Pavilion (German Pavilion for the 1929 International Exposition in Barcelona, demolished in 1930, rebuilt in 1959 to the original design, Figure 5.5) of Ludwig Mies van der Rohe (1886–1969). The design of the Barcelona Pavilion is a composition of horizontal and vertical planes tangent to each other, reducing the architectural vocabulary to the bare minimum, abstracting it for the purpose of representing the absolute and the *uitbeelding*. There are no enclosed spaces: the form of the architecture contradicts the function of the building, and the fourth dimension of time is introduced in the continuous flow of space, as in the Spatial Diagrams of Theo van Doesburg. Mies was perhaps also influenced by the pinwheel plans of the Prairie Style houses of Frank Lloyd Wright, as published in the Wasmuth Portfolio, which are also designed to avoid enclosed spaces.

The architecture of Mies is a departure from the traditional anthro-pocentric or figural architecture, the idea of the building as a body, symmetrical, proportioned according to the body. The Barcelona Pavilion and the Concrete Country House project of 1923 are asymmetrical, non-hierarchical, and unstable, challenging the traditional gestalt body image and organic continuity. Architecture as text, writing, or simulation, replaces architecture as mimesis, or as imaging of the human subject. The object, the architectural form, is disassociated from the human subject; the form of the architecture contradicts the function of the building to accommodate human activity, and it contradicts the metaphysical function of the building to reaffirm individual embodied or cultural historical identities. The architecture is a tabula rasa for a utopian society, and a pure form of abstraction expressing the transcendental idea, and the spiritual absolute.

The subject is elided in the text of the architecture as the asymmetry, fragmentation, and dispersal of the forms dominates over a mimesis of form based on gestalt or body identification. Mimesis is the basis in the formation of

Figure 5.5 **Ludwig Mies van der Rohe, Barcelona Pavilion, 1929**

the individual ego in perception for the identity of the subject as an ideal, unified and total; it is the basis for the reflection of the subject in the form of the self-consciousness of reason, and the basis of the disjunction in conscious thought between forms as they are perceived, as the construct of reason in perception, and forms as they exist prior to the intervention of the subject, as in the a priori categories of intuition of Kant. The concept of abstract form outside of mimesis, outside of both *natura naturata* and *natura naturans*, is thus the concept of form in relation to what is other to conscious reason, or the concept of form in relation to the absolute, the synthesis of the real and ideal, what is perceived and what is thought. Mies' architecture accomplishes the same thing as De Stijl as inspired by Hegel, in the representation of the absolute outside the real. Mies' architecture subverts the symbolic relation between human being and object, and in so doing establishes a relation between subject and object in the dialectic of the perception and thought, the dialectic of the self-consciousness of reason, the interpersonal relation and identification, and the matrix of language into which the subject is inserted, in the *Zeitgeist* of the culture.

Mies' architecture is a product of the transcendental idealism of Schelling and Hegel, in the definition of reason in relation to that which is other to it, and the necessity of the self-alienation of reason in the identity of spirit, that which Mies seeks to express in architecture. In disjoining the text, the matrix of language, from the body of the subject, the architecture both reasserts the interdependence of body and language and redefines the subject in the freeing of language from the body, from the constructs of mimesis and gestalt identification. In the text of Mies there is differentiation and no representation, suggesting the divided subject which is not present in the mimetic construct. Mies' architecture can be seen as a psychoanalytic architecture as well, but one which is formulated within the context of Modernism, reflective of the divided subject of twentieth-century experience, but only anticipating the divided subject of psychoanalysis. There is no reason to discount the influence of Freudian psychoanalysis itself on Mies' work, or on the work of Theo van Doesburg and the De Stijl movement from which Mies' early work is evolved. The work of the avant-garde in Europe in the early twentieth century reflects the psychoanalytic subject, one which has been divided and self-alienated by the events occurring around it, such as technological war and media, new matrices of industry and communication, etc., and also one which has been redefined by the discoveries of Freud, in the science of psychoanalysis. Mies' architecture represents a necessary sustaining of the practice of architecture, which must contradict itself by displacing its own metaphysic in order to be a form of artistic expression; as in the tradition of Schelling and Hegel, architecture must contradict, even parody, its function, in order to be art, to express spirit.

Architecture as a form of expression must be "simultaneously becoming independent of itself," and it must become a "free imitation of itself," as Schelling expressed in *The Philosophy of Art* (Schelling 1989 [1859]: §107). As soon as architecture "attains through appearance both actuality and utility without intending these *as* utility and as actuality," that is, as soon as the cut is made between the signifier and the signified, the form and the idea, then it becomes "free and independent art." Because of the physical complicity in architecture between form and function, signifier and signified, architecture is the least representative of all the arts. In *The Philosophy of Art* (§111), because of the functional necessity of the forms of architecture, because of their physical presence, architecture is the least able among the arts to express the dialectic between the conceptual and the physical, or mind and matter. Architecture can only be art when it is both an enactment of necessity and an enactment of a freedom from that necessity; both an enactment of material reality (the real) and an enactment of the transcendence of material reality (the ideal, the *nous poietikos*). It is only in that way that architecture can express a dialectic between the objective and subjective, the universal and particular.

According to Peter Eisenman, in order for architecture to overcome its physical limitations in expression, an absence must be introduced in its presence, as in the use of metonymy in language, where the definition of one word is elided in a metaphorical comparison with another word. "If we want to make a wall more of a sign—that is, more rhetorical—we have to reduce its traditional opacity, that is, its traditional elemental, structural, and aesthetic content," as in the Barcelona Pavilion. "This requires the introduction of an absence in the *is* of architecture, an absence in its presence," Eisenman writes in the essay "Architecture and the Problem of the Rhetorical Figure" (Eisenman 2004a: 204).

A perfect example of this is the "Miesian Corner," the corner found in buildings designed by Mies, on the campus of the Illinois Institute of Technology in Chicago (Classroom Building, 1945–6, Figure 5.6; similarly at Crown Hall, 1950–6, Figure 5.7; or the Seagram Building in New York, 1954–8), which consists of a right-angle steel plate which is inserted into a brick frame at the corner of the building for the purpose of both covering the fire-proofed steel column and mimicking the steel column as the corner. The steel plate is placed above ground level, above courses of bricks, so that there is no possibility that it can be mistaken for a structural element, although it has the form and location of a structural element. The presence of the steel column as a corner structural element is absent in the welded steel plate, which acts metonymically in the text of the architecture. The form of the architecture contradicts the function of the building. In order to be art, architecture must contradict its structural necessity in form, in order to express the absolute, spirit, in the tradition of the transcendental idealism of the German philosophers, the tradition of which Mies van der Rohe was a product. The false column also appears on Crown Hall (Figure 5.7) on the IIT Campus. Crown Hall is suspended

Figure 5.6 **Ludwig Mies van der Rohe, IIT Classroom Building, 1945–6**

from hanger beams, creating an open interior space, a universal Socialist space, and I-columns are attached to the curtain wall to give the appearance of structure, their form contradicting the structural function of the building.

If architectural forms can be fragmented and recombined in the same way, to form formal catachreses (misapplications or misuses of words), which introduce absences into presences in words, in the process of fragmentation and recombination, then architecture can be invested with the same rhetorical function that is found in language. The architectural forms would be divested of their complicity with their signified, with what they express metaphysically, in their function and necessity, and would become independent of themselves, as in the theory of Schelling. Architecture would have the potential to depart from its expectations both physically and metaphysically (in anthropocentrism, for example), and to further contain the absence which is in the presence of reason and perception, revealing the relation between the real and the ideal, the absolute. The contradiction between form and function in the architecture expresses the contradiction between reason and perception, in the *Vorstellung* and in the phenomenal world.

Unexpected correspondences between architectural forms bring into question the relation between the architectural forms and their functional necessity, while they are generated from that functional necessity. The architectural forms satisfy Schelling's criterion for art in that they both satisfy their functional necessity and contradict their functional necessity at the same time, by blocking the relation between the signifier and the signified, the form and the idea. The unexpected correspondences provoke a misreading, in the impossibility of the self-consciousness of reason, which becomes a tenet of post-Hegelian thought in psychoanalysis. The physical presence of the forms of architecture is both reinforced and denied, as presence is constantly reinforced and denied in language,

Figure 5.7 **Ludwig Mies van der Rohe, Crown Hall, 1950–6**

resulting in the misreading of the subject in relation to its self-definition in reason. In psychoanalysis, it is impossible for reason to know itself, self-consciousness is an illusion, and it is impossible for the subject to know itself.

The absence in the presence of the forms is a *chôra*, which constitutes a trace in the presence of the forms. The form of the Barcelona Pavilion, based on the necessity of containment, denies the possibility of containment, in the same way that reason itself, based on the necessity of containment (in the Kantian sense of an a priori intuition or apperception of a totality of being), denies the possibility of containment. Reason is predicated on the necessity of the universal, as is revealed in language, but the universal itself comes to be seen as an impossibility. Reason is denied containment because of the holes in language, the metonymical and rhetorical absences and catachreses. Eisenman argues that the trace of presence, or the absence of presence, is automatically contained in any site on which a building is situated. "Any site contains not only presences, but the memory of previous presences and the immanences of a possible presence" (p. 207); thus "the introduction of this trace, or condition of absence, acknowledges the dynamic reality of the living city," and the dynamic reality of the human subject.

In composing a building, traces of previous buildings or site conditions may be incorporated into the architecture, but the reproduction of those traces would then be purposefully dislocated from the site, for the purpose of preserving the reproductions in the architecture as rhetorical figures, in mimesis, but blocking them from their origin or metaphysical associations. The temporal dislocation and blocking of the metaphysical signification of architectural forms in metonymic or rhetorical strategies can be found throughout the history of architecture. Alberti's façade for the Church of Sant'Andrea in Mantua (Figure 3.2), for example, introduced both an imperial triumphal arch and a pagan temple front to the façade of a Catholic church, in combination, for the first time, challenging the traditional form of the church in relation to its metaphysical function, and challenging the assumed metaphysical relation between an architectural form and the idea or association which it communicates. The basilica of the Christian church is a pre-existing dislocation, combining the nave and side aisles of the Egyptian hypostyle hall with colonnades from Greek stoas.

All invention in architecture involves some form of dislocation or displacement, as invention in language, in metaphor and metonymy, involves dislocation and displacement. In the dislocation of the metaphysic, "architecture can be considered, paradoxically, contradictory to building, to its institutionalizing presence," as Eisenman writes in "Misreading Peter Eisenman" (Eisenman 2004a: 222), in the contradiction between form and function, as for Schelling, architecture as art must be a "parody of the mechanical building arts" (Schelling 1989 [1859]: §111). Architecture must be an imitation of the act of building, the act of sheltering, in its allegorical representation, as the elevations of Sant'Andrea do not support the barrel vault which appears to rest on them (as in St. Peter's in Rome), and the springer poles in the elevations of Lincoln Cathedral do not support the tierceron vault above them. The contradiction between form and function reveals the absence in the presence, the transcendental idea in reason, the Absolute Spirit in being.

It is impossible for architecture as art or expression to take building seriously in its imitation of it; architecture must be a parody of necessity because of the disjunction between thought and language in the blocking of the signifier from the signified, the disjunction between the real and ideal. This can be seen in the Glass House by Philip Johnson (1906–2005), built in New Canaan, Connecticut, in 1949–50. In the Glass House, the welded steel plate that was designed by Mies to mimic the steel column, which was unavailable to represent the structural function of the building, becomes the structural element. The house is presented as a parody of the necessity of the relation between form and function in architecture, and a parody of the metaphysic of architecture. A form which was designed as ornament, in imitation of structure, is used as structure. Such a play of forms is characteristic of mannerism in architecture, as was seen in the Palazzo del Tè of Giulio Romano in the late Renaissance. At the Palazzo del Tè (Figure 3.4), the possibility of the ornamental elements as structure (as occurs in the Glass House) is negated, as pieces of the entablature are "slipped" below the entablature, so that the entablature could not be a horizontal support, and columns are removed from underneath pediments, leaving the pediments floating on the façade. The architecture is revealed to be a parody of itself in its imitation of itself. This was accomplished by Romano in the use of linguistic tropes as applied to architecture, from the *Rhetoric* of Aristotle.

In *Of Grammatology* (1967), Jacques Derrida (1930–2004) described the instituted trace in language as maintaining language as a structure of differences in the Saussurean sense of a lack of relationship between the signifier and the signified in the word. The presence of absence in the trace is not a metaphysical presence, but rather a structural presence in the science of the letter. The trace makes signification possible, as is shown by Jacques Lacan in the *point de capiton* in the sliding of the signifying chain, the point at which absence is made present in the correlation between signified and signifier. In its modeling of the signifying chain, architecture can be seen as a structure of differences, through which signification is produced, in the combination and displacement of architectural forms. The trace is "where the relationship with the other is marked" (Derrida 1976 [1967]: 47), as described by Derrida, the crossing of the bar between signifier and signified at the *point de capiton*, and, as in the metaphoric chain, "the movement of the trace is necessarily occulted, it produces itself as self-occultation. When the other announces itself as such, it presents itself in the dissimulation of itself." The trace is thus never present, it is only present as absence. The other, that which is inaccessible to reason, is only known as absence in conscious thought (the unconscious), in the structural mechanisms of language, making possible and precluding the possibility at the same time of presence. The other can be seen as the absolute.

Similarly, in the *Phenomenology of Spirit* of Hegel, spirit, described as the inner being of the world, assumes objective form and enters into relations with itself. Spirit becomes externality or otherness, and exists for itself. Spirit doubles itself in its otherness, and it is through the doubling of itself as otherness or externality that it participates in the particular. Spirit becomes object, but as object it is immediately negated; it becomes self-reflected in the object which is the product of its doubling, as reason itself is reflected in the object in perception which is the product of its doubling in self-consciousness. Spirit can be seen as the absence which allows for presence in language. The synthesis of spirit and object, objective and subjective, is the ideal of the absolute. The trace is an absolute for Derrida, a form of an archetypal principle. In the Miesian Corner, the trace in the absence may be seen as the archetypal principle in the structure of differences, as in the *point de capiton* in the relation between the signifier and the signified, which is still a metaphysical presence of absence.

For Derrida it is the otherness retained within the trace which is the necessary condition for the movement of differences, as for Hegel it is the otherness of spirit in matter which is the necessary condition for the dialectic between the subjective and objective. Derrida described language as a play of differences and deferrals, called *différance*. The play of language caused by the lack of a relationship between the signifier and the signified in the word defers the possibility of meaning. The trace is *différance*, which is the condition of the movement which produces differences. *Différance* is spirit, which negates itself in its doubling of itself in otherness. Although *différance* (spirit) "does not exist, although it is never a being-present outside of all plenitude, its possibility is by rights anterior to all that one calls sign (signifier/signified, content/expression, etc.), concept or operation, motor or sensory" (Derrida 1976 [1967]: 62); in other words, the absolute.

Like the spirit of Hegel, *différance* is anterior to and inaccessible to the laws of reason in language, which are predicated on objective self-doubling and negation, the production of difference. *Différance* "founds the metaphysical opposition between the sensible and intelligible, then between signifier and signified, expression and content, etc." It is the ground for the possibility of the dialectic of the metaphysic, which is given by the structure of language. The metonymical or rhetorical figure in the text of architecture, as the enactment of *différance*, contains the metaphysic within it, and the Subjective Spirit of Hegel, in the absence contained within the linguistic structure, within the limits of conscious reason, and contains the trace as well, which is the presence (as absence) of the absolute. The trace does not participate in the dialectic or the metaphysic; it is neither real nor ideal, sensible nor intelligible, but is anterior to all, the ground on which reason operates in language, according to Derrida (p. 65).

Writing in architecture, architectural composition, can never be purely phenomenological or conceptual, but both, as in the Hegelian synthesis, and neither; that is, the synthesis must always contain a negation, as it does for Hegel, and a dialectic. The conceptual must negate the physical form, as in language the trope or rhetorical figure overcomes the lack of sense (in metaphor and metonym, for example), and the physical form must negate the conceptual, as in language the trope conceals the signified. In that way a sort of dialectic is enacted in *différance*, which can be applied to architectural composition.

A mechanism which results from the spacing of Derrida's *différance* in writing is the "graft." A graft is an intervention into the pre-existing structure of a language, as in the welded steel plate inserted by Mies into the corner of the steel frame building in the writing of architecture, for the purpose of exposing the limitations of the structure of language, and overcoming them. The graft begins with oppositions, differences in the structure of language, the opposition of signifiers, and then proceeds to the displacement of those oppositions, in particular the displacement of metaphysical oppositions, which rely on the pre-inscribed correspondence between the signifier and the signified. Signifiers in language are taken out of the oppositions in which they are generated, and are recombined in ways which expose the absences which the metaphysical oppositions concealed. For Eisenman, design in architecture should "move the act of architecture from its complacent relationship with the metaphysic of architecture by reactivating its capacity to dislocate" ("Misreading Peter Eisenman") (Eisenman 2004a: 214).

Le Corbusier

The cantilevered overhangs of the Robie House in Chicago (1910, Figure 5.8) and Fallingwater (Kaufmann Residence, Bear Run, Pennsylvania, 1935) of Frank Lloyd Wright (1867–1959) depend on concealed steel beams. As Wright said in "The Art and Craft of the Machine," a talk given to the Chicago Arts and Crafts Society at the Hull House in 1901, the architect should take advantage of new technology without allowing the technology to dictate the architecture. Thus the form must contradict the function. The cantilevered overhang made possible by industrial technology is a symbol of the rejection of industrial technology, in favor of guild production, and the creativity of the individual, in the Arts and Crafts tradition. The contradiction between form and function represents the contradictory relationship between the freedom and creativity of the individual and the dictates of industrial and technological society.

The exact opposite can be found in the architecture of Le Corbusier (Charles-Édouard Jeanneret, 1887–1965). The early villas, such as the Villa Savoye (Poissy, 1928), exemplars of the *machine à habiter*, the house as a machine, employ painted wood panels to appear as machined parts. Here the technology dictates the architecture, and the architect does not take advantage of new technology. The form contradicts the function in the opposite manner. The Purist ideals are achieved through smoke and mirrors; it is easy to understand how they were so easily abandoned by Le Corbusier in his later career, in favor of Surrealist forms, in which the form of the architecture also contradicts its function. Surrealist forms, as at the Chapel of Notre Dame du Haut at Ronchamp (1955, Figure 5.10), are dream images, formed through the mechanisms of condensation and displacement in dream construction, as described by Sigmund Freud in *The Interpretation of Dreams*. Rational objects and perceptions are transformed into irrational forms, as

Figure 5.8 **Frank Lloyd Wright, Robie House, 1910**

the form of the dream contradicts the function of the perception or thought from which it is derived. Form often contradicts function in dreams.

In Le Corbusier's Villa Stein at Garches (1927, Figure 5.9), the regular grid of the building corresponds to the vertical divisions of the space of the elevation, in section, and the horizontal divisions of the space of the plan; the intersections and overlapping of these grids create irregular and unexpected spaces, as in the overlay of oblique and curved lines in the two-dimensional grid of a Cubist painting. As observed by Colin Rowe and Robert Slutzky in their essay "Transparency: Literal and Phenomenal" of 1955–6, the result is a "contradiction of spatial dimensions" (Rowe and Slutzky 1976: 169), and there is a "continuous dialectic between fact and implication. The reality of deep space is constantly opposed to the inference of shallow; and, by means of the resultant tension, reading after reading is enforced" (p. 170). Le Corbusier sets up an expectation of symmetry in elevation which gives way to asymmetry in plan.

The dialectic between frontality and recession is the same dialectic which occurs in the Cubist composition, given by the regular grid and the oblique and curved lines suggesting volume. Thus, "this gridding of space will then result in continuous fluctuations of interpretation." The mind of the observer or inhabitant will continuously juxtapose the different spaces and grids created in the building, in different imagined relationships. In that way sensible form and space are translated into intelligible form and space. The architecture of the building is constructed and exists in the mind of the observer, as in the lineament of Leon Battista Alberti. The form of the architecture depends on a conceptual organization underlying the physical presence of the building, a "deep structure." In the contradiction of spatial dimensions and the dialectic between fact and interpretation, the form of the architecture contradicts the functional and structural requirements of the building.

Figure 5.9 Le Corbusier, Villa Stein, 1927

The simultaneous perception of different spatial locations was defined as "transparency" by Gyorgy Kepes in *Language of Vision* in 1944: "Transparency means a simultaneous perception of different spatial locations. Space not only recedes but fluctuates in a continuous activity. The position of the transparent figures has equivocal meaning as one sees each figure now as the closer, now as the further one" (Kepes 1944: 77). This transparency, which Rowe and Slutzky called "phenomenal transparency," is a product of the Cubist composition, in the construction of a space in which objects have ambiguous relationships in terms of foreground, middleground, and background, and in terms of the point of view of the observer. It is also a product of the desire on the part of the Cubist painters to portray the sensible world as infinitely variable in a space which fluctuates in a continuous activity. Like the forms of the objects themselves, the spatial relations between the objects are the subject of the conceptual organization in the mind of the observer, rather than an attempt to imitate nature. Thus phenomenal transparency is a conceptual transparency, a construct of the imagination, a product of the ideal as opposed to the real, like the a priori categories of Kant, and a form of abstraction in the expression of the absolute as the dialectic between the real and the ideal, in the contradiction between form and function.

The aerodynamic shape of the roof of the Chapel of Notre Dame du Haut at Ronchamp (Figure 5.10) contradicts its function in relation to the building. The building is composed of sinuous shapes which mimic the landscape, and non-machined materials, stone and concrete, representing a rejection of the earlier Purist *machine-à-habiter*, a rejection of the pre-war positivism and belief that industrial technology would bring about a better future. The sinuous, organic shape of the roof was only made possible by the most advanced technology in aerodynamic design. Each of the elevations of the building is treated differently, creating a contra-diction of spatial dimensions and a dialectic between fact and interpretation, a spatial organization of phenomenal transparency in the mind of the viewer. A gutter spout is sculpted in the form of the horns of the Minotaur, a symbol of Surrealism, and other Surrealist forms are found in the building and the landscape around it. The sculpted Surrealist forms, in contrast to Le Corbusier's earlier Purist paintings of objects resolved to ideal geometries by machines, look like the forms in the paintings of the early Surrealist painter Joan Miró (1893–1983). The forms of Miró can be described as organic and biomorphic, and hybridized and disconnected, as in forms in dreams. The hybridized and disconnected forms of Miró are the product of the mechanisms of condensation and displacement, the principal methods of dream formation, according to Sigmund Freud.

The formation of images in dreams was described by Sigmund Freud (1856–1939) in *The Interpretation of Dreams* (1900) and *On Dreams* (1901). The dream is not the unconscious, although it is seen to reveal the structures of the unconscious, and Freud's analysis is of the memory of the dream rather than the dream itself; the dream is thus seen as a mnemic residue, or memory trace, of perception. The content of the memory of the dream, the dream image, is the "manifest content" of the dream, and the product of the conceptual analysis of the dream is the "latent content," or dream thought, of the dream. The latent content of the dream is not a content of the memory of the dream itself, but something which is ascribed to it by conscious thought. Dreamwork is the process which transforms the latent content of the dream into the manifest content, the process by which the dream is generated from unconscious thought. The structure of unconscious thought contains linguistic constructions, as the unconscious

Figure 5.10 **Le Corbusier, Notre Dame du Haut at Ronchamp, 1955**

is structured like a language (in the words of Jacques Lacan). The relations of the linguistic constructions can be found in the relations between images in the manifest content of the dream.

Freud sees a direct relationship between the dream thought and the dream content in the same way as there is a direct relationship between the signifier and the signified in the structural linguistics of Ferdinand de Saussure, as two sides of a piece of paper, and the transcription between the two is governed by a linguistic syntax, a complex system of rules which operates according to a logic which does not always correspond to conscious reason. The mechanisms of representation, as they are developed between the dream thought and the dream image, are different from conscious mechanisms of representation in the intersection of perception and language, although the mnemic residues of dream memories are derived from those of external perception, and the linguistic mechanisms of representation in the unconscious are derived from conscious language. Unconscious mechanisms are seen as a variation of conscious mechanisms not under the control of conscious reason.

Dream thoughts and dream images are for Freud, in *The Interpretation of Dreams*, "two versions of the same subject-matter" presented in two different languages in a transcript "whose characters and syntactic laws it is our business to discover by comparing the original and the translation" (Freud 1965 [1900]: 311–12). Dream images are seen as a "pictographic script, the characters of which have to be transposed individually into the language of dream thoughts" in a signifying relation. Relations between dream images depend on relations between dream thoughts in a syntactical matrix. There is no direct relationship between sequences of images in dreams and thought processes in the dream thoughts, which leads Freud to a conclusion which would suggest that there is no unconscious thought per se, but only mimetic repetitions and reproductions of thoughts which correspond to mimetic reproductions of images in perception, the mnemic residues.

The mechanism of the transposition from dream thoughts to dream images is labeled "imagination," and the "mental activity which may be described as 'imagination'" is "liberated from the domination of reason and from any moderating control" (p. 116). Dream imagination "makes use of recent waking memories for its building material," in mimesis and repetition, and "it erects them into structures bearing not the remotest resemblance to those of waking life." Dream imagination is "without the power of conceptual speech" and has "no concepts to exercise an attenuating influence," thus being "obliged to paint what it has to say pictorially." The linguistic structure of the dream image is seen as "diffuse, clumsy and awkward"; it is missing the organization of conscious reason, while its forms are mimetic of conscious reason. Dreams have "no means at their disposal for representing these logical relations between the dream-thoughts" (p. 347), or for representing logical relations between conscious thoughts, the relations created by syntactical rules.

Thinking does not occur in the dreams themselves either, according to Freud; any thought processes which might be perceived in memories of dreams are only a mimicking of thought processes which occur in the dream thoughts, which are themselves a mimicking of conscious thought processes. Thus "what is reproduced by the ostensible thinking in the dream is the subject matter of the dream thoughts and not the mutual relations between them, the assertion of which constitutes thinking" (pp. 347–8). Dream images constitute a kind of false façade and a form of deception; they are as the luminous embroidered veil in the Allegory of the Cave in the *Republic*, hanging between the finite and the infinite, between the real and ideal, between the images which are mnemic residues of images in sensible perception, and the thoughts in the unconscious which are mnemic residues of conscious rational thoughts. The form of the dream image can easily contradict the function of the dream thought, as Surrealist forms in architecture contradict the practical or conceptual function of the building.

The memory of the dream image enacts the same dialectic as is found in metaphysics in conscious thought, the disjunction between that which is perceived and that which is conceived, the real and the ideal. The dream image can thus express the absolute. Any thought activity represented in dreams is represented as having already been completed, according to Freud, so thought activity, whether conscious or unconscious, is crystallized into a structure in the dream, made abstract, and made synchronic. A contradiction in a dream cannot correspond to a contradiction in a conceptual sequence which is a product of the dream analysis. The logic of the dream is independent of conscious logic. Any correspondence between conceptual structures would only be an indirect one. Different dreams vary in the clarity of their correspondence with conceptual structures; some seem to correspond fairly clearly, which can easily be a deception, and others make no sense at all. Chronological sequences occur in dreams as imitations of chronological sequences in conceptual thought; they have no logic of their own, and any correspondence with conceptual chronological sequences is an accident.

Diachronic sequences, as they are understood in conscious reason, may as a result be compressed into synchronic events or images, in condensation, or they may be fragmented, or reversed, in displacement. There is a dialectic between the mechanisms of conscious and unconscious thought—between the hierarchy, unity, sequence, and progression of conscious thought and the fragmentation, disjunction, contingency, alternation, slippage, and oscillation of unconscious thought, all of which can be found to be characteristics of dream composition. The simultaneity of the conscious and unconscious necessitates an "oscillating" reading, as in phenomenal transparency in architecture. The presence of the unconscious is revealed as the absence in conscious discourse, as that which is incompatible with conscious reason in the subject, which results in a continuous oscillation of presence, in language and architecture. The structuring of dream images as described by Freud corresponds fairly closely to linguistic structures, in that the unconscious mimics language. The rules of collocation in dream images correspond to the rules of collocation in language.

Dream images are distinct from one another in the same way that words are distinct from one another in a sentence, and the logic behind the combination of dream images is usually evident, a structural logic, as one that corresponds to the logic behind word combinations in sentences. Dreams seem to obey a grammatical and syntactical structure, regardless of whether a sense can be derived from them which corresponds to conscious reason. In that way dream images can be seen as pictorial equivalents of signifiers; they operate independently of the dream thoughts to which they are attached, and any signification which they produce is a product of their combinations as systems of differences in a syntax, as in the structural linguistics of Ferdinand de Saussure or the *différance* of Jacques Derrida. Dreams have no intention of communicating anything, according to Freud, so it is most likely that they produce no signification. Such communication would require a recognizable syntactical structure that corresponds to conscious logic, which does not exist in dreams, despite the periodic correspondences and similarities which are reproduced in imitation of relations in logic.

One example of the inability of dreams to correspond to conscious reasoning, in addition to the lack of distinction between the synchronic and diachronic, is the simultaneity of contraries and contradictions. Opposite forms are combined into a single form, in condensation, or appear as the same form, or a form might be replaced by its opposite, or represented by its opposite. There is no distinction between positive and negative, no sign of any conclusion that might be drawn from conceptual thought as given in the syntactical structure of language. Representation in dreams, according to Freud, is often facilitated by replacement, as in condensation, or a metaphor in language. Displacement has been seen to be a mechanism in architectural composition. This is one of many examples in Freud's dream interpretation which points to the linguistic structuring of dream images.

The two principal mechanisms of the formation of dream images are displacement and condensation. Displacement is responsible for the fact that dream images do not correspond to conscious reason, and causes the dream to be seen as a distortion, or perversion, of reason, a deceptive façade, as in archi-tecture. Displacement can be seen as a primary mechanism of both metaphor and metonymy in language; it results in a figurative or poetic signification in language which goes beyond its literal function and introduces the irrational within the rational, the presence of the absence of reason. In such a mechanism, the dream can be seen as a form of tropic language whose logical sense is removed from rational discourse.

The other principal mechanism in dream formation is condensation, which involves the coincidence of opposites, the representation of two contrary ideas by the same structure, as well as the diachronic combined into the synchronic, and "collective and composite figures," as in paintings by Miró, or the Surrealist architecture of Le Corbusier. Condensation is the most active mechanism in dream formation, as "in dreams fresh composite forms are being perpetually constructed in an inexhaustible variety," as described by Freud in *On Dreams* (Freud 1952 [1901]: 30). In condensation the dream image is over-determined by material in the dream thoughts. A single dream image may be the combination of several pictorial or linguistic forms which have no apparent relation to each other. The condensation and displacement which Freud observes as characteristics of the dream image lend to the theory that the dream is a pictorial language, a pictographic script, a derivation of the *Vorstellung*, and that the unconscious is structured like a language.

As a result of the complex network of psychical relationships which produce the dream images, and the mechanisms of condensation and displacement, dreams are composed of "disconnected fragments of visual images, speeches and even bits of unmodified thoughts," which "stand in the most manifold logical relations to one another" which are seen for example as "foreground and background, conditions, digressions and illustrations, chains of evidence and counterarguments" (p. 40), as in the contradiction of spatial dimensions, the dialectic between fact and interpretation, the spatial organization of phenomenal transparency, and the Surrealist forms resulting from condensation and displacement in the architecture of Le Corbusier. Displacement, condensation, fragmentation, and the coincidence of opposites are products of the complex network of logical relations in dream thoughts, which is too complex to correspond to a logical structure. In the process of the dream formation, "the logical links which have hitherto held the psychical material together are lost" (p. 41).

Terragni

In the Casa del Fascio (1932–6, Figure 5.11) and the Casa Giuliani Frigerio (1939–40, Figure 5.12) by Giuseppe Terragni (1904–43) in Como, Italy, the seemingly irrational arrangement of balconies, railings, and windows on each façade is the product of

Figure 5.11 **Giuseppe Terragni, Casa del Fascio, 1932–6**

rational compositional devices carried out to organize the buildings—the shifting and rotating of the nine square grid at the Casa del Fascio, and the overlay of additive and subtractive or centrifugal and centripetal plans at the Casa Giuliani Frigerio, as analyzed by Peter Eisenman in "From Object to Relationship II: Giuseppe Terragni, Casa Giuliani Frigerio," published in *Perspecta* 13, *The Yale Architectural Journal*, in 1971.

A student of Colin Rowe, Eisenman employed similar analytical devices. The compositions of Terragni's buildings are ascribed the same discrepancy between formal disposition and conceptual arrangement, as enacted by certain sets of dialectical relations between the architectural forms and their relationships, as in Cubist paintings and the architecture of Le Corbusier. The buildings of Terragni display the same "contradiction of spatial dimensions" and "dialectic between fact and implication" as described by Rowe and Slutzky in "Transparency: Literal and Phenomenal." The reading of the buildings involves the same "simultaneous perception of different spatial locations" or "transparency" as described by Gyorgy Kepes in *Language of Vision*. The spatial relations between objects are seen as the subject of the conceptual organization in the mind of the observer.

The dialectic between form and concept was reformulated by Eisenman in the terms of Chomskian linguistics. The architectural forms (columns, lintels, frames, balconies, doorways) and the perceived appearance of their relation-ships in space (juxtaposed, overlapping) were designated the "surface aspect" of the composition by Eisenman, as in the elevation or plan of the Villa Stein, in the analysis of Rowe, or the grid and oblique lines of the Cubist compositions. The underlying conceptual relations between the architectural forms, as deter-mined by the architect (mathematical and geometrical constructs and proportions,

Figure 5.12 **Giuseppe Terragni, Casa Giuliani Frigerio, 1939–40**

additive and subtractive, centripetal and centrifugal compositional devices), and as constructed in the mind of the perceiver (frontality as opposed to spatial recession in phenomenal transparency, solid as opposed to void in the spatial recession, axial relations) were designated the "deep aspect."

In Chomskian linguistics, the surface aspect of a language is the phonetic form or physical signal, the signifying element of the word as sign, as in the structural linguistics of Ferdinand de Saussure, while the deep aspect is a "corresponding mental analysis," as described in Chomsky's *Language and Mind* (Chomsky 1968: 16), that arises in response to the physical signal of the phonetic form. In Chomskian linguistics, the sign only contains a signifier and not a signified, as it would in Saussurean linguistics, because, first, the corresponding mental analysis consists only in sets of extended signifiers prompted by the phonetic signal, and second, because the phonetic signal only operates in a given syntax, and not of its own. In architecture, forms are either pure signifiers, with no signifying element, as in Chomsky's phonetic signal, or they are signs, in the Saussurean sense, containing both signifier and signified. A form as pure signifier in architecture would be a vertical, horizontal, or diagonal line, or a geometrical figure in two or three dimensions; in other words, pure geometry, which is the language, or linguistic structure, of architectural composition. The purified syntax of geometry becomes the vocabulary of communication and expression in Modernist architecture, in the absence of ornament, and the absence of the symbol. Terragni's architecture and, subsequently, Peter Eisenman's architecture continue the utopian purification of De Stijl in the enactment of a universal language devoid of signifieds, symbols, or cultural particularities.

In the analysis of Peter Eisenman, the result of the dialectic between form and concept is a "transformational relation" between the contradictory forms of the "surface structure" or façade and the "deep structure" or conceptual organization, using terms borrowed from Noam Chomsky, in the same way that there is a transformational relation between syntax in language and the associated meaning. In structural linguistics, Ferdinand de Saussure established that the relationship between the signifier, the word, and the signified, the meaning or idea, is arbitrary at best. The "transformational relation" functions as the *point de capiton* of Lacan, the point at which the bar between the signifier and signified is crossed, and signification or communication is achieved. In this case the signified is the "deep structure" itself, the conceptual syntax of the architectural forms.

An abstract geometrical figure of itself has no signifying function in architecture, unless the figure has an ascribed association. Geometries are no longer symbolic, like they were in the Renaissance. Architectural vocabulary elements such as columns, lintels, doors, or windows can always be seen to have signifying capacity in relation to architectural functions; for example, a column under a lintel suggests that the column is supporting the lintel, the form of a door suggests the possibility to walk through it. The vocabulary of architecture, without ornament or symbol, has a very limited capacity for signification, and can only signify something in relation to its functional purpose. Given the limitations of the purified vocabulary of Modernist architecture in the twentieth century, what is architecture capable of communicating or expressing? How can architecture be seen as a form of art?

Even in its limited vocabulary, in Modernist architecture the form of the architecture can still contradict the function of the building. The contradiction between form and function can be enacted in any kind of architecture, and is shared by any architecture in history, including Modernist and contemporary computer-generated forms. The contradiction between form and function can be seen as the one continuous thread throughout the history of architecture which defines architecture as a form of art and enables architecture to communicate an idea which is not related to the functional requirements of a building. Eisenman's investigation of the syntactical relations of the architectural forms of Terragni, and his subsequent use of them in his own architecture, provide a basis for possibilities of communication and expression in abstracted Modernist forms. The element that Terragni's buildings and all of Eisenman's buildings have in common is the contradiction between form and function.

For Chomsky the deep aspect of language consists of interrelating propositions and ideas, networks of signifiers, that are not articulated in the phonetic signal but are generated by it, and are generated by a matrix of underlying relations from the signal. The deep aspect consists of a network of formal regularities organized by a conceptual framework, which might be described as the unconscious. The relationship between dream images and dream thoughts, like the relationship between form and conceptual organization in architecture, can be seen as a relationship between surface aspect and deep aspect. Eisenman's analysis of the deep aspect of architecture consists of the implied relationships of conceptual space generated by the surface aspects or forms, beginning with the dialectical relations described by Rowe and Slutzky in phenomenal transparency (frontality/recession, luminosity/opacity), and continuing with the dialectical relations of solid/void, additive/subtractive, centripetal/centrifugal, and axial/contiguous in the architecture of Terragni. Eisenman explained that the deep aspect in architecture is "concerned with conceptual relations which are not sensually perceived; such as frontality, obliqueness, recession, elongation, compression, and shear, which are understood in the mind. These are attributes which accrue to relationships between objects, rather than to the physical presence of the objects themselves" (Eisenman 1971: 38). In language, the deep aspect is concerned with conceptual relations which do not exist in the phonetic signal, but which are generated from the phonetic signal itself or from its location in a syntax, and transferred to the conceptual relations. In this sense, the transference would be the obverse of the transference of relations between dream thoughts and dream images.

While in painting, three-dimensional spatial relationships are generated from two-dimensional graphic forms and relationships, as in the two-dimensional grid and straight and curved lines which create an "oscillation of readings" in the Cubist painting, in architecture the conceptual spatial relationships can be generated from either planar or spatial forms and relationships or syntaxes. In architecture, the spatial relationships constructed in the mind in phenomenal transparency or deep structure must be differentiated from the actual spatial relationships present in the sensual perception or surface structure of the architecture. The transformational relation, the transference from the surface aspect to the deep aspect, involves the process of "apperception," as described by Eisenman, involving the combination of multiple perceptions, and the differentiation between the physical and the conceptual spatial relationships. Apperception, as described by Plotinus, Benedict de Spinoza (1632–77), or Kant, involves the transference from the phenomenal world to the world as it is constructed in the mind, according to *nous poietikos* or the categories of a priori intuition in the forming of concepts.

In the *Enneads* of Plotinus, perceptual experience is multiple and fragmented, as individual objects have no necessary connections in size or position; those connections are constructed in the mind, as in the thought of George Berkeley or the phenomenal transparency of Colin Rowe. In the process of perception, all of the objects of perception and all of the acts of perception are unified to form a coherent whole or totality which structures the world as it is perceived; the surface aspect is a product of the deep aspect, and dream images are a product of dream thoughts. The fragmented objects of perception "become like partless thoughts" when they "reach the ruling principle" (Plotinus 1966: IV.7.6), that is, they are organized as concepts, and their resultant appearance is determined by concepts in *nous poietikos*, as in a priori intuition.

For Berkeley, the quality of distance is not immediately perceived, but is a judgment which is learned through an accumulation of sense perceptions, or apperception, in relation to discursive thought. Distance is perceived through the mediation of signs or representations, abstractions in apperception, which immediately and unconsciously produce concepts, as in a priori intuition. The sign is a conception, but it is hidden from consciousness in the act of perception. The formation of the object as a *species apprehensibilis* (an intelligible form) or signified (in a deep aspect) is hidden in the perceptual experience of the object as a *species sensibilis* (sensible form, signifier or sign) in a surface aspect. The intelligible under-standing of architecture is hidden in the perception of the building.

Spinoza distinguished between three kinds of knowledge, based in sense, reason, and intuition. Sense knowledge is derived from individual objects perceived through the senses in a fragmentary and confused manner without any conceptual order, in immediate sensory experience. Reason is derived from symbols, according to Spinoza, from which ideas are formed in the imagination. The symbols of Spinoza can be seen as the signifieds of Saussure. The vocabulary elements of architecture, as signifiers in a syntax, become symbols or signifieds from which ideas or concepts are derived. Spinoza's reason involves shared ideas about the properties of the objects of sensation and perception. Reason provides a conceptual order to the fragmentary objects of perception, a kind of apperception. The third kind of knowledge, intuition, is a kind of *nous poietikos*, involving *principia essendi*, the principles of the essence of objects, which for Kant are unknowable.

According to Kant in the *Critique of Pure Reason*, sensible objects can only be known by means of intuition. The capacity for receiving representations is the source of intuition, which allows sensible objects to be conceptualized. Thought is related to intuition and perception through representation by signs, as in the symbols of Spinoza. Sensible objects can only be thought of as representations. In that sense the surface aspect of architecture is already a product of the deep aspect. The vocabulary forms of architecture are representations, as are objects in perception, or words in language. Perceived sensations cannot arrange themselves or assume composite forms; in order for the physical world to be perceived as a totality, or for a building to be perceived as a totality, the forms must exist a priori in the mind, and be seen as separate from forms as perceived. In the pure forms of sensuous intuition which exist in the mind a priori, the "manifold content of the phenomenal world is arranged and viewed under certain relations" (Kant 1990 [1781]: 22), according to Kant, in apperception. The very definition of architecture is the a priori ordering of the phenomenal world according to space and time, geometry and mathematics. Architecture itself is a form of apperception before it is perceived, so all architecture communicates at the very least an idea, a basic philosophical truth about human thought and experience.

According to Kant, space is not a concept which is derived from outward experience, nor from relations between external phenomena. Perceptions of phenomenal space are predetermined by a priori concepts. The communication of the idea of architecture depends on a priori intuition in perception, rather than in sensory perception or reason based in perception. Architecture cannot be conceived without space; as space is an a priori concept, architecture must be seen as an a priori concept, as understood in the mind as a product of apperception, in a disjunction from perception itself. Objects are perceived as representations by a priori intuition, as forms. Forms are perceived as representations in intuition. A priori cognition is made possible by a synthesis of the manifold of conceptions in relation to the "unity of apperception" (p. 86), according to Kant, the synthesis of the multiple perceptions of objects. Reason is architectonic, in a constructed totality. The synthesis is transcendental and purely intellectual, and is figurative as opposed to conjunctive, as it is the product of intuition rather than discursive reason.

The transformational relation of Eisenman is a method for "deriving and relating specific forms to formal universals. These transformational devices translate formal regularities into specific forms" (Eisenman 1971: 40), as described by Chomsky in *Cartesian Linguistics*. Transformational devices require certain mental operations and "grammatical transformations," as the grammar of architecture must, like the grammar of language, or its syntax, "contain a system of rules that characterize deep and surface structures and the transformational relation between them," as described in *Language and Mind* (Chomsky 1968: 30). The transformational relation is for Eisenman a means to define the conceptual link between the particulars of forms and relationships of architectural vocabulary elements and the underlying structure of those forms and relationships. An example of the transformational relation is "pictorial ambiguity." Pictorial ambiguity is the simultaneity of opposites in perception, the oscillation of readings in phenomenal transparency, or the product of condensation in the formation of dream images. In pictorial ambiguity, apperception is enacted in the process of perception.

In language, ambiguity arises from the conflict between the "denotative and the connotative" (Eisenman 1971: 41), the denotative being the signifier in the phonetic signal, and the connotative being the network of signifiers generated by it, or also the figural as opposed to the literal in language. Ambiguity in meaning arises from the location of a word in a sentence in relation to other words, and in the possibility of a figural as opposed to a literal use of a word. Ambiguity in language can act as a transformational device, because it reveals the underlying structure upon which the generation of meaning depends, the deep aspect, or a priori intuition.

In the Casa Giuliani Frigerio (Figure 5.12), pictorial ambiguity is identified in the simultaneous occurrence of both an additive and subtractive compositional process and centripetal and centrifugal organizations of forms, and in the dialectics of planar/recession, solid/void, horizontal/vertical, and in the juxtaposition of forms generated by the superimposition and shifting of grids in plan. Pictorial ambiguity is seen as a compositional strategy in architecture to transform conceptual structures into formal structures, and to allow formal structures to be read as conceptual structures. Pictorial ambiguity enacts the dialectic of thought in perception and what is perceived, and the contradiction between form and function in perception, and the contradiction between form and function in architecture.

The dialectics parallel the dialectics between the diachronic sequences of conscious reason and the synchronic characteristics of dream images, a contradiction which reveals the unconscious, as a priori intuition is revealed in relation to discursive reason. Eisenman observed of the buildings of Terragni that "the meaning of their facades, plans and sections can be read as displacements from an architecture of origin, hierarchy, unity, sequence, progression, and continuity to one of fragmentation, disjunction, contingency, alternation, slippage, and oscillation" (Eisenman 2005: 75). The buildings stage the relation between the rational and the irrational, and between conscious and unconscious thought. Through the use of the transformational devices of simultaneous centrifugal and centripetal, and additive and subtractive organizations, which locate the *point de capiton* of Lacan, the point at which the unconscious is made present in the absence of the subject, and the point at which a relation between a surface structure and a deep structure is revealed, the buildings stage the simultaneity of conscious thought and unconscious production as manifest in dreamwork.

The dialectic between the two mechanisms consists of the dialectic between the hierarchy, unity, sequence, and progression of conscious thought and the fragmentation, disjunction, contingency, alternation, slippage, and oscillation, all of which can be found to be characteristics of dream composition and unconscious thought. The simultaneity of the conscious and unconscious necessitates an oscillating reading of the architecture; the presence of the unconscious is revealed as that which is incompatible with conscious reason in the subject, which results in a continuous oscillation of presence, as language itself, as Derrida and Lacan have shown, is a continual oscillation of presence and absence in the play of signifiers and the relation between signifier and signified. The oscillating readings of the architecture demonstrate that there are absences in the architectural syntax, just as there are absences in the syntax of language, which reveal the unconscious.

According to Lacan, the unconscious is inaccessible, and can only be known in absence, in the gaps in consciousness, and in language. The gaps in the phenomena of consciousness are the holes and scotomata of Lacan in the human subject, "everything that the ego neglects, scotomizes, misconstrues in the sensations that make it react to reality, everything that it ignores, exhausts, and binds in the significations that it receives from language," as described in *Écrits* (Lacan 1977 [1966]: 22). The goal of psychoanalysis, for Freud, was to fill in those gaps in consciousness in order to have access to unconscious processes. In *An Outline of Psycho-Analysis*, "we infer a number of processes which are in themselves 'unknowable' and interpolate them in those that are conscious to us" (Freud 1949 [1940]: 83). The ego is seen as being split by Freud: there is an ego given by perception in consciousness, and an ego given by language. In consciousness the two egos are indistinguishable, as language is a product of perception, and works in conjunction with perception to actualize consciousness. In *The Ego and the Id*, the ego is defined by Freud as the organization of mental processes, and the unconscious is defined as that which is repressed in consciousness in its scotomata, its gaps and voids.

The dialectical relations which are present in the Casa Giuliani Frigerio are present in the design by Le Corbusier for the Villa Shodhan in Ahmadabad (1951–6, Figure 5.13), which appears to be a concrete version of a nine-square grid exercise. The oscillation of readings and pictorial ambiguity at the Villa Shodhan includes overlapping and discontinuous fragments, the interweaving of horizontal and vertical, solid and void, symmetry and asymmetry, axial and centrifugal, and

Figure 5.13 **Le Corbusier, Villa Shodhan, 1951–6**

the spacing of forms resulting from the shifting of grids in plan, which suggest a deep aspect, or conceptual reading of the architecture. The building displays the same dialectic as Terragni's buildings, between the conceptual organization and the material presence, to produce the same relationships in the signification of the building.

The formal composition of the Villa Shodhan is combined with elements that formed the theoretical basis of the architecture of Le Corbusier's late career: the *béton brute* (rough-formed concrete), *brise soleil* (angled wall to take advantage of the sun), and landscaped terrace (to connect the villa to its surroundings). These elements were developed by Le Corbusier after World War II to produce a more humanistic and less positivistic, less machine-oriented architecture, along with the Surrealist vocabulary. The Villa Shodhan also displays the indigenous patterns of forms and living spaces associated with its surrounding region, thus absorbing a local cultural identity into a structuralist matrix, the particular into the universal, in a contradiction between form and function.

The dialectical relations of Terragni are also present throughout the architecture of Peter Eisenman, in the staging of the contradiction between form and function, and the communicative potential of Modernist architecture. Eisenman sees himself as a Modernist, but his architecture introduces a new level of complexity, resulting from his analysis of the architecture of Terragni. Complexity is seen as a characteristic of Postmodernist architecture as opposed to Modernist architecture, as a result of the theme of a manifesto of Postmodernist architecture, Robert Venturi's *Complexity and Contradiction in Architecture*.

Chapter 6

Postmodernism: complexity and contradiction

Venturi

Robert Venturi's manifesto, written in 1962, calls for complexity and contradiction in architecture, because human beings are complex and contradictory, but the book provides no formal analysis of architecture. Ambiguity is cited as an important component of the complexity and contradiction of architecture, because architecture "is form *and* substance—abstract *and* concrete—and its meaning derives from its interior characteristics," its deep structure, "and its particular context" (Venturi 1966: 20). The dialectics of form and substance, abstract and concrete, texture and material, result in "oscillating relationships, complex and contradictory," which are the source of ambiguity and tension. The very fact that an architectural form can contain both a signifier and a signified, like a word in language, results in ambiguity, as ambiguity is a necessary element of language. The dialectics of form and concept and the resulting oscillating reading seem also to have been influenced by the phenomenal transparency of Colin Rowe.

The manifesto by Venturi is described as an apology for his own architecture, the best-known example of which is the Residence in Chestnut Hill, Pennsylvania, or the Vanna Venturi House (1962, Figure 6.1), which is an icon of Postmodernist architecture as historicist pastiche. The design for the façade consists of a pediment broken down the middle, below which is a lintel in the center intersected by the trace of an arch, and bands of small windows on either side. The obvious precedent for the house is the Casa del Girasole (1947, Figure 6.2) by Luigi Moretti, on Via Parioli in Rome, where Venturi researched his manifesto. The façade of the Casa del Girasole combines the Classical pediment, the tripartite division of the Renaissance palazzo, and the Five Points of Le Corbusier, including ribbon windows and a roof terrace, in a historicist composition in the tradition of Leon Battista Alberti, who combined the tripartite division of the Florentine palazzo with the Roman orders for the Palazzo Rucellai (Figure 3.1), and a temple front and triumphal arch for the façade of Sant'Andrea in Mantua (Figure 3.2).

Figure 6.1 **Robert Venturi, Vanna Venturi House, 1962**

Moretti's building is featured in Venturi's manifesto, in the section on ambiguity. The multiple historicist references create an oscillating reading, an ambiguity in the relation between the form of the architecture and the function of the building, and a split down the middle of the building (which results in an asymmetrical pediment) creates a visual ambiguity as to whether there are two buildings or just one. The split and asymmetrical façade contradict the historicist references of which they are composed. In a detail on the side of the house, a sculpted leg stands in for a window jamb, creating a pun on the word "jamb" (*jambe*) as an architectural vocabulary element, as if it were a part of the body, in the tradition of Renaissance humanism. On multiple levels, Moretti's building questions the relationship between form and function in architecture.

Robert Venturi's design for the Residence in Chestnut Hill is historicist architecture: a building is designed with a reference to a specific building in the past, but altered for the purpose of making a commentary on the contemporary cultural context. A precedent for Venturi's approach to the design of the building can be seen in paintings of Édouard Manet (1832–83) in Paris. *Le Déjeuner sur l'Herbe* (1863) is a reference to the *Pastoral Concert* (c.1510) of Tiziano Vecellio (c.1485–1576), drawing a parallel between the Venetian Renaissance and Parisian society in the nineteenth century, as they are both peaceful, prosperous, leisurely, decadent cultures. The new social class in Paris, the bourgeoisie, aspire to the leisurely learning of the Renaissance humanists. A theme in the painting by Titian, found throughout the Venetian Renaissance, is the juxtaposition of the sacred and profane, represented by the clothed humanist musicians contrasted with the naked wood nymphs. The theme is re-appropriated by Manet, as a naked courtesan in the foreground is contrasted with a woman in the background who is dressed in white and in a pond, suggesting the waters of baptism. Manet suggests that the

Figure 6.2 **Luigi Moretti, Casa del Girasole, 1947**

bourgeois culture in Paris has in common with Renaissance Venice the dichotomy of the sacred and profane.

Venturi's house suggests that complexity and ambiguity are charac-teristics shared by the United States in the early 1960s and Italy following World War II in the period of La Dolce Vita—growth, prosperity, leisure, and self-indulgence—but in an increasingly complex modern world of media bombardment and confusion, as represented in works by Robert Rauschenberg (1925–2008), such as *Buffalo II* (1964). Postmodernist architecture is a media architecture: the buildings are designed to be reproduced in photographs, and the success of the building depends on the success of the form of the building in the photograph, and not on the function of the building. In architecture for media, form contradicts function. In the house by Venturi, the forms which are appropriated from the Casa del Girasole are abstracted and minimalized, to turn them into vocabulary elements of a more universal language, in the dialectic between the particular and abstract which reveals the absolute in the limitations of thought and knowledge.

Eisenman

In the early house compositions of Peter Eisenman, architectural form is seen as a "marking or notational system," as Eisenman describes in the essay "Cardboard Architecture: House I and House II" in *Eisenman Inside Out: Selected Writings, 1963–1988*. Form and space in the architecture are "structured so that they would produce a set of formal relationships which is the result of the inherent logic in the forms themselves" (Eisenman 2004a: 29); the logic of the physical relation-ships is correlated with the logic of the conceptual relationships which are derived from them, as the deep structure is derived from the surface structure. In order to do that, the forms and relationships in the composition must be divested of their symbolic function in architecture, or their function in relation to the structural or functional requirements of the building. The form must contradict the function. If a vertical post is seen in combination with a horizontal slab, for example, the pairing cannot be other than a symbol of a structural system. Such vocabulary elements in the composition must be divested of their symbolic function if they are to function as pure signs in a given syntax, and thus contribute to the production of a set of conceptual relationships which would constitute a deep structure. The visual indication of the function must thus be contradicted by the form.

In the Barenholtz Pavilion in Princeton (House I, 1967–8), a column does not support anything. The Falk House, in Hardwick, Vermont (House II, 1969–70, Figure 6.3), has two structural systems, of columns and walls, creating a "nonfunc-tional redundancy" in which "each system's function was to signify its own lack of function," as Eisenman explains in *House of Cards* (Eisenman 1987: 174), in an architecture which is an "imitation of itself as the art of need" in the words of Schelling. Later, in the IBA Housing in Berlin (1981–7), the grid on the façade does not correspond to the structure of the building. In the Wexner Center for the Arts at Ohio State University (1983–9, Figure 6.4), a column does not reach the floor, and inserted fragments of historical building types make no sense in relation to the structural and functional requirements of the building. The fragments of historical building types contradict the geometrical organization of the building established by

Figure 6.3 **Peter Eisenman, Falk House (House II), 1969–70**

the abstract grid structure, as if to represent the contradictory relationship between rational thought and sense experience in perception. The conceptual organization contradicts the physical organization of the building; form purposefully contradicts function to demonstrate the presence of the idea of the architecture, what Alberti called the lineament, in relation to the material presence of the architecture, so that the architecture can be a form of art, communicating an idea disconnected from its material presence, in poetic expression.

Certain compositional procedures in the design of the early houses of Eisenman can be directly related to the use of metaphor and metonymy in language, and can be directly related to the structuring of the unconscious in psychoanalysis. In the description of the compositional process of House I in "Cardboard Architecture: House I and House II," the first step was to structure form and space in such a way that they could produce a set of formal relationships reflective of an inherent interior formal structure, as in language. In order to do this, the forms used had to be divested of their usual associations (the structural function of a column, for example), in order that they could function as pure marking devices in a formal system. In a metaphor, the primary signifier is divested of its associated signified in order to allow the shifting of the signifier in the metaphor to produce signification. In the composition of House I, the traditional forms associated with structure are used in a non-structural way. "It is actually not possible to determine how the structure functions from looking at the columns and beams" (Eisenman 2004a: 30).

There are many examples in the history of architecture of the use of architectural vocabulary elements as metaphors. In Alberti's Sant'Andrea, the fluted pilasters on the walls of the nave, organized in the *rhythmische travée* of paired columns in a bay alternating with the arches which front the vaults of the chapels,

Figure 6.4 **Peter Eisenman, Wexner Center, 1983–9**

are only a decorative device in correspondence with the orders of Classical architecture, as they have been stripped of their structural function. This particular use
of the Classical column, which was never intended to be a non-structural pilaster
or a decorative device, is metaphorical, in the elision of the structural function of
the column, or the primary signified. The use of the pilaster becomes a metaphor
of the relation between the Classical orders and the structure of theology in the
Renaissance: the church is held up by modern buttressing techniques which are
visually inaccessible, but it is adorned, in a deceptive way, with Classical ornament,
made to appear as the support structure, which was adopted by the Church for
historical justification. The architectural vocabulary elements are used as figures of
speech in rhetorical language, constituting a text of the culture.

The same composition is found in Carlo Maderno's nave of St. Peter's
Basilica in Rome, and in Francesco Borromini's worship space of San Carlo alle
Quattro Fontane (Figure 3.6), for the purpose of demonstrating that the material
world is a false veil or scaffold which hides the true reality of forms known only
to intelligence, in the Renaissance synthesis of Platonic cosmology and Catholic
theology, and the mysticism of the Counter Reformation. In the metaphor, the
function of the forms and patterns in the architectural composition is elided, and
as a result it is very difficult to read the forms in relation to the architecture itself,
in relation to the structural and functional requirements of the building. Alberti and
Borromini produced linguistically complex architectural forms which were reflective
of the complex epistemologies of their cultures, which involved contradiction
and ambiguity. They pushed the boundaries of architecture as a form of poetic
expression, by employing devices borrowed from language, including metaphor,
in the same way that Postmodernist architects have done in response to similarly
complex cultural epistemologies involving contradiction and ambiguity.

Such is the case with Eisenman. In House I, all of the "apparent
structural apparatus—the exposed beams, the freestanding columns—are in fact
non-structural. When this is understood, a first step has been taken to unload,
albeit in a very primitive way, their structural meaning," namely, the signified or
metaphysic of architecture in the symbolism of its vocabulary elements. As a result,
"while the apparent physical fact is the same whether they are load-bearing or not,
their meaning has changed because they are in fact not load-bearing, and thus the
intention implied in their use in a particular location must now be considered in a
different way" (Eisenman 2004a: 30). It is Eisenman's purpose, then, in the use of
metaphor, to disassociate the traditional architectural signifiers from their traditional
signifieds, so that the signifiers can signify something else, which is the structure of
signification itself. In order to do that, the architectural forms must signify nothing;
they must be prevented from signifying anything. This is accomplished by the
placing of the forms in a particular syntax. The architecture is modernist in that it
has no reference to anything outside of itself; it is also mannerist in that it is self-
referential. Modernist art and architecture are purely subjective; the work turns its
focus inward, to the philosophical and psychological basis of the expression of the
subject, in relation to subjective experience.

In order to disassociate the signifiers from the signifieds in Eisenman's composition, "the formal structure was in a sense over-stressed or over-articulated so that it would become a dominant aspect of the building." The formal structures were derived from the analysis of Terragni's buildings; they are thus in a sense historicist. "One means to over-stress such a structure was to suggest two simultaneous structures which overlay and interact," as in the overlay of centrifugal and centripetal in the Casa Giuliani Frigerio (Figure 5.12). "These were based on a simple combination of two pairs of formal references: planes and volumes on the one hand, frontal and oblique relationships on the other," as in the phenomenal transparency of Colin Rowe. As derived from the Casa Giuliani Frigerio, Eisenman employs the particular dialectics of frontality/recession and solid/void, and the pictorial ambiguity of two simultaneous systems, similar to the use of the gerund in language, in order to further the metaphorical use of the architectural forms and to further divest them of their signification.

The gerund in language is often the source of ambiguity in meaning, as in the phrase "the shooting of the hunters," an example given by Noam Chomsky. The transformation of an active verb into a neutral noun, like the transformation of an active architectural vocabulary element into a neutral architectural vocabulary element, stripped of its function, results in the loss of a clear relationship with the subject in the syntax. Such a reification of the formal system of architectural elements reaffirms their status as phonetic entities, or the equivalent in the language of forms, in a network of signifiers which have been cut off from a direct identification with corresponding signifieds, as in the *différance* of Jacques Derrida. The formal elements are left to enact a different process of signification, which corresponds to the Chomskian distinction between a surface structure and a deep structure as a distinction between a network of phonetic signifiers and a network of abstract signifiers functioning as signifieds, which connect at certain anchoring points through metaphor and metonymy, as in the *point de capiton* of Lacan, and are otherwise left to shift (Saussure) or slide (in the *glissement* of Lacan) in a self-referential form of signification, which is defined by Lacan as *signifiance*, and involves the play of differences and subsequent deferrals in the *différance* of Derrida.

In House I, Eisenman assigns the role of the trace of absence of Derrida in *différance*, or the *point de capiton* of Lacan, the point of connection between the signifier and the signified in the *glissement*, to a series of rectilinear columns and beams. "In the first instance, the space is conceived of as a layering or plaiding (cross layering) of planes. The rectilinear columns and beams are placed so that they will read as a residue of these planes," as a trace, then "the round columns are used to mark the intersections of two planes, which might possibly be read as joined at this intersection, thus forming volumes if the columns were square." As a result, "the round column prevents the possible interpretation of columns as residual 'corners' of volumes." The rectilinear columns and round columns function as metonyms, as their functional signification has been elided and replaced by a syntactical signification in a conceptual rather than functional organization. There is no longer a direct relation between their form, acting as signifier, and their structural function, which would be their expected signified meaning, and their presence becomes nonsensical in relation to the structural function of the building; the form contradicts the function. The original signified of the column, as structural device in the form of the column itself, is retained in combination with the new signified, as marking device in the location of the column, as in a metaphor, and the distinction between the signifying chain and the signified is retained, enacting the *glissement* or *signifiance* of Lacan.

Signifiance is a type of production in language, as opposed to signifi- cance, which retains the distinction or separation between the signifier and signified, avoiding significance or meaning in language, as in the arbitrary play of signifiers in the *différance* of Derrida. *Signifiance* is the subjective, self-referential communicative potential of language without the signified or the production of what is taken to be meaning. Like the *différance* of Derrida, it proposes to eliminate the metaphysical in language, but that is impossible, as both systems depend on the presence of an absence, the trace or the *point de capiton*, the absence which reveals the unconscious, the gap in consciousness, or that which cannot be known. The metaphysical or the production of meaning also cannot be eliminated from language because words are necessarily symbolic in their cultural context, as is particularly the case of metaphor and metonymy.

A different kind of signification is produced in the play of signifiers, in a process of shifting or sliding, in which each signifier resists a direct identification with a signified, or a corresponding network of signifiers. The metonymy of the form of the column as marking device, divested of its primary signification, is a transfor- mational device enacting a transformational relation between the surface structure (the architectural forms as pure signifiers in a syntax) and the deep structure (the conceptual organization of the forms and the underlying matrix of rules which govern communication in language). The use of the "floating" column as a trans- formational device in the composition of House I is a historicist reference to the transformational relations perceived by Eisenman in the Casa Giuliani Frigerio, that is, the formal elements of the architecture which connect the physical structure with a conceptual structure. Eisenman's use of the column as first a metaphor (a direct comparison, in this case between the form of the column and a marking device, without losing the structural symbolism of the column) and then a metonym (an indirect comparison in which the meaning of one element is elided, in this case the structural symbolism of the column, when it is placed in a non-structural position) is thus the trope of the transformational relation. In language, a metaphor is a simple comparison to give a word a new meaning, as in "the world is a stage." A metonym is a comparison in which the meaning of one word is lost, as in "the leg of a table," and the word assumes a new meaning in relation to the other word. In the use of the metaphor and metonym in architecture as transformational devices, the architecture becomes a catechism of condensation and displacement in the language of the unconscious and the formation of dreams, as condensation and displacement are the mechanisms of metaphor and metonymy.

The metonymic function of the column allows two simultaneous compositional systems to be disassociated from one another, as in the metonym "the leg of a table," the retention of both signifieds disassociates the words from each other and renders the phrase senseless as a combination of signifiers. The column functions as the preposition between subject and object and as the location of the anchoring point, or *point de capiton*, which is a location of the presence of an absence, in the disjunction between signifiers, and which ties the phrase to a network of conceptual signifiers or deep structure in a particular way. The simultaneity of two compositional systems overlapping in the architecture is itself a metaphor, and a transformational device, as in the Cubist painting, for the physical/ conceptual or signifier/signified dialectic. The metaphysic of the dialectic, as in language, is retained in the trace, or the "residue" of the planes which is marked by the columns, in the pictorial ambiguity. Eisenman explained that "the intention was to use the columns and beams to mark two systems without giving preference to either," the structural and organizational or conceptual.

The interaction of a layering of planes with a diagonal shifting of volumes makes it difficult to read the organizational system in relation to the structural system, or to the syntax of forms, enacting a dialectic between the physical and the metaphysical, in the same way that the forms of dreams are difficult to read in relation to the dream thoughts, as a result of the mechanisms of condensation and displacement, or metaphor and metonymy. The disengagement of the structural and organizational systems from each other, in the metonymic process, takes place in the mind, as in the lineament of Alberti or the phenomenal transparency of Rowe. The activity takes place in the mind because it is a perceptual activity translated to a linguistic activity, as perceptions are a product of a priori intuition, or the formation of the *species apprehensibilis*, in the same relation as between the dream image and the manifest content of unconscious thought.

The simultaneity of two or more formal compositional systems linked by marking devices, which act as transformational devices, can be found in Alberti's façade for Sant'Andrea in Mantua (Figure 3.2), and Borromini's plan for San Carlo alle Quattro Fontane (Figure 3.6). The façade of Sant'Andrea is composed of the layering of two separate architectural types, the temple front—with pediment, entablature, and colossal pilasters—and the triumphal arch, with a large central arch, a small entablature running along the base of the central arch, and minor arches on either side above and below the entablature, separated from the central arch by small fluted pilasters. The layering of the two types is metonymic: the temple form signifies paganism, and the triumphal arch signifies imperialism, as each form is symbolic. The combination of the two forms produces a metonymic concept equivalent to "the imperialism of religion," signifying the ambitions of the Catholic Church in the Renaissance in secular as well as religious affairs. The residue or trace of the layering of the architectural types, the anchoring point which enacts the signification and the transformational relation from the form to the concept, is the doubling of the columns and entablature in each type at different scales. The relation between column and entablature shared by each type, the temple front and triumphal arch, simultaneously marks each system and is the point at which the transformation from form to concept occurs, as in House I the relation between column and beam is shared between the structural and organizational systems, functioning as a trace and transformational device.

In the plan of San Carlo alle Quattro Fontane, sixteen columns are used to mark the footprint of the elevations around the worship space, in a historicist reference to Bramante's Tempietto. The columns are residues, traces, or markers of the intersection or simultaneity of several formal systems that are combined in the plan. Four pairs of the columns are located on the four sides of a rectangle which circumscribes an oval, in Borromini's drawings. If the columns from each of those pairs are paired with the adjacent columns on the adjacent sides, then the resulting four pairs of columns define lines that are drawn tangent to the oval at the point where the lines are drawn perpendicular to lines that are projected through the center point of circles bisecting the oval, from the corner point of a diamond circumscribed around the oval. The lines created by the second pairing of columns chamfer the rectangle at the corners, creating an octagon. The remaining four pairs of columns are located by drawing arcs between the first four pairs and around the corners of the diamond, and intersecting the arcs with lines drawn through the centers of the sides of the rectangle, from the intersection of the oval and the first lines projected from the corners of the diamonds.

The columns in the plan are traces of the intersection of the construction of a series of geometries: the oval created by two circles, the octagon created by the circumscribed rectangle, and the cross created by the center points of the sides of the rectangle. The three geometries symbolize the Trinity, and the superimposition of systems creates a series of polygonal figures set in relation to circles and an oval. The relation between the polygonal figure and the circle is an allegory of the relation between human intelligence and divine intelligence. The geometries have symbolic functions as well as signifying functions, as in the façade of Sant'Andrea, to represent cultural ideas. The columns are the marks or traces which enact the transformational relations between formal and conceptual systems, and which provide the anchoring point in the metonymic process. They are the hinge of the dialectic between the physical and the conceptual. The dialectic in the Renaissance between human intelligence and divine intelligence can be applied to the dialectic of conscious and unconscious thought in psychoanalysis, and of signifier and signified in linguistics, as all depend on the functions of language.

All systems of signification, in language or formal compositions, have a deep structure, and the deep structure conditions the way in which words or visual forms are understood or perceived, as in a priori intuition. It is the responsibility of the architect to address this issue in architecture and to understand the ways in which the language of architecture engages philosophical, linguistic, and psychoanalytic structures. All conscious perception and experience are structured by unconscious thought processes which create a matrix, grammar, or set of rules which determine the possibilities of conscious perception and experience. Architecture should challenge those possibilities in the design, perception, and experience of architecture, so that architecture is an expression of human identity. According to Eisenman, "[t]he capacity to understand" the relation between the formal and the conceptual in architecture "does not depend entirely on the observer's particular cultural background, his subjective perceptions, or his particular mood at any given time, all of which condition his usual experience of an actual environment, but rather it depends on his innate capacity to understand formal structures" (p. 33), the a priori intuition or the underlying matrix of conscious experience. Architecture is thus seen by Eisenman as a kind of universal language, in the utopian tradition of De Stijl.

In *Positions*, Derrida describes *différance* as "a structure and a movement that cannot be conceived on the opposition presence/absence" (Derrida 1981 [1972]: 27), or signifier/signified. *Différance* is the "systematic play of differences, of traces of differences, of the spacing by which elements relate to one another." The spacing is the "production, simultaneously active and passive … of intervals without which the 'full' terms could not signify, could not function." *Différance* is the mechanism of the production of differences in signification in the absence of a direct relationship between signifier and signified, in the linguistic structure introduced by Saussure. The play of differences "involves syntheses and referrals that prevent there from being at any moment or in any way a simple element that is present in and of itself and refers only to itself. Whether in written or in spoken discourse, no element can function as a sign without relating to another element which itself is not simply present" (p. 26). No element of language, in the relation between signifiers and signifieds, is simply presence or absence, but is rather difference and trace. In the architecture of Eisenman, the presences and absences are represented by the traces of the structural and metaphorical functions of the architectural vocabulary elements, in particular the columns and beams.

For Lacan, a signifier is defined by the rules of the interactions of the system of networks between form and thought. The value of the signifier is deter-mined at a certain point in the flux of the interaction of networks, the flux of the play of differences, which is the "anchoring point." The anchoring point (*point de capiton*) is the point at which "the signifier stops the otherwise determinate sliding of signification" (Lacan 1977 [1966]: 303). The anchoring point, as a transforma-tional device, is necessary for a relationship between the signifier in visual form and the signifier in the conceptual organization, and it reveals the presence of the unconscious, and the metaphysical gap in language. The communication of the idea occurs retroactively: the concept must be anticipated in order for it to be commu-nicated. Thus, "the diachronic function of this anchoring point is to be found in the sentence, even if the sentence completes its signification only with its last term, each term being anticipated in the construction of the others, and, inversely, sealing their meaning by its retroactive effect," defining the trace and the metaphysical gap. The anchoring point is the point at which the constructed signification intersects a corresponding signification in the network of signifiers in thought, or the conceptual organization. Signification is a diachronic event, but is produced at a synchronic point, resulting in the metaphysical gap. Signification is only produced retroactively, when the synchronic structure of the identification between form and concept intersects with the diachronic structure of speech and thought.

According to Lacan, the anchoring point in the sentence must stop the *glissement* or sliding of signifiers in order for the sentence to signify something. A metaphor produces signification by substituting the name of one thing for something else, but it is only in the combination of the two names that an idea is formed. If the world is a stage, the idea of the stage must be subsumed under the sign of the world; a shift or *glissement* takes place in which the signified is trans-ferred from one signifier to another, in what is called *signifying substitution*. It is the process of combination and condensation which produces the signification, which occurs at the anchoring point of the phrase, the point at which the condensation intersects with the equivalent network of signifiers in thought, as it is anticipated, and the idea is retroactively produced in the gap between the two networks, the metaphysical gap, which is also the point of combination. The anchoring point in the metaphor is the point at which "sense emerges from non-sense" (p. 158), the rational emerges from the irrational in conscious thought. In the *glissement*, the idea of the "world" has been effaced or hidden, and replaced by the idea of the stage. The effaced signified remains as a trace, and occupies the metaphysical gap between speech and idea, or between visual form in perception and conceptual organization in thought.

The metonym, in contrast, is a displacement, a change of name (*metonoma*), the substitution of a descriptive term with another which has no relation to the subject term, as in the leg of the table. In metonymy, as opposed to metaphor, the initial signified, the "body" of the table in this case, is not eliminated or effaced; it is retained as necessary to produce the signification in relation to the substituted signifier. The division between the signifier and signified is maintained, because the substituted signified has not been elided. In the metonym there is a certain resistance to signification. A metonym is literally irrational, because it involves a displacement or substitution as well as a condensation or combination. In the displacement, the substituted signified must be maintained, and the *point de capiton* is delayed in the process of signification, and requires an additional association between signifieds in order to take place. Metaphor and metonymy, condensation and displacement, are the compositional mechanisms used by Eisenman in a self-referential syntactical architecture, in the tradition of the purified language of De Stijl, in order to represent human identity, to understand the mecha-nisms of thought, language, and perception in the twentieth century. In order to represent these mechanisms, the form of the architecture contradicts the function, in program and structure.

Figure 6.5 **Renzo Piano and Richard Rogers, Pompidou Center, 1972–7**

Late Capitalism

The Pompidou Center in Paris (1972–7, Figure 6.5), also known as the Beaubourg, designed by Renzo Piano and Richard Rogers, is an icon of Postmodernist archi- tecture, because it celebrates technology, displays the excess of Late Capitalism, includes a historicist reference, and questions the relation between form and function in architecture. All of the functions that are usually found on the interior of the building, covered over by a dressing or costume, are moved to the exterior, including structure, transportation, and the heating and ventilating equipment. The traditional "form" of the building, the ornament or composition of the façade, or the visual clues to the organization of the building, are replaced by the traditional "function" of the building itself. The functional elements become the form, and are painted and transformed for aesthetic display. The painted functional elements conceal the reason for their presence on the exterior, which is to allow for universal, open space on the interior, to maximize exhibition space.

Postmodernism is associated with Late Capitalism, the phenomenon in capitalist economic development in post-World War II first world countries, where production exceeds consumption, resulting in a culture of excess. Postmodernist buildings display excess—not an excess of ornament, but an excess of materials in relation to the function of the building. The technology displayed on the exterior of the Pompidou Center is in excess of the requirements of the building. Other icons of Postmodernist architecture, such as the Guggenheim Museum in Bilbao (1998), the Walt Disney Concert Hall in Los Angeles (1999–2003), and the Pritzker Pavilion in Chicago (2004, Figure 6.6) by Frank Gehry, or the Denver Art Museum (2006) by Daniel Libeskind, display an excess of materials in relation to the structural and functional requirements of the building. This often results in unused space between the sculptural cladding and the structure of the building, and in the case of the art museums, a disjunction between the forms of the architecture and the function of the building to display the art. The building itself is intended as a work of art, thus the form contradicts the function. At the Walt Disney Concert Hall and Pritzker Pavilion, the forms express the rhythms and crescendos of the music which is performed within, in excess of the programs or structures of the buildings. The forms express a metaphysical idea, a poetic spirit, not connected to the material presence of the architecture.

Renzo Piano worked for the Italian neorationalist architect Franco Albini (1905–77), whose design for La Rinascente department store in Rome (1957–61) displays the internal functions of the building on the exterior. A steel frame structure is placed on the exterior of masonry construction, using the same brickwork as in the nearby Aurelian wall. The building also has a tripartite vertical division in reference to the Renaissance palazzo. Heating and cooling ducts are indicated by protrusions in the masonry. The design for the Pompidou Center is a reference to La Rinascente, which in turn incorporates Classical and Renaissance references, like the Casa del Girasole of Moretti, in the spirit of historicism and Postmodernism.

The Piazza d'Italia in New Orleans (1978), designed by Charles Moore, is also an icon of Postmodernism, as it displays historicist references and an excess of materials. Architectural forms such as colonnades, temple fronts, and campaniles were executed in synthetic and artificial materials, stainless steel and incandescent

Figure 6.6 **Frank Gehry, Pritzker Pavilion, 2004**

and neon lighting, and brightly painted, to displace the historicist references into the Postmodernist culture of excess and artificiality. The references to Italian forms were designed to appeal to the Italian-American community in New Orleans, but it was found to be more offensive than anything else; coupled with the fact that the rest of the surrounding development was never completed, the complex fell into disuse, and became a "postmodern ruin." As a ruin, the complex displayed the void at the center of a culture of excess and artificiality, and of materialism and consumerism, as displayed by the sculptural ensembles of Duane Hanson (1925–96) such as *The Tourists* (1970) or *The Shoppers* (1976), where obese Americans in polyester clothing are weighed down by material possessions which bring them no satisfaction. In the excess of Late Capitalism, desire is manufactured by advertising, which convinces consumers that there is a need for something completely unnecessary, and the individual becomes disconnected from actual needs and desires. The identity of the subject falls victim to excess and advertising, and to its own artificially stimulated needs and desires, prompting messages in conceptual art such as Jenny Holzer's famous phrase, "Protect Me From What I Want."

There is a culture-wide contradiction between form and function in Postmodernist culture, between the appearance and cultural identity of the individual and the function that the individual plays in the culture. While the Piazza d'Italia complex fell into disuse because it failed in its function, it became an often-reproduced image in magazines, which led to its restoration in 2004, except for the campanile which was removed. The Piazza d'Italia is media architecture: it is successful if it is reproduced in magazines, not if it functions well as architecture. The Postmodern ruin was rescued by the very means of media and consumerism in Postmodernism; although it was restored, it remains a ruin as architecture, in relation to the function of architecture. The form of the architecture contradicts the function as the form of advertisement and consumption contradicts the function of a society.

The Gehry House in Santa Monica (1978), by Frank Gehry (Frank Owen Goldberg), is an icon of both Postmodernism and deconstructivism in architecture. It displays materials in excess of the structural or functional requirements of the building, in this case materials found in a junkyard, the type of materials normally found on the interior of the building, arranged aesthetically on the exterior, as at the Pompidou Center. It displays the dramatic angles of Russian constructivist architecture and agitprops, the formal basis adapted for deconstructivist architecture (while the forms are stripped of the political and social associations), and the house displays a tenet of deconstruction, the philosophical basis adapted for deconstructivist architecture. The architecture of Zaha Hadid—for example, the Vitra Fire Station in Weil am Rhein, Germany (1993)—similarly strips the constructivist aesthetic of any political connotations, and presents a form in excess of any function. The goal of deconstruction as a form of literary criticism was to analyze a literary text in order to find the flaw in the argument of the text, to find the point at which the text fails, in the same way that deconstruction used structural linguistics to find the point at which the production of meaning in language fails, in the disjunction between the signifier and the signified.

As the materials of the interior of the California bungalow in Santa Monica appear to explode out to the exterior, in the aesthetic prop designed by the architect, the failure of the architecture is revealed. The materials fail in their structural function, and the design of the house fails in relation to the traditional organization of a house, which includes a dressing or costume over the functional materials. As at the Pompidou Center, the interior functional materials become the costume, but here their structural or functional associations are stripped from them, and they become pure excess and artificiality, and dysfunctional as architecture. Like the form of the Rooftop Remodeling Project in Vienna (1988) by Coop Himmelblau (Wolf Prix and Helmut Swiczinsky), it appears as if an infection has violently exploded out of the body of the building, and the traditional concept of the building as a body, and the traditional relation between the form and function of the building, have been exposed as false metaphors, as representing an artificially constructed and false meaning, as in the *différance* of Jacques Derrida. At the Gehry House, the form contradicts the function in both Postmodernist and deconstructivist motifs.

Tschumi

At the Parc de la Villette (1982–98, Figure 6.7) in the nineteenth arrondissement in Paris, Bernard Tschumi demonstrated that there is an inherent disjunction in architecture between form and function, in this case showing that there is no relation between the visual forms of Russian constructivist architecture, reconstructed here out of context, and the political ideologies of the Bolshevik Revolution which they were designed to represent. Such a disjunction was inspired by the deconstruction of Jacques Derrida, Tschumi's collaborator on the project, and *différance*, language defined as nothing more than a system of differences which perpetually defers any possibility of meaning.

In Tschumi's design for the Parc de la Villette, thirty-five "follies," small buildings designed to house various functions, are placed at the nodal points of an orthogonal grid to represent those points at which the rational structure of human thought, as represented by the orthogonal grid, is escaped in "madness" or excess, or in the unknowable aspects of intellect, the Classical *nous*, *pronoia*, or the unconscious in psychoanalysis. The follies are composed of diagonals and abstract geometries, painted red, to reference the constructivist architecture in Russia during the Bolshevik Revolution. The constructivists used the diagonal line as a method to agitate political consciousness; abstracted geometrical forms represented the tabula rasa which was the goal of the utopian movement, a revolutionary clean slate for a new social beginning; and the color red symbolized Communism, the political mechanism of a utopian society. Tschumi employed those devices in the follies in Parc de la Villette to illustrate that the forms themselves are not inherently connected to any of those ideas, that there is only an arbitrary relation between

Figure 6.7 **Bernard Tschumi, Parc de la Villette, 1982–98**

function and form, or the functional and metaphysical roles that architecture plays, which is established by language, and revealed by the disjunction between signifier and signified, in language and architecture.

The arbitrary relation between the form and function in Tschumi's architecture is based on the core idea in the deconstruction of Jacques Derrida, developed from structural linguistics, that there is no relation between a signifier and a signified in a word in language, that is, between the sound of a word and the idea or meaning attached to it. For Derrida, the lack of a relation between signifier and signified prevents the possibility of the production of meaning in language, and the possibility of a metaphysic in language. The follies or *folies* of Tschumi are placed as "nodal points" on a grid system and act as punctum points on the grid, introducing gaps or lacunae in the signifying structure of the grid. Derrida described the "punctum" as the point in a space that punctures the space and becomes heterogeneous to it, deferring the space and becoming unlocatable in it, thus haunting the space, as a *chôra*.

The *folies* are small structures whose architectural form has no relation to their function, creating a disjunction between symbol and reality, between sign and being, thought and language. Tschumi described the *folies* as "transference grafts" which allow access to space, like a *chôra*, beginning with the ambivalence of the form, the in-between. The architecture creates a place which is in "constant production, in continuous change; its meaning is never fixed but is always deferred, differed, rendered irresolute by the multiplicity of meanings it inscribes," as described by Tschumi in *Architecture and Disjunction* (Tschumi 1994: 201). A dialectic is created between the grid and the *folies* similar to the dialectic between the regular grid and the oblique and curved lines in the paintings of Paul Cézanne and the Cubists.

The project at La Villette "aims to unsettle both memory and context, opposing many contextualist and continualist ideals that imply that the architect's intervention necessarily refers to a typology, origin, or determining signified." This is accomplished through the hybridization of forms, the continual transformation between forms, as Plato described the elements of matter: "There is in fact a process of cyclical transformation. Since therefore none of them ever appears constantly under the same form, it would be embarrassing to maintain that any of them is certainly one rather than another" (Plato 1965: 49–50). Thus "in general we should never speak as if any of the things we suppose we can indicate by pointing and using the expressions 'this thing' or 'that thing' have any permanent reality: for they have no stability and elude the designation 'this' or 'that' or any other that expresses permanence." The *folies* at La Villette avoid such determinations given by fixed typologies in architecture.

The grid of the *folies* takes the form of the *chôra*, the permanent Same in constant fluctuation, but itself never determined by the changing forms. The meaning as given by the forms of the *folies* is never direct but always deferred and differed, as in *différance*. Meaning is dislocated and deregulated, and the signifying function of architecture, its ability to function as a language, is rejected. Relations between signifieds and signifiers are arbitrary, as in the structural linguistics of Ferdinand de Saussure; concept and language are disjoined, as in the deconstruction of Derrida, opening the space of the *chôra*, the deferred presence, in *différance*. The *folies* unsettle memory and context in their "programmatic instability," forcing the subject outside the familiar shelter of language, outside the familiar shelter of architectural typologies which are symbols of shelter and symbols of origin, or *archê*, as in *archê*-tecture. La Villette is a Postmodern place of transformations, deregulations and in-between spaces, rather than a Modernist place of autonomous and independent, fixed identities.

According to Tschumi in *Architecture and Disjunction*, the "internal contradictions of architecture had been there all along," in particular the contradiction between the concept of space and the experience of space. Architecture has never been able to establish a direct relationship between the construction of spaces and the programs that are established in the spaces. Tschumi quotes Étienne-Louis Boullée, in *Essai sur l'art*, to illustrate the inherent disjunction in architecture between the signified and signifier, lineament and matter: "This production of the mind, this creation is what constitutes architecture, that which we now can define as the art to produce any building and bring it to perfection" (Tschumi 1994: 34). Architecture is defined as the ideas in the mind of the architect, so "the art of building is thus only a secondary art that it seems appropriate to call the scientific part of architecture." The construction of the architecture is a science appropriated by architecture in order to realize its structure and space. The experience of the space, based on the architectural construction, is in conflict with the concept of the space as developed in the idea of the architecture, so architecture has both a surface structure and a deep structure, as described by Eisenman.

In *Toward a New Architecture* (*Vers une Architecture*), Le Corbusier similarly defined architecture as distinct from the construction of a building. "Architecture is a thing of art, a phenomenon of the emotions, lying outside questions of construction and beyond them" (Le Corbusier 1960 [1923]: 23). While construction only serves the purpose of holding things together, the purpose of architecture is to "move us"; the architect "affects our senses to an acute degree and provokes plastic emotions." We are moved by the order in the architecture which we perceive to be in accordance with the order within us and the order of the cosmos, as in Renaissance humanism. "Architectural emotion exists when the work rings within us in tune with a universe whose laws we obey, recognize and respect." This is true of any kind of architecture, from Classical to Modernist, deconstructivist to bioconstructivist.

The architectural object itself is pure language according to Tschumi, and architectural composition is an "endless manipulation of the grammar and syntax of the architectural sign" (Tschumi 1994: 36). Forms only refer to other forms, and not to functions. Forms contradict functions. In Kantian terms, space is an a priori form imposed by the mind to the perception of the external world. In Berkleian terms, the perception of space involves a gradual construction, as in the phenomenal transparency of Colin Rowe. As an a priori category of consciousness independent of matter, space is seen as an instrument of knowledge, according to Tschumi, rather than an experiential component of the perceived world. Space is a representation of an idea, in Kantian terms, a thought or a signified, rather than a signifier in constructed form. A single space can thus only be understood in relation to other spaces, and all spaces can only be understood as subdivisions of "space" in general, which is a necessary a priori concept which grounds perceptual experience. Space is thus a vocabulary element in language, and functions syntactically to organize experience. As for Kant, space is not an inherent quality of the perceived world, and it is impossible to reconcile the function of space with the concept of space in architecture. There is an inherent contradiction between architecture as an empirical event, a sensual experience, and architecture as a "dematerialized or conceptual discipline with its typological and morphological variations" (p. 83).

Architecture is thus a "thing of the mind" rather than a "pictorial or experiential art" (p. 84), in which its vocabulary elements, "facades, arcades, squares" (p. 90), even architectural concepts, "place a veil between what is assumed to be reality and its participants," as does language itself. Language and architectural language have come to be seen as primarily fragmented, beginning with the redefinition of language in relation to dreams and the subconscious in psychoanalysis. Architectural forms can only be seen as series of fragments in an architectural composition, which "make up an architectural reality" (p. 95), as in the *folies* at the Parc de la Villette. In architecture there are two sets of fragments, the real fragments of the architectural construction and the virtual fragments of the architectural concept, as in phenomenal transparency, elaborating the disjunction between function and form. The relations between the fragments, both real and virtual, constitute traces, or signs of transference, in the play of signifiers. Experience is constituted in the "in-between," in the *différance* or *glissement* of the signifiers in the architectural language, within language itself.

Architecture sets into motion the operations of the subconscious in the formation of language in relation to perceptual experience. The operation of architecture is thus the operation of desire, desire created by the unconsummated relationship between conscious reason and the unconscious, and by the relations between the fragments of language, which preclude the possibility of fulfillment or wholeness, and create a perpetual cycle of incompletion in the relation between language and reality, or architecture and reality. The *folies* at the Parc de la Villette preclude any possibility of a relation between architecture and program or architecture and meaning; they constitute a "system of relations between objects, events, and people" (p. 178), and allow for "the development of a change, a point of intensity," but they can only be seen as "pure trace or play of language" (p. 203), as can architecture in general.

Peter Eisenman described a strategy of dislocation and deferral in architecture in "Architecture as a Second Language: The Texts of Between." If several grids or typologies are superimposed, differing in scale, axial progression, and origin, then the origin associated with architecture is dislocated. The typologies are not necessarily architectural; an "immanent text" might be introduced which is "authorized by the program and by the site" but not by the architecture, and thus becomes a "strategy for dislocation." The scale and axial progression of the grids is continuously dislocated, creating "the architectural analogue to the rhetorical figure *catachresis*" (Eisenman 1989: 72), a paradoxical figure of speech or incorrect word, the punctum in language which exposes the disjunction between thought and language and opens a negative space of deferral as in *différance*. The multiple grids produce a typology of transformations and ambivalences rather than fixed identities, as at La Villette. In a "system which contains its own contradictions," meaning is freed from symbolic representation, from the signifying structure of language in architectural forms.

Peter Eisenman and Jacques Derrida, having been introduced by Bernard Tschumi, collaborated on a project for a garden at La Villette which was named *Choral Works*, based on the *chôra* of Plato's *Timaeus*. In the *Timaeus*, the *chôra* is a place which is not a place; it is becoming, rather than being, thus challenging the metaphysical concept of place. The challenge was to represent non-place by place in architecture, thus challenging the metaphysical confirmation of place which is at the core of the function of architecture. Eisenman and Derrida produced a model of the project, using the form of the winnowing basket described by Plato in the *Timaeus* as the process of becoming. Derrida expressed that *chôra* is "something that cannot be represented, except negatively. ... It is a space that cannot be represented, so it is a challenge to anything solid, to architecture as something built" (Kipnis and Leeser 1997: 12). The negative space of the *chôra* is represented in the project in the form of the winnowing basket or sieve as described by Plato in *Timaeus* 52, the instrument by which chaos is transformed to matter, in a state of agitation. The *chôra* is inserted into a superimposition of multiple grids or typologies as the punctum in the field of signification, the lacuna in the continuity of being and the shelter of language.

The space created by Eisenman and Derrida is the space of *différance*, the space defined as a "becoming-space which makes possible both writing and every correspondence between speech and writing, every passage from one to the other." The *chôra* is defined as a becoming space in the *Timaeus* as well, being "the nurse of all becoming and change," and "a space which is eternal and destructible, which provides a position for everything that comes to be." *Chôra* is the place (which is not a place) where the Idea is transformed into the material, or the intelligible into the sensible; *différance* is the place (which is not a place) where the intelligible is transformed into the sensible as speech is transformed into writing. *Différance* as defined by Derrida is the "origin or production of differences," which is not a static structure or inscribed in a closed system, and which presents the possibility of structure in its systematic and regulated transformations beyond the usual concept of structure. The irregular form of the sieve is placed in the regular grid by Eisenman and Derrida to enact the role of *différence* in the relation between the sensible and intelligible, as a transformational device, similar to the way in which the oblique and curved lines were inserted into the regular grid of late Cézanne and Cubist paintings, as observed by Colin Rowe and Robert Slutzky in the essay "Transparency: Literal and Phenomenal." *Différance* is the system of transferals which a person constantly experiences between concept and word, or intelligible and sensible, which is constantly enacted in architecture.

For Derrida, the sign, which generates semiotics in language, is a "deferred presence," as in *différance*. The space of *différance*, like the space of Plato's *chôra*, is the space of the in-between, a trace of relationships, and it is this intelligible space which makes form possible and facilitates its coming into being, as in the agitation of the winnowing machine in the *Timaeus*. Sensible form is only a copy or a reflection of intelligible form, as constructed form in architecture is only a copy of an idea, as it cannot exist outside the intelligible space of *différence*. The distribution and play of differences is defined by Derrida as "spacing," which is the transformation between intelligible and sensible forms, as represented by the sieve. Spacing necessarily involves the disruption of a structure, creating an internal displacement and a discontinuity, a contradiction between form and function, an "irreducible alterity," as Derrida and Eisenman hoped to create in their project for La Villette. Spacing "is the index of an irreducible exterior, and at the same time of a *movement*, a displacement that indicates an irreducible alterity." Every autonomous element in language and metaphysics, every sign or symbol, contains within it the possibility of spacing. Every place contains folded within it the possibility of its own disruption or alteration, as every particular is an unstable and variable manifestation of the universal in Platonic thought. The space of *différence* is "the non-place or non-lieu which would be the 'other' of philosophy. This is the task of deconstruction," according to Derrida.

At the Parc de la Villette, and in the function of language, the signifier is removed from the sign, and is divested of its traditional linguistic function. The resulting algorithm is seen as a "hole" in signification, and is composed of purely differential logic, based on the "logic of the signifier." The signifier is seen as being constituted by a principle of opposition in a synchronic collection of elements. From Plato, mathematics is based on the perception of opposites in sensible reality, in particular day and night. According to Jacques Lacan, "If linguistics enables us to see the signifier as the determinant of the signified, analysis reveals the truth of this relation by making the 'holes' in meaning the determinates of its discourse" (Lacan 1977 [1966]: 299). It is the gaps in discourse—the lacunae, the scotomata, the *méconnaissance* (inability to know or understand, misconstruction or failure to recognize)—which determine the relation of discourse to the subject, as traces of the bar between the signifier and the signified, between language and the subject, and which determine the relation between conscious and unconscious thought.

The organization of the play of the signifier in *signifiance* is based on the presence of the holes in signification. This is also represented in architecture by the *folies* designed by Bernard Tschumi. The *folies* are placed as nodal points on an orthographic grid and act as punctum points on the grid, representing gaps or lacunae in the signifying structure of the grid. The holes or *folies* are seen as the *chôra*, which again is described by Derrida as "something that cannot be represented, except negatively. ... It is a space that cannot be represented, so it is a challenge to anything solid, to architecture as something built" (Kipnis and Leeser 1997: 12). The *chôra* is described in the *Timaeus* as "space which is eternal and indestructible, which provides a position for everything that comes to be, and which is apprehended without the senses by a sort of spurious reasoning and so is hard to believe in," thus "we look at it indeed in a kind of dream and say that everything that exists must be somewhere and occupy some space, and that what is nowhere in heaven or earth is nothing at all" (Plato 1965: 52). The *chôra* is as the One of Plotinus, beyond being, inaccessible to being, but participating in all being and becoming.

The *chôra* is a space which is other than space, which allows for the becoming of space, as *signifiance* of Lacan is, in the science of the letter, signification which is other than signification, and which allows for the becoming of signification. The *chôra* is only given in a dream, that is, in unconscious thought, as it is interpreted in the mechanisms of language. According to Plato, "because of this dream state we are not awake to the distinctions we have drawn and others akin to them, and fail to state the truth about the true and unsleeping reality," that, "whereas an image, the terms of whose existence are outside its control in that it is always a moving shadow of something else, needs to come into existence in something else if it is to claim some degree of reality, or else be nothing at all," in the space between language and perceptual experience. The *chôra* is the becoming place of the image as signification, in language or architecture: the transference between perception and language. It is the place of the transformation of the manifest content of a dream (the dream thought) into a dream image; and it is the space beneath the signification of both the image and the signifier in language, the space which is the absence of the subject in the intellect, the absence of the signified, the void around which desire in language circulates, which is continually enacted in architecture.

The anchoring point of Lacan, the *point de capiton*, in the *glissement* of *signifiance*, is a *chôra*, a place which is not a place. Like the *chôra* of Plato, the anchoring point of Lacan is presented as a myth, a necessary construction of reason, as knowledge of the unconscious is a myth. As Jean-Luc Nancy and Philippe Lacoue-Labarthe describe it, in *The Title of the Letter*, "there is no signi-fication which is not always already sliding outside of its alleged proper meaning" (Nancy and Lacoue-Labarthe 1992 [1973]: 54). In Lacan's words, quoted in *The Title of the Letter* from a 1958 seminar, "between the two chains ... that of the signifiers in relation to the circulation of traveling signifieds which are always in the process of sliding," the "anchoring point I am speaking about ... is mythical, for no one has ever been able to pin a signification onto a signifier." The anchoring point, like the bar between the signifier and signified, is an *archê*, an *apeiron*, a source of origin which does not exist.

The *apeiron* (of Anaximander, for example) is a *chôra* which exceeds the physical and temporal permutations of matter, as the anchoring point in the tropic sequence is that point which exceeds the mechanisms of language and introduces the crossing of the bar between the signifier and the signified as a mythological event. The anchoring point, as the *chôra*, provides a receptacle for the process of change (the tropic *glissement*) in language. The anchoring point is the zero point (the hole) in the flux of signification (*signifiance*) in language, the point at which the network of signifiers both passes along the bar and crosses over it, the point at which the signifiers in language leave an impress which produces signification, as a transformational relation.

The concept of the signified is not excluded from Lacanian linguistics, but it is displaced within the process of signification, as is the metaphysic. The signifier is initially that which resists the possibility of signification, or posits a bar between signifier and signified. In the metonymic process, the bar is maintained between signifier and signified; the signifiers slide along the bar, and the presence of the elided signified is manifest as absence, or lack of being, within the chain of signifiers itself, in the nonsensical or irrational quality of the metonym. In the metaphoric process, the bar is crossed in the elision of the second signified, in the positing of a presence of an absence in relation to the chain of signifiers, that which allows the chain of signifiers to create signification. The crossing of the bar is the myth of reason introduced by the anchoring point in the sliding of the signifiers, which introduces the void of signification as an element in the signifying process. The crossing of the bar is constituted by the substitution of one signifier for another and the elision of the proper signified. It is thus a process of negation, and in particular the negation of the subject in language, which results in the void at the center of the being of the subject, the void around which desire circulates in language.

Substitution in metaphor renders "signification inaccessible to the conscious subject," according to Lacan (Lacan 1977 [1966]: 166), while metonymy enacts a perpetual desire which is always a desire for that which is not there, the absence in being which metonymy stages. As Lacan says, the "signifying game between metonymy and metaphor, up to and including the active edge that splits my desire between a refusal of the signifier and a lack of being, and links my fate to the question of my destiny," is a game which, "in all its inexorable subtlety, is played until the match is called, there where I am not, because I cannot situate myself there," in the *chôra*, the void at the center of language and being. The result in the psyche is "the radical excentricity of the self to itself with which man is confronted" (p. 171), an excentricity which can be applied to language and architecture. The void or gap (*écart*) which has been identified in signification in language or architecture can only be associated with a creation of a gap in the subject (*s'écarte*), a tearing or dehiscence, and that which is torn away (*écartelé*) within the subject. Signification is not possible without the presence of absence, the absence of both the subject and being, which are both necessarily negated in the signifying chain. Language, and the language of architecture, are the product of a human subject which is not present to itself, which is dictated by unconscious processes, thus the conscious subject is a product of language. The conscious subject is assured of its presence in language even by its absence, and the negation of being; language, and architecture as described by Tschumi, are thus the veil which reaffirms the participation of the conscious subject in the world through perception, but which is an illusion.

Chapter 7

Bioconstructivism: topological theory

Sanford Kwinter and Greg Lynn published several essays in *Assemblage Magazine* in the 1990s in which they attempted to lay a theoretical groundwork for computer-generated architectural design. In the essay "Landscapes of Change: Boccioni's *Stati d'animo* as a General Theory of Models" (*Assemblage* 19, 1992), Kwinter proposed a number of theoretical models which could be applied to computer-generated forms. These included topological theory, epigenesis, the epigenetic landscape, morphogenesis, catastrophe, and catastrophe theory. Topological theory entails transformational events or deformations in nature which introduce disconti-nuities into the evolution of a system. Epigenesis entails the generation of smooth landscapes, in waves or the surface of the earth, for example, formed by complex underlying topological interactions. The epigenetic landscape is the smooth forms of relief which are the products of the underlying complex networks of interactions. Morphogenesis describes the structural changes occurring during the development of an organism, wherein forms are seen as discontinuities in a system, as moments of structural instability rather than stability. A catastrophe is a morphogenesis, a jump in a system resulting in a discontinuity. Catastrophe theory is a topological theory describing the discontinuities in the evolution of a system in nature.

In contrast to the calculus of Newton and Leibniz, where trajectories of bodies are plotted against an immobile space, the coordinates of which are described in numerical terms such as x and y, topology describes transformational events or deformations that result in discontinuities in the evolution of a system. Topological mapping is not determined by the gridded quantification of a substrate space, but rather by singularities, occurrences of self-generation or immanence, in the flow of space of which the mapping is a part. The simplistic singularities of flows on a plane are combined to create complex and variegated forms. Attractors and separatrices create topological formations, as in the epigenetic landscape. The Aristotelian concept of epigenesis was revived in Conrad Waddington's *Strategy of the Genes* in 1957, as a biological metaphor for cell reproduction, and recently in Helmut Müller-Sievers *Self-Generation* in 1997. The epigenetic landscape displays the relation between phenotypes or phenomenal forms and the morphogenetic fields in which their formation takes place. The multiplicities of the valleys in the landscape correspond to the possible trajectories of bodies, or the shapes formed, as in the continuous multiplicities of the monads of Leibniz.

Form evolves along a pathway through surface differentiations, represented by the potential trajectory of a ball along the surface. The path of the ball is subject to external forces, so the evolution of the form is not predetermined. The modulations of the epigenetic landscape create default scenarios that frame the evolution of the form, which is only virtual, as the product of the complex convergences of vectors or forces. Through time, the form evolves as a singularity which corresponds to a phenomenal force in the real world. Forms and forces in the real world do not "exist" as such but are rather actualized or unfolded in time as morphological events or differentiations. A phenomenal form or force is an interruption of the continuous flux of possibilities, a disturbance of a continuum. In morphogenesis, all forms are seen as discontinuities in a system. Morphogenesis refers to the biological process that causes an organism to develop its shape. In catastrophe theory, a dynamical system is composed of a distribution of differences or potentials. Potentials operate along vectors in vector fields. For example, a book falls from a shelf to the floor, caused by gravity, along a vector in a vector field defined by attractors, the shelf and the floor. The catastrophe is the mutation of a system to a different level of organization; for example, the replacement of the shelf by the floor as the attractor. The momentary stability of the book on the shelf, amidst the flux of vectors and attractors, can be seen as a form.

A form is a structurally stable moment in the evolution of a dynamic system, at the point of its passing to a structurally instable moment. A system is dynamic if it is continually transforming from stability to instability. The form is the equilibrium at the threshold in a dissipative system. All forms in the phenomenal world are products of the mapping of thresholds between stability and instability in dissipative or dynamic systems. A form should be seen as an event. Forms and forces in the phenomenal world mirror the virtual forms and forces modeled in topological or virtual space. Every form or force enfolds within it a multiplicity of possibilities of forms and forces, as in the monad of Leibniz. The catastrophe is the point at which a system flips to a different organization, and a different form is produced.

In DNA cell reproduction, forms evolve along vectors through topological space, but external forces cause flips in the organization of the system, causing all resultant life forms to be unique. This can be modeled geometrically, and applied to architecture. For example, units of geometries can be organized in sequences, and be programmed to unfold in self-generation, but the width and length of the geometrical units, in the context of the sequence, may cause a divergence in the direction of the generation, a catastrophe which causes its reorganization. The resultant form of the system, its moment of stability, disguises its organizational logic, as do life forms.

The form as event or catastrophe evolves in relation to a control space or attractor, which is the Cartesian parameter space. The trajectory projected into the space above the plane is a virtual universal unfolding, resulting in a cusp or catastrophe set. The combination of continuous and discontinuous behaviors results in unpredictable unfolding through time in the event space or catastrophe surface, producing virtual event-forms or catastrophes. Greg Lynn applied topological theory and catastrophe theory to the design for the Cardiff Bay Opera House competition project in 1994. In *Animate Form*, Lynn described form as a virtual force or vector in a trajectory, resulting in immanence and singularity. Form is defined by "multiple interacting vectors that unfold in time" (Lynn 1999: 11). The vectors enter a topological space which is "differentiated by gradients of force." Architectural form is redefined as it is "modeled as a participant immersed within dynamical flows." Topological space is described as an "animate field" (p. 32). The shape of a body in space is transformed as it evolves through series of gradient spaces to topological space.

Lars Spuybroek's Oblique World Trade Center proposal of 2001 displays complex tectonic structures and topological surfaces that are generated from a multiplicity of analogical vector forces and interactions. Tectonic surfaces are modeled on radiolarians, the multi-cellular and perforated skeleton of silica, and surfaces in nature which are formed from the rigidification of flexible structures. The flexible surfaces produce event-forms in topological space which blur the traditional distinctions in architecture between surface and support, column and beam, forms which are now seen as moments of structural instability in morphogenesis.

These preliminary attempts to establish a theoretical basis for computer-generated design were discontinued in the first decade of the twenty-first century, especially after both *Assemblage* and *ANY Magazine* came to an end in 2000. Many have proclaimed the end of these architecture journals to be symptomatic of the "death of theory" in architecture. Emphasis has been placed instead on the development of the technological means of architectural production, in particular computer programs, at the expense of the development of a theoretical or conceptual basis for architectural form-making. As Nikolaos-Ion Terzoglou writes, for example, "Architecture has concentrated mainly on technological means and instrumental procedures that, in certain cases, manage empty forms without conceptual content" (Terzoglou 2012: 172). The discipline of architecture has increased its dependence on other forms of technological production, and has increased its identity as a "service industry" at the end of the twentieth century. Terzoglou continues: "The rapid technological evolution of our current 'Hypermodern Times' ... leads to a social structure which is governed mainly by specialization, instrumental reasoning and technocratic-economic parameters" (p. 168). The acceleration of economic production has made it increasingly difficult for an architect to express an idea in a building, outside its constructional necessities, and increasing specialization among disciplines, in both academia and professional practice, has made it increasingly difficult for an architect to have control over the design and construction of a building. "This situation has marginalized architecture as a form of mental expression and spatial imagination. An almost exclusive and one-dimensional emphasis on material and technological means reduces the ontological complexity of architecture and often leads to results which lack mental depth and spiritual purposes."

This situation has been aggravated by architectural theorists themselves, proclaiming the death of architectural theory, and seeking to liberate architecture from any mental depth or spiritual purpose, any mental expression or spatial imagination, in deference to the necessity of technological advancement. In Detlef Mertins' essay "Bioconstructivisms," in *NOX: Machining Architecture* (2004), materialism is proclaimed as the new basis for architectural theory. Self-generation and immanence replace predetermination and transcendence in a celebration of the material, and material technology, in exclusion of human intellectual development. An important element of bioconstructivism is autopoiesis or self-generation, taking advantage of digital modeling and computer programs to imitate the capacity for organisms in nature to organize themselves, or for unorganized or fluid material to consolidate itself, based on the inner active principle of the organism, an "essential force" or "formative drive" which contradicts the mechanistic theories of Galileo, Descartes, and Newton. The monad of Leibniz, for example, can self-generate in "integrals" from pre-existing sets of variables, resulting in "continuous multiplicity."

While "a history of generative architecture has yet to be written" (Mertins 2004: 361), structural linguistics and deconstruction, in their emphasis on the pure signifier and the priority of syntactical relations, are seen as having led to the "shift from metaphysics to epistemology," and the pure materialism of self-generation and immanence, which are paradoxically seen as guaranteeing "transcendental apriority" and "cognitive necessity and universality." This kind of stylistic reductionism and materialism needs to be avoided in architecture. Self-generation needs to be combined with predetermination, and the metaphysical needs to be combined with the immanent. As Mertins himself said, quoting Helmut Müller-Sievers, "Only if they are self-produced can the categories guarantee transcendental apriority and, by implication, cognitive necessity and universality" (p. 361). The denial of the possibility of the metaphysic cannot lead to transcendental apriority. The materialist epistemology of bioconstructivism on its own has no theoretical basis, and no potential to develop architecture as a form of human expression.

In bioconstructivism, architectural history has been for the most part abandoned, which is the case in general in current architectural education. Historical styles have come to be understood as "residual transcendent authorities no longer commensurate with the present" (p. 362), the present entailing the abandonment of architectural design to mechanical production and technological advancement, and the abandonment of the desire on the part of the human being to express an idea in the current hypertechnological dystopia. Predetermination (the a priori concept or the expression of an idea) and transcendence (the metaphysical in language) are avoided, in deference to self-generation and immanence in the bioconstructivist model, because of the "new urgency under the conditions of industrialization and mass production" (p. 363). Hypertechnological production neglects intellectual and spiritual development, and the potential for human expression and creativity.

Similarly, Jane and Mark Burry, in *The New Mathematics of Architecture* (2010), celebrate the submission of architecture to the materialism of technological production. Complex geometries are incorporated into architectural design, expanding the vocabulary of architecture, but the new vocabulary thus far does not contribute to the expansion of architecture as a form of the communication of ideas or poetic expression. The new computer-generated forms based on complex geometries are mute forms, technological marvels servicing technological advancement, but revealing nothing about the human condition or human identity, other than its servitude to technology. The new mute forms have "transcended the metaphysical" (Burry and Burry 2010: 8), as self-generated and immanent, and they have evolved beyond the "dead geometries" of the "rectilinear dogma of Modernism" (pp. 10–12). The excitement over technological development supersedes the value of history, philosophy, and intellectual development, the humanistic elements of architecture and expression in the arts which resonate with the core of human identity, which have lasting value as expressions of the human condition, of human experience and existence in the world.

A redeeming quality of bioconstructivism is that it involves the engagement in architecture of generative models from nature, which is in the tradition of the *natura naturans* in architecture, the imitation of the forming principles of nature, as opposed to the *natura naturata*, the direct imitation or mimesis of the forms. As was seen in the first chapter, according to Plotinus in the *Enneads*, it is the purpose of all the arts to not just present a "bare reproduction of the thing seen," the *natura naturata*, but to "go back to the Ideas from which Nature itself derives" (Plotinus 1952: V.8.1), in the *natura naturans*. As was seen, the contrast between *natura naturans* and *natura naturata* was explored in the writings of Johann Winckelmann, Francesco Algarotti, and Quatremère de Quincy in the eighteenth century. In Winckelmann's *History of the Art of Antiquity* (2006 [1764]), architecture is more ideal than the other arts because it does not imitate objects in nature. Its forms are instead derived from the rules and laws of proportion, which are abstract concepts. In Algarotti's *Saggio sopra l'architettura* (1784), architecture "must raise itself up with intellect and must derive a system of imitation from ideas about things that are the most universal and farthest from what can be seen" (Lavin 1992: 107).

In the *Encyclopédie méthodique* (1788) of Quatremère de Quincy, architecture is described as more ideal, intellectual, and metaphysical than the other arts, because architecture must convert the qualities of the forms of nature into its own forms, and it must imitate the spirit of the forms of nature, in the universal idea, rather than a particular form (1:495), as in biomimesis. Architecture should imitate natural forms analogically and metaphorically, rather than literally. Quatremère describes architecture as imitating the ideas from which nature derives, like Plotinus, rather than natural forms as given by sense perception. The model for this type of imitation in abstraction was the primitive hut of Marc Antoine Laugier, described in the *Essai sur l'architecture* (1775). While the cave is a model for architecture in the imitation of the forms of nature, and the tent is a model for architecture in the construction of forms not connected to nature, the primitive hut is the perfect model for architecture in the construction of forms in the imitation of the principles of nature. In *De l'architecture égyptienne*, Quatremère described the primitive hut as the product of the perfection in the human intellect of the forming principles of nature, and it was that perfection which made Classical architecture possible. In this way the origins of architecture are linked to the present, in bioconstructivism.

Laugier saw the primitive hut as a purely natural model, but Quatremère argued, in *Encyclopédie méthodique* (1:454), that the primitive hut was already an abstraction in human intellect, derived from the principles of nature. While Laugier saw the primitive hut as a model that could be directly reproduced in architecture, for Quatremère it could only be indirectly reproduced, since the wood of the hut would have to be transformed into the stone and marble of Greek buildings. According to Quatremère, Classical architecture was based on an underlying conceptual organization of abstracted forms and principles from nature, in the *natura naturans*, as in bioconstructivism.

A project which shows the potential for the tenets of bioconstructivism to be integrated with a genuine theoretical basis for computer-generated design, which does not abandon architectural history or the historical function of architecture as a form of poetic expression, is a design for a theater by Amy Lewis in a Graduate Architecture Design Studio (a 515, 6 c.h.) directed by Associate Professor Andrew Thurlow at Roger Williams University, School of Architecture, Art and Planning, in Spring 2011 (Figures 7.1 and 7.2).

In the design by Amy Lewis there is a dialectic between the form and the function, a contradiction between the forms and the structural and functional requirements of the building. There are, on the one hand, the methodologies of

Figure 7.1 **Amy Lewis, Endless Dreamscape, Andrew Thurlow Studio, 2011**

bioconstructivism and biomimesis, the focus on immanence and self-generation, and there is, on the other hand, the methodology of poetic expression, of transcendence and predeterminism, in the contradiction between the form and the function, and the presence of the metaphysic in the allegorical or metaphorical. There is the focus on the signifier and the syntactical, and the play of differences in signs, and there is also the narrative and the representational. There is an enactment of the syntactical relation between dream thoughts and dream images from the dreamwork of Freud, through the mechanisms of condensation and displacement. The title of the project is "Endless Dreamscape." The building appears as an epigenetic landscape, contradicting the topological forces which predetermine it, in the same way that a Renaissance façade would be both a summation and a contradiction of the structural and functional relationships of the building.

The forms in Amy Lewis' project display the catastrophic jumps in epigenetic processes, resulting in the contradiction between form and form as well as the contradiction between form and function. The forms display the "modifications, perturbations, changes of tension or of energy" (Kwinter 1992: 52) of matter, as described by Henri Bergson. The forms display the vocabulary of "waves, fields, and fronts" of epigenesis. The forms display topological flows which are "scattered, accelerated, accreted, collided" (p. 53) into diverse surfaces or developmental fields. The forms display a dialectic between the stable and continuous and the unstable and discontinuous. The discontinuity of the forms is a sign of morphogenesis. Catastrophic mutations take place between different levels of activity and organization. The presence of forms as "structurally stable moments within a system's evolution" (p. 59) is subsumed into a process of evolution or mutation. Moments of structural stability are juxtaposed with moments of structural instability, to represent the contradiction inherent in self-generation or emergence.

The composition can be seen as a "dissipative system," a dynamic evolving system of matter. The composition can be seen as a catastrophe because each singular form can be seen to be the product of a multiplicity of forces, singular and multiple causes simultaneously. The combinations of multiple and contradictory forms result in irregular and discontinuous formal relationships which create a dynamic, emerging composition. Trajectories of forms suggest development and change, and transformation through time. The trajectories incorporate realized forms as well as forms which are not yet actualized, but are present as traces, as enfolded "in between" the realized forms. The unrealized forms are related to the actualized forms in a continuum of contradictions. The architectural composition should be seen as an "event," as an occurrence in nature, both biomimetically and allegorically, involving continuity and interruption, singularity and multiplicity, predetermination and immanence. The self-generation of the forms situates the unpredictable within the predictable, as can be found in DNA cell reproduction.

Within a continuity, the morphogenesis of the forms results in structural changes (as represented by the forms), which occur during the developmental process of an organism in nature. The forms in the composition display the transformational events or deformations that result in discontinuities and contradictions, according to topological theory. The forms display the dynamic of morphogenesis, as a system of discontinuities, involving the simultaneous transformation of every individual parts of a system. The emergence of a singular form within the system, in catastrophe theory, is a moment of structural instability rather than a moment of structural stability.

In Amy Lewis' composition (Figure 7.2), moments of structural instability are juxtaposed with moments of structural stability. In the morphogenesis of the catastrophe, certain configurations will remain stabilized, while other configurations will point toward destabilization, or structural instability. Equilibrium is juxtaposed with disequilibrium. The singularity of the surfaces of the forms in the epigenetic landscape contradicts the complex network of interactions of topological forces from which they result, in a contradiction between form and function. Actions in the environment on unstable, unstructured forms, and undifferentiated structures, result in stable, structured forms and differentiated structures. Traditionally, architectural forms such as the post and lintel or column and entablature are seen as representing structural stability and continuity, but in catastrophe theory and epigenesis they are seen as interruptions of structural stability and continuity. The stasis and the flux are juxtaposed in this project.

Amy Lewis' project illustrates that theory is not "dead" in bioconstructivism and computer-generated design, that predetermination and the metaphysic, representation and signification, can be reconciled with immanence and self-generation, syntax and the play of signifiers, and that architectural history can still have relevance in bioconstructivism and other models of computer-generated design, in the incorporation of formal typologies into generative systems. As in all stages in architectural history, form can contradict function in a bioconstructivist architectural composition, so that the architecture continues to be a form of poetic

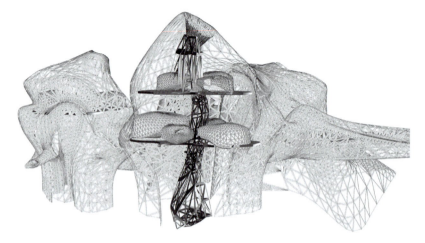

Figure 7.2 Amy Lewis, Endless Dreamscape, Andrew Thurlow Studio, 2011

expression, and the expression of an idea external to the structural and functional requirements, through allegory or signification.

The project calls to mind the dictates of Louis Sullivan, that form should follow function in the creative process of the architect, but not that the form of the building should follow the function of the building, its functional or structural requirements, and that "the essence of things is taking shape in the matter of things" in nature (Sullivan 1947: 208). As was seen in Chapter 5, form follows function in the expression of life, in the processes of birth and growth, and in the dialectics of birth and death, organic and inorganic, physical and metaphysical. Form follows function in the emotional expression of life, wherein "the same emotional impulse shall flow throughout harmoniously into its varied form of expression" (p. 188). Form follows function in architecture insofar as the function of architecture is to express a metaphysical idea.

All forms in architecture "stand for relationships between the immaterial and the material, between the subjective and the objective—between the Infinite Spirit and the finite mind" (p. 45), according to Sullivan. Function in architecture is a "phase of that energy which we have called the Infinite Creative Spirit" (p. 99), the essence of the creative process of architecture, its emotional needs. Function is assimilated in order to express a creative impulse. As Amy Lewis said to the author, "the architect still exists in the realm of the poet, who seeks to describe the nature of a beast he can never hope to know or understand, but merely define in his own rudimentary conceptualization or philosophical truth."

The design of a building is the expression of a transcendental idea which manifests itself in form through nature. Architecture imitates nature insofar as nature forms itself by universal principles, in bioconstructivism as well as in prior theoretical approaches. A building, as an organism, while it is developed according to the methods of nature, cannot be an imitation of any particular work of nature, but must rather be the expression of an idea of nature. Architecture is poetry, as poetry is the expression of an idea in matter. According to Sullivan, the functional and structural requirements of a building play no role in the art of architecture, because they have no relationship with nature, but only with the technological progress and material development of society. Architecture is based on the visual appearance of a natural organism, which best expresses the essence of nature.

The essence of the building, the expression of the transcendental idea, the relationship between the human mind and nature, is likewise expressed in the composition by Amy Lewis. The design involves an interweaving of the mimesis of organic forms and constructed geometries, to represent the dialectic between a priori reason (predetermination) and sense experience (immanence). The dialectic between the objective, in the rational organization of the building, and the subjective, in the incongruities and inconsistencies, is also represented. As in Sullivan's architecture, the dialectical method is used in multiple ways, in juxtaposition and contradiction: subjective/objective, appearance/essence, rational/emotional, geometrical/organic, horizontal/vertical, form/function. The juxtapositions evoke the "Rhythm of Life" and the "Rhythm of Death," the rhythms of growth and aspiration interwoven with the rhythms of decadence and destruction, and the rhythms of Eros and Thanatos. The vertical movements and the striving in the forms for the detachment from the constraints of the material are juxtaposed with the horizontal movements and the confinement to the material, the grounding of the concept in the matter. As it is biomimetic, Amy Lewis' project is anthropomorphic, metaphorically, as if it is a body striving to lift itself off the ground, and to release itself from material constraints, of outline and gravity. The dialectical relations evoked in the composition of the building have no connection with the structural or functional requirements of the building.

The dialectic of the building in architecture, like the dialectic of the human being, involves the understanding of the processes of nature and the ability to transfer those processes into visual form, establishing the rhythm of the relationship between the human being and nature. The dialectic is a form of *Einfühlung*, or empathy, the act of inner imitation, *natura naturans*, carried out in bioconstructivism. The dynamism injected into the architectural vocabulary elements, the organic and geometrical forms, and the horizontal and vertical movements, projects the struggle between body and mind, material and spiritual, onto the building. The *Einfühlung* involves the dialectic of the rhythm of life and death.

The human mind defines itself in its translation of that which is external to it, as in the transposition of the essence of nature to visual form. Language, and the visual language of architecture, are a function in mind of the translation from the external to the subjective, and from the particular to the universal. The essence of nature is transposed to visual form metaphorically. The nature of the sign in language is that the particular becomes subject to the universal in the transition of the perceived object into the word or form, and the simultaneous transition of the word or form into the idea. The formulation of language is a process of the externalization of perception into the particulars which mask the unified universality of existence and render existence fragmented, in the same way that the instinct for self-preservation in the organic being renders the universal impossible in a nature composed of fragmented particulars. Amy Lewis' composition stages these relationships—between the human mind and nature, particulars in perception and universals in thought, words, or visual forms and ideas.

The transition from nature to mind is a "coming-to-itself of mind out of its self-externality in Nature," in the words of Hegel (Hegel 1971 [1830]: § 381). The transition from nature to idea occurs in mind; it is not a natural transition, not governed by the Principle of Sufficient Reason. Perception is constructed by reason, and ideas in mind are constructed by mind in self-consciousness. While reason and logic are governed by necessity, in cause and effect, language (the scaffolding of reason), which is an abstraction of perception in mind (a transition from "the singleness of sensation to the universality of thought"), is a construct of mind in its development toward self-consciousness. Language and the language of visual forms in architecture are elements in the mediating process of nature in mind, which begins to disappear in the development of self-consciousness. Architecture, in any form, from a Classical temple to a bioconstructivist composition, is capable of expressing and representing that process, in the relation between the human being and nature, between perception and language, and between form and function in both visual form and the human mind. The processes and relationships are most completely revealed in the contradiction between form and function.

The contradiction between form and function is inherent in architecture, language, philosophy, and human identity. Architecture, like poetry, requires the contradiction between form and function in order to be artistic expression, in order to express the human condition, in the contradiction between mind and matter, thought and perception. This simple lesson, included in architectural education, can result in great architecture. Architecture is not about making empty formalist compositions with new technologies, or, as Alberto Pérez-Gómez writes, the "mindless search for consumable novelties disconnected from history" (Pérez-Gómez 2012: 164). As Sullivan put it in the "Kindergarten Chats," the architect has to be more than a "peddler of fashions" (Sullivan 1947: 39). Architecture is about the expression of ideas. Architects need to resist the mindless conformity imposed by consumerism and technology. As Amy Lewis said to the author, "because the technology exists to prescribe a certain tectonic ideal does not mean it should become the motive power behind design and the teaching of our craft."

The use of the computer has increased the conformity imposed by technology on the architectural profession. The discipline of architecture is currently servicing media markets and flooding them with novel "blobs" and other forms which communicate or express nothing, and books and magazines are being filled by corresponding apologies by "architectural theorists" who celebrate the "death of theory" in architecture, under the threat of conformity imposed by techno-logical production and the corresponding necessity of technological development and novelty, and offer nothing as an alternative. Perhaps the "death of theory" in architecture will lead to the death of architecture as an autonomous profession. Architecture will complete its dissolution into a service industry, and be absorbed by various types of media production. Buildings will continue to be built, but archi-tects will play no creative role in their design, as suggested by Mario Carpo in *The Alphabet and the Algorithm* (2011).

Contemporary "architects" and "architectural theorists" have already begun to abandon architecture, and are profiting from the dissolution of the very practice in which they purport to engage. Architectural schools teach construction, structure, construction management, computer operations, and sustainable practices, but they rarely teach architecture as an art, the design of a building for the purpose of expressing an idea external to its structural and functional require-ments. Symptomatic of this is that architectural history is currently disappearing from architecture schools, as it is supposedly irrelevant to computer-generated design. Doctoral programs in architectural history as an autonomous discipline are becoming fewer, and there are fewer positions for architectural historians. The death of architectural history as a discipline is complicit with the death of architecture as art. The lack of architecture as a form of expression of ideas, along with the lack of art, literature, and philosophy in a society, means a lack of human intellectual development in favor of the priority of empty consumerism and the disposable novelties of technological development and entertainment, shadows on the wall.

The potential for architecture to be a form of artistic or poetic expression should not be forgotten. Through its forms, architecture can express and communicate aspects of human identity that even language cannot express. While the role of architecture in culture has changed dramatically in the last five hundred years, with the advent of the printing press, the Industrial Revolution, and now the computer, architecture can still play the same roles that it played historically, in the expression and representation of cultural identities and values, philosophies, cosmologies, and psychologies. If nothing else, history can provide models for architects to express ideas through architecture. The uniqueness of architecture as a form of expression lies in the dual presence of its functional requirements combined with the visual affects of its sculpted forms. In other words, architecture is unique because of the relationship between form and function which it necessarily entails. This relationship can be exploited by architects, not only as a conformance, in the traditional "form follows function," but also as a contradiction, as suggested by this book. The contradiction between form and function can in fact lead to greater potentials for architecture to express and communicate fundamental elements of human existence, and allow architecture to have more value in people's lives and identities. That is the hope of this book.

Bibliography

Agudin, L.M. (1995) *The Concept of Type in Architecture: An Inquiry into the Nature of Architectural Form*, Zurich: Swiss Federal Institute of Technology.

Alberti, L.B. (1988 [1452]) *De re aedificatoria* (*On the Art of Building in Ten Books*), trans. J. Rykwert, N. Leach, R. Tavernor, Cambridge, MA: The MIT Press.

—— (1972 [1435/1464]) *On Painting* and *On Sculpture*, trans. C. Grayson, London: Phaidon.

Alexander of Aphrodisias (1979) *The De Anima of Alexander of Aphrodisias*, trans. A.P. Fotinus, Washington, DC: University Press of America.

Alexandrakis, A. (ed.) (2002) *Neoplatonism and Western Aesthetics*, Albany: State University of New York Press.

Alfarabi (1967) *The Letter Concerning the Intellect*, trans. A. Hyman, in A. Hyman, J.J. Walsh (eds.), *Philosophy in the Middle Ages: The Christian, Islamic, and Jewish Traditions*, New York: Harper and Row.

Anselm of Canterbury (2008) *The Major Works*, B. Davies, G.P. Evans (eds.), Oxford and New York: Oxford University Press.

Aquinas, T. (1990 [1274]) *Summa Theologica*, trans. Father L. Shapcote, Chicago: Encyclopaedia Britannica.

Aristotle (1985) *Nicomachean Ethics*, trans. T. Irwin, Indianapolis: Hackett Publishing Company.

—— (1952a) *Metaphysics*, trans. W.D. Ross, in *The Works of Aristotle*, Chicago: Encyclopaedia Britannica.

—— (1952b) *On the Soul* (*De anima*), trans. J.A. Smith, in *The Works of Aristotle*, Chicago: Encyclopaedia Britannica.

Arnheim, R. (1977) *The Dynamics of Architectural Form*, Berkeley: University of California Press.

Averroes (1967) *Long Commentary on De Anima*, trans. A. Hyman, in A. Hyman, J.J. Walsh (eds.), *Philosophy in the Middle Ages: The Christian, Islamic, and Jewish Traditions*, New York: Harper and Row.

Bandyopadhyay, S., Lomholt, J., Temple, N., and Tobe, R. (eds.) (2010) *The Humanities in Architectural Design: A Contemporary and Historical Perspective*, London and New York: Routledge.

Behne, A. (1996 [1926]) *The Modern Functional Building*, trans. M. Robinson, Santa Monica: The Getty Research Institute for the History of Art and the Humanities.

Bergdoll, B. (1994) *Karl Friedrich Schinkel: An Architecture for Prussia*, New York: Rizzoli.

—— (1990) "The *Dictionnaire raisonné*: Viollet-le-Duc's Encyclopedic Structure for Architecture," in E.-E. Viollet-le-Duc, *The Foundations of Architecture: Selections from the Dictionnaire raisonné*, trans. K.D. Whitehead, New York: George Braziller.

Berkeley, G. (1963) *Works on Vision*, C.M. Turbayne (ed.), New York: The Library of Liberal Arts.

Blake, P. (1974) *Form Follows Fiasco: Why Modern Architecture Hasn't Worked*, Boston and Toronto: Little, Brown and Company.

Borsi, F. and Portoghesi, P. (1991) *Victor Horta*, trans. M.-H. Agüeros, New York: Rizzoli.

Boullée, É.-L (1968) *Architecture: Essai sur l'art*, Paris: Hermann.

Brand, D.J. (trans.) (1981) *The Book of Causes* (*Liber de Causis*), New York: Niagra University Press.

Brentano, F. (1977 [1874]) *The Psychology of Aristotle: In Particular His Doctrine of the Active Intellect*, trans. R. George, Berkeley: University of California Press.

Burry, J. and Burry, M. (2010) *The New Mathematics of Architecture*, New York: Thames and Hudson.

Caillois, R. (1993) "Mimicry and Legendary Psychasthenia [1937]," trans. J. Shepley, in *October* 31, Cambridge, MA: The MIT Press.

—— (1990 [1981]) *The Necessity of the Mind*, trans. M. Syrotinski, Venice, CA: The Lapis Press.

—— (1938) *Le Myth et l'Homme*, Paris: Gallimard.

Campbell, C. (1967 [1715]) *Vitruvius Britannicus, or, The British Architect*, New York: B. Blom.

Carpiceci, A.C. (1997) *Art and History of Egypt*, trans. E. Pauli, Florence: Bonechi.

Carpo, M. (2011) *The Alphabet and the Algorithm*, Cambridge, MA: The MIT Press.

Chomsky, N. (1968) *Language and Mind*, New York: Harcourt Brace Jovanovich, Inc.

Culler, J. (1982) *On Deconstruction: Theory and Criticism after Structuralism*, Ithaca: Cornell University Press.

Cusanus, N. (1972 [1443]) *De coniecturis*, Hamburg: In Aedibus Felicis Meiner.

Davidson, H.A. (1992) *Alfarabi, Avicenna, and Averroes, on Intellect*, Oxford: Oxford University Press.

Dernie, D. and Carew-Cox, A. (1995) *Victor Horta*, London: Academy Editions.

Derrida, J. (1981 [1972]) *Positions*, trans. A. Bass, Chicago: University of Chicago Press.

—— (1976 [1967]) *Of Grammatology*, trans. G.C. Spivak, Baltimore and London: The Johns Hopkins University Press.

Descartes, R. (2003) *Discourse on Method and Related Writings*, trans. D. Clarke, New York: Penguin Books.

—— (1998) *The World and Other Writings*, trans. and ed. S. Gaukroger, New York: Cambridge University Press.

Diani, M. and Ingraham, C. (eds.) (1989) *Restructuring Architectural Theory*, Evanston: Northwestern University Press.

Doig, A. (1986) *Theo van Doesburg: Painting into Architecture, Theory into Practice*, Cambridge and New York: Cambridge University Press.

Eastwood, B.S. (1964) *The Geometrical Optics of Robert Grosseteste*, University of Wisconsin, Ph.D. Thesis.

Eidlitz, L. (1977 [1881]) *Nature and Function of Art, More Especially of Architecture*, New York: Da Capo Press.

Eisenman, P. (2006) *The Formal Basis of Modern Architecture*, Baden: Lars Müller.

—— (2005) "Giuseppe Terragni: A Critical Analysis," in P. Noever (ed.), *Barefoot on White-Hot Walls* (*Barfuss Auf Weiss Glühenden Mauern*), Ostfildern: Hatje Cantz Verlag.

—— (2004a) *Eisenman Inside Out: Selected Writings, 1963–1988*, New Haven and London: Yale University Press.

—— (2004b) "The End of the Classical: The End of the Beginning, the End of the End," in *Eisenman Inside Out: Selected Writings, 1963–1988*, New Haven and London: Yale University Press.

—— (2004c) "Notes on Conceptual Architecture: Toward a Definition," in *Eisenman Inside Out: Selected Writings, 1963–1988*, New Haven and London: Yale University Press.

—— (1989) "Architecture as a Second Language: The Texts of Between," in M. Diani, C. Ingraham (eds.), *Restructuring Architectural Theory*, Evanston: Northwestern University Press.

—— (1987) *House of Cards*, Oxford and New York: Oxford University Press.

—— (1971) "From Object to Relationship II: Giuseppe Terragni, Casa Giuliani Frigerio," *Perspecta* 13, *The Yale Architectural Journal*, pp. 37–65.

Emmons, P., Hendrix, J., and Lomholt, J. (eds.) (2012) *The Cultural Role of Architecture: Contemporary and Historical Perspectives*, London and New York: Routledge.

Ficino, M. (1985 [1484]) *Commentary on Plato's Symposium on Love*, trans. S. Jayne, Dallas: Spring Publications.

—— (1964 [1474]) *Platonic Theology: On the Immortality of Souls*, Paris: Humanities.

Fiero, G.K. (2002) *The Humanistic Tradition, Volume V*, Boston: McGraw Hill.

Fludd, R. (1619) *Microcosmi Historia*, Oppenheim: Johannes Theodore de Bry.

Francesca, P. della (1942) *De Prospectiva Pingendi*, Firenze: Sansoni Editore.

Frankl, P. (1962) *Gothic Architecture*, Harmondsworth: Penguin Books.

Freud, S. (1965 [1900]) *The Interpretation of Dreams: The Standard Edition*, trans. and ed. J. Strachey, New York: Avon Books.

—— (1962 [1927]) *The Ego and the Id: The Standard Edition*, J. Strachey (ed.), trans. J. Riviere, New York: W.W. Norton.

—— (1952 [1901]) *On Dreams: The Standard Edition*, trans. and ed. J. Strachey, New York: W.W. Norton.

—— (1949 [1940]) *An Outline of Psycho-Analysis: The Standard Edition*, trans. and ed. J. Strachey, New York: W.W. Norton.

Grosseteste, R. (1996) *On the Six Days of Creation* (*Hexaëmeron*), trans. C.F.J. Martin, British Academy, Oxford: Oxford University Press.

—— (1981) *Commentarius in Posteriorum Analyticorum Libros*, P. Rossi (ed.), Firenze: Olschki.

—— (1964) "On Lines, Angles, and Figures, or the Refraction and Reflection of Rays" (*De Lineis, Angulis et Figuris*), trans. B.S. Eastwood, in *The Geometrical Optics of Robert Grosseteste*, University of Wisconsin, Ph.D. Thesis.

—— (1942) *On Light* (*De Luce*), trans. C.C. Riedl, Milwaukee: Marquette University Press.

—— (1503) *Libellus Linconiensis de Phisicis Lineis Angulis et Figuris per quas omnes Acciones Naturales Complentur*, Nurenburge.

Harvey, J. (1972) *The Medieval Architect*, New York: St. Martin's Press.

Hegel, G.W.F. (1993) *Introductory Lectures on Aesthetics* (*The Introduction to Hegel's Philosophy of Fine Art*, 1886), M. Inwood (ed.), trans. B. Bosanquet, London: Penguin Books.

—— (1977 [1807]) *Phenomenology of Spirit*, trans. A.V. Miller, Oxford: Oxford University Press.

—— (1971) *Hegel's Philosophy of Mind, Being Part Three of the Encyclopedia of the Philosophical Sciences* (1830), trans. W. Wallace, Oxford: Clarendon Press.

Hendrix, J.S. (2011) *Architecture as Cosmology: Lincoln Cathedral and English Gothic Architecture*, New York: Peter Lang Publishing.

—— (2006) *Architecture and Psychoanalysis: Peter Eisenman and Jacques Lacan*, New York: Peter Lang Publishing.

—— (2005) *Aesthetics and the Philosophy of Spirit: From Plotinus to Schelling and Hegel*, New York: Peter Lang Publishing.

—— (2004) *Platonic Architectonics: Platonic Philosophies and the Visual Arts*, New York: Peter Lang Publishing.

—— (2003) *Architectural Forms and Philosophical Structures*, New York: Peter Lang Publishing.

—— (2002) *The Relation Between Architectural Forms and Philosophical Structures in the Work of Francesco Borromini in Seventeenth-Century Rome*, Lewiston, NY: Edwin Mellen Press.

Hersey, G.L. (1976) *Pythagorean Palaces, Magic and Architecture in the Italian Renaissance*, Ithaca: Cornell University Press.

Hitchcock, H.-R. and Johnson, P. (1996 [1932]) *The International Style*, New York: W.W. Norton.

Huysmans, J.-K. (1959 [1884]) *À Rebours* (*Against Nature*), trans. R. Baldick, London: Penguin Books.

Hyman, A. and Walsh, J.J. (eds.) (1967) *Philosophy in the Middle Ages: The Christian, Islamic, and Jewish Traditions*, New York: Harper and Row.

Jacq, C. (1998) *I grandi monumenti dell'antico Egitto*, Milano: Mondadori Editore.

Kant, I. (1990 [1781]) *Critique of Pure Reason*, trans. J.M.D. Meiklejohn, Amherst, NY: Prometheus Books.

Kennedy, R.W. (1950) "Form, Function and Expression: Variations on a Theme by Louis Sullivan," *Journal of the American Institute of Architects*, VIV, November, No. 5, New York: The Octagon.

Kepes, G. (1944) *Language of Vision*, Chicago: Paul Theobald.

Kipnis, J. and Leeser, T. (eds.) (1997) *Chora L Works: Jacques Derrida and Peter Eisenman*, New York: Monacelli Press.

Kircher, A. (1666) *Obeliscus Aegyptiacus*, Roma: Ex Typographia Veresii.

—— (1653) *Oedipus Aegyptiacus, Tomi Secundi*, Roma: Ex Typographia Vitalis Mascardi.

—— (1650a) *Obeliscus Pamphilius*, Roma: Typis Ludovici Grignani.

—— (1650b) *Musurgia Universalis*, Roma: Ex Typographia Haeredum Francisci, Corbelletti.

—— (1636) *Prodromus Coptus Sive Aegyptiacus*, Roma: Propaganda Fide.

Bibliography

—— (1633) *Primitiae Gnomonicae Catoptricae*, Avenione: Ioannis Piot Ex Typographia.

Kwinter, S. (1992) "Landscapes of Change: Boccioni's *Stati d'animo* as a General Theory of Models," *Assemblage* 19, Cambridge, MA: The MIT Press.

Lacan, J. (1977 [1966]) *Écrits: A Selection*, trans. A. Sheridan, New York: W.W. Norton.

Laugier, M.-A. (1977 [1753]) *An Essay on Architecture* (*Essai sur l'architecture*), trans. W. and A. Herrmann, Los Angeles: Hennessey & Ingalls.

Lavin, S. (1992) *Quatremère de Quincy and the Invention of a Modern Language of Architecture*, Cambridge, MA: The MIT Press.

Layzer, D. (1990) *Cosmogenesis: The Growth of Order in the Universe,* New York: Oxford University Press.

Le Corbusier (1960) *Toward a New Architecture* (*Vers une Architecture*, 1923), trans. F. Etchells, New York: Praeger Publishers.

Lynn, Greg (1999) *Animate Form*, New York: Princeton Architectural Press.

Menocal, N.G. (1981) *Architecture as Nature: The Transcendentalist Idea of Louis Sullivan*, Madison: The University of Wisconsin Press.

Mertins, D. (2004) "Bioconstructivisms," in L. Spuybroek (ed.), *NOX: Machining Architecture*, London: Thames and Hudson, pp. 360–9, reproduced in Departmental Papers (City and Regional Planning), Department of City and Regional Planning, University of Pennsylvania.

Mirandola, G.P. della (1956 [1486]) *Oration on the Dignity of Man*, trans. A.R. Caponigri, Chicago: Regnery Gateway.

Müller-Sievers, H. (1997) *Self-Generation: Biology, Philosophy, and Literature Around 1800*, Palo Alto, CA: Stanford University Press.

Nancy, J.-L. and Lacoue-Labarthe, P. (1992 [1973]) *The Title of the Letter: A Reading of Lacan*, trans. F. Raffoul and D. Pettigrew, Albany: State University of New York Press.

Neutra, R.J. (1969 [1954]) *Survival Through Design*, London and New York: Oxford University Press.

Noever, P. (ed.) (2005) *Barefoot on White-Hot Walls* (*Barfuss Auf Weiss Glühenden Mauern*), Ostfildern: Hatje Cantz Verlag.

Padovan, R. (2002) *Toward Universality: Le Corbusier, Mies and De Stijl*, London: Routledge.

Panofsky, E. (1991 [1927]) *Perspective as Symbolic Form*, trans. C.S. Wood, New York: Zone Books.

Paul, S. (1962) *Louis Sullivan: An Architect in American Thought*, Englewood Cliffs, NJ: Prentice-Hall.

Pérez-Gómez, A. (2012) "The Relevance of Beauty in Architecture," in P. Emmons, J. Hendrix, and J. Lomholt (eds.), *The Cultural Role of Architecture*, London and New York: Routledge.

Pevsner, N. (1943) *An Outline of European Architecture*, Harmondsworth: Penguin Books.

Plato (1973) *Phaedrus*, trans. W. Hamilton, London: Penguin Books.

—— (1965) *Timaeus*, trans. D. Lee, London: Penguin Books.

—— (1955) *The Republic*, trans. D. Lee, London: Penguin Books.

—— (1952) *The Dialogues of Plato*, trans. B. Jowett, Chicago: Encyclopaedia Britannica.

Plotinus (1991) *The Enneads*, trans. S. MacKenna, London: Penguin Books.

—— (1966) *Enneads*, trans. A.H. Armstrong, Cambridge, MA: Harvard University Press.

—— (1952) *The Six Enneads*, trans. S. MacKenna and B.S. Page, Chicago: Encyclopaedia Britannica.

Proclus (1970) *A Commentary on the First Book of Euclid's Elements*, trans. G.R. Morrow, Princeton, NJ: Princeton University Press.

Pseudo-Dionysius (1987) *The Complete Works*, trans. C. Luibheid, New York: Paulist Press.

Rodenbach, G. (1993 [1892]) *Bruges-la-Morte*, trans. T. Duncan, London: Atlas.

Rowe, C. (1976) *The Mathematics of the Ideal Villa and Other Essays*, Cambridge, MA: The MIT Press.

Rowe, C. and Slutzky, R. (1976) "Transparency: Literal and Phenomenal," in C. Rowe, *The Mathematics of the Ideal Villa and Other Essays*, Cambridge, MA: The MIT Press.

Schelling, F.W.J. von (1989 [1859]) *The Philosophy of Art* (*Die Philosophie der Kunst*), trans. D.W. Stott, Minneapolis: University of Minnesota Press.

Schroeder, F.M. (2002) "The Vigil of the One and Plotinian Iconoclasm," in A. Alexandrakis (ed.), *Neoplatonism and Western Aesthetics*, Albany: State University of New York Press.

Scott, G. (1980 [1914]) *The Architecture of Humanism*, London: The Architectural Press.

Snow, C.P. (1993 [1959]) *The Two Cultures*, London: Cambridge University Press.

Spinoza, B. de (2006) *The Essential Spinoza: Ethics and Related Writings*, M.L. Morgan (ed.), trans. S. Shirley, Indianapolis and Cambridge: Hackett Publishing Company.

Spuybroek, L. (ed.) (2004) *NOX: Machining Architecture*, London: Thames and Hudson.

Steinberg, L. (1977) *Borromini's San Carlo alle Quattro Fontane: A Study in Multiple Form and Architectural Symbolism*, New York: Garland Publishing.

Sullivan, L.H. (1947) *Kindergarten Chats and Other Writings*, New York: Wittenborn, Schulz, Inc.

Terzoglou, N.-I. (2012) "Architectural Creation between 'Culture' and 'Civilization'," in P. Emmons, J. Hendrix, and J. Lomholt (eds.), *The Cultural Role of Architecture*, London and New York: Routledge.

Tschumi, B. (1994) *Architecture and Disjunction*, Cambridge, MA: The MIT Press.

Twombly, R. (ed.) (1988) *Louis Sullivan: The Public Papers*, Chicago and London: The University of Chicago Press.

Venturi, R. (1966) *Complexity and Contradiction in Architecture*, New York: The Museum of Modern Art.

Vesely, D. (2004) *Architecture in the Age of Divided Representation: The Question of Creativity in the Shadow of Production*, Cambridge, MA: The MIT Press.

Vidler, A. (1992) *The Architectural Uncanny: Essays in the Modern Unhomely*, Cambridge, MA: The MIT Press.

Viollet-le-Duc, E.-E. (1990) *The Foundations of Architecture: Selections from the Dictionnaire raisonné*, trans. K.D. Whitehead, New York: George Braziller.

Vitruvius (1931 [27 BC]) *De architectura* (*On Architecture*), trans. F. Granger, Cambridge, MA: Harvard University Press.

Waddington, C.H. and Kacser, H. (1957) *The Strategy of the Genes: A Discussion of Some Aspects of Theoretical Biology*, London: George Allen & Unwin.

White, H. (1973) *Metahistory: The Historical Imagination in Nineteenth-Century Europe*, Baltimore and London: The Johns Hopkins University Press.

Whitman, W. (1902) *Poems of Walt Whitman (Leaves of Grass)*, New York: T.Y. Crowell.

Wigley, M. (1993) *The Architecture of Deconstruction: Derrida's Haunt*, Cambridge, MA: The MIT Press.

Winckelmann, J.J. (2006 [1764]) *History of the Art of Antiquity*, trans. H.F. Mallgrave, Los Angeles: Getty Research Institute.

Ziegler, R. (2002) *Beauty Raises the Dead: Literature and Loss in the Fin de Siècle*, Newark: University of Delaware Press, London: Associated University Presses.

Zurko, E.R. de (1957) *Origins of Functionalist Theory*, New York: Columbia University Press.

Illustration credits

Figure 1.1 Pyramids at Giza, 2589–2504 BC, photo by John Hendrix

Figure 1.2 Parthenon, 447–438 BC, photo by John Hendrix

Figure 1.3 Colosseum, 72–80, photo by John Hendrix

Figure 1.4 Pantheon, 125–8, photo by John Hendrix

Figure 2.1 Hagia Sophia, 532–7, photo by Walker Shanklin

Figure 2.2 Katholikon, Hosios Loukas, 1012, Madison Digital Image Database

Figure 2.3 Alhambra, muqarnas dome, 1354–91, Madison Digital Image Database

Figure 2.4 Durham Cathedral choir, 1104, photo by John Hendrix

Figure 2.5 Canterbury Cathedral choir, 1174–9, photo by John Hendrix

Figure 2.6 Lincoln Cathedral, St. Hugh's Choir, 1200–39, photo by John Hendrix

Figure 2.7 Lincoln Cathedral nave, 1235–45, photo by John Hendrix

Figure 3.1 Leon Battista Alberti, Palazzo Rucellai, 1455, photo by John Hendrix

Figure 3.2 Leon Battista Alberti, Sant'Andrea in Mantua, 1470–6, photo by John Hendrix

Figure 3.3 Michelangelo, Porta Pia, 1562, photo by John Hendrix

Figure 3.4 Giulio Romano, Palazzo del Tè, 1527, photo by John Hendrix

Figure 3.5 Federico Zuccari, Palazzo Zuccari, 1592, photo by John Hendrix

Figure 3.6 Francesco Borromini, San Carlo alle Quattro Fontane, 1638, photo by John Hendrix

Figure 4.1 Karl Friedrich Schinkel, Schauspielhaus, 1818–21, Madison Digital Image Database

Figure 5.1 Louis Henry Sullivan, Wainwright Building, 1890, Balthasar Korab courtesy of the Library of Congress

Figure 5.2 Louis Henry Sullivan, Bayard (Condict) Building, 1899, Madison Digital Image Database

Figure 5.3 Victor Horta, Tassel House, 1893, © Photo Bastin & Evrard

Figure 5.4 Gerrit Rietveld, Schröder House, 1924, photo by Tom Sherman

Figure 5.5 Ludwig Mies van der Rohe, Barcelona Pavilion, 1929, photo by Rebecca Sargent

Figure 5.6 Ludwig Mies van der Rohe, IIT Classroom Building, 1945–6, photo by John Hendrix

Figure 5.7 Ludwig Mies van der Rohe, Crown Hall, 1950–6, photo by John Hendrix

Figure 5.8 Frank Lloyd Wright, Robie House, 1910, Balthasar Korab courtesy of the Library of Congress

Figure 5.9 Le Corbusier, Villa Stein, 1927, © 2013 Artists Rights Society (ARS), New York/ADAGP, Paris/FLC

Figure 5.10 Le Corbusier, Notre Dame du Haut at Ronchamp, 1955, © 2013 Artists Rights Society (ARS), New York/ADAGP, Paris/FLC

Figure 5.11 Giuseppe Terragni, Casa del Fascio, 1932–6, photo by John Hendrix

Figure 5.12 Giuseppe Terragni, Casa Giuliani Frigerio, 1939–40, photo by John Hendrix

Illustration credits

Figure 5.13 Le Corbusier, Villa Shodhan, 1951–6, © 2013 Artists Rights Society (ARS), New York/ADAGP, Paris/FLC

Figure 6.1 Robert Venturi, Vanna Venturi House, 1962, Madison Digital Image Database
Figure 6.2 Luigi Moretti, Casa del Girasole, 1947, photo by John Hendrix
Figure 6.3 Peter Eisenman, Falk House (House II), 1969–70, photo by John Hendrix
Figure 6.4 Peter Eisenman, Wexner Center, 1983–9, photo by John Hendrix
Figure 6.5 Renzo Piano and Richard Rogers, Pompidou Center, 1972–7, photo by Tom Sherman
Figure 6.6 Frank Gehry, Pritzker Pavilion, 2004, photo by John Hendrix
Figure 6.7 Bernard Tschumi, Parc de la Villette, 1982–98, photo by Tom Sherman

Figure 7.1 Amy Lewis, Endless Dreamscape, Andrew Thurlow Studio, 2011, photo by Amy Lewis
Figure 7.2 Amy Lewis, Endless Dreamscape, Andrew Thurlow Studio, 2011, photo by Amy Lewis

Index